A Handbook of Military Law

Reference Manual

A Handbook of Military Law

Reference Manual

(Revised and Updated Edition)

Wing Commander (Dr) U C Jha (Retd)

Dr Kanika Sharma

Vij Books
New Delhi (India)

Published by

Vij Books
(Publishers, Distributors & Importers)
4836/24 (Third Floor), Ansari Road, Darya Ganj
New Delhi - 110002
Phones: 91-11-43596460, Mob: 98110 94883
e-mail : contact@vijpublishing.com

First Edition: 2011, ISBN: 978-93-80177-33-5

Second Revised and updated edition : 2013, ISBN: 978-93-82652-04-5

Third Revised and updated edition: 2016, ISBN: 978-93-85563-63-8

Fourth Revised Edition : 2020, ISBN: 978-81-942851-3-7

Fifth Revised and updated edition: 2026, ISBN: 978-93-7794-020-1

ISBN: 978-93-7794-020-1 (Paperback)

In the memory of

Colonel T C Banerjee

Contents

Preface

The military the world over has an independent criminal justice system. This system performs dual functions: it strives to ensure both discipline and justice. As an instructor of military law, I felt the need for a handbook which would contain the essentials of military criminal law and serve as a ready reference for all the officers of the Indian Army. This book discusses not only military law as spelt out in the Army Act, 1950, but also as elaborated under various subordinate legislations. Besides, it touches upon related civilian legal codes that a military officer must be aware of.

The book has been divided into 16 chapters. The first six chapters are devoted to the Army Act and Rules. Important definitions, rights and privileges, conditions of service, jurisdiction, military crimes, administrative action, grievance redress, summary punishments and the court martial process have been elaborately explained in these chapters. Chapter 7 deals with the provisions relating to the court of inquiry. Chapter 8 covers the composition, jurisdiction and power of the Armed Forces Tribunal, which became effective in August 2009 and has been instrumental in dispensing justice in more than 1000 cases in a short span of one year.

Chapters 9, 10 and 11 cover provisions contained in the criminal justice system (BNS, POSCO, BNSS and BSA), as they relate to the personnel of the Indian Army. The Criminal Courts and Court Martial (Adjustment of Jurisdiction) Rules, 1978 have also been discussed in Chapter 10.

Besides carrying out its primary task of defending the country against external aggression, the Indian Army has conducted counter-insurgency campaigns in the northeastern states and Kashmir. There has been protracted and malicious propaganda against the Armed Forces (Special Powers) Act, or AFSPA, under which the armed forces get protection while being engaged in counter-insurgency operations. The AFSPA has been called a draconian legislation that gives the members of the Army a licence to kill. In an attempt to clear this misconception, Chapter 12 discusses the duties of the armed forces in aid to civil power and the provisions of the AFSPA, as well as the rulings of the higher courts relating to it. It also covers the role and functioning of the National Human Rights Commission in relation to the armed forces.

The Inter-services Organisations (Command, Control and Discipline) Act was passed by the Parliament in 2023 and is effective from May 10, 2024. It empowers the Commander-in-Chief or Officer-in-Command of Inter-services Organisations to exercise disciplinary or administrative control over the service personnel under their command, irrespective of their service. Existing Inter-services Organisations will be deemed to have been constituted under this Act. These include the Andaman and Nicobar Command, the Defence Space Agency, and the National Defence Academy. The central government may constitute an Inter-services Organisation which has personnel belonging to at least two of the three services: the army, the navy, and the air force. These may be placed under the command of an Officer-in-Command. These organisations may also include a Joint Services Command, which may be placed under the command of a Commander-in-Chief. The Inter-services Organisations (Command, Control and Discipline) Act, 2023 and its Rules of 2025 are discussed in Chapter 13 of the book. These rules enhance tri-service integration, reduce duplication in proceedings, and ensure unified control without altering individual service regulations.

A statutory right to information under the Right to Information Act, 2005 is one of the most significant reforms in public administration in India in the last 75 years. It has become an important tool for upholding the spirit of openness, transparency and accountability even in the armed forces. Chapter 14 of the book covers provisions of the Act and the decisions of the Chief Information Commissioner in matters relating to the Army.

As the distinction between 'international' and 'non-international' wars is getting increasingly blurred, armed conflicts in modern times are becoming more and more complex. The laws of armed conflict or the laws of war have been covered in Chapter 15. The chapter includes the salient features of the four Geneva Conventions of 1949 as well as laws related to the protection of prisoners of war. The responsibility of the commander during armed conflicts has also been discussed in this chapter.

Starting from Korea in 1950, the Indian Army has participated in 45 United Nations (UN) missions, and nearly 180,000 Indian peacekeepers have so far served under the UN flag. India has been the largest contributor to UN mission since inception. The range of tasks under UN peacekeeping operations has expanded significantly in response to shifting patterns of conflict. UN peacekeepers must have a clear understanding of the principles and rules of international humanitarian law (IHL) and observe them in situations where they apply. These have been covered in the last chapter of the book.

This book has not been written for lawyers and is not intended to be a manual on military law. It has been designed for the use of personnel of the armed forces, especially the Indian Army, who would like to know something about their legal rights and responsibilities. It also covers the syllabus of Part B and D of the promotion examination and DSSC/TSOC entrance examination.

This is the fifth revised and updated edition of the book. It includes provisions contained in the Protection of Children from Sexual offences Act, 2012 and the Sexual Harassment of Women at Workplace (Prevention, Prohibition and Redressal) Act, 2013.

It is hoped that the book will provide valuable assistance to the officers of the Indian Army: in day-to-day functioning of the unit, for promotion examinations, in investigations of charges, in the exercise of their judicial powers or for the conduct of trials by court martial.

I am thankful to M/s Vij Books India Pvt Ltd for shaping the book.

This book is dedicated to the soldiers of the Indian Army.

-U C Jha

- Kanika Sharma

Abbreviations

AFSPA	Armed Forces (Special Powers) Act, 1954
AFT Act	Armed Forces Tribunal Act, 2007
AA	Army Act, 1950
AO	Army Order
AR	Army Rules, 1954
AWL	Absent without Leave
BNS	Bharatiya Nyaya Sanhita
BNSS	Bharatiya Nagarik Suraksha Sanhita
BSA	Bharatiya Sakshya Adhiniyam
CAT	UN Convention against Torture, 1984
Ch.	Chapter
CIC	Chief Information Commission
CPC	Civil Procedure Code, 1908
CO	Commanding Officer
COAS	Chief of the Army Staff
DCM	District Court Martial
DV Act	Domestic Violence Act, 2005
FIR	First Information Report
GCM	General Court Martial
ICC	International Criminal Court
ICCPR	International Covenant on Civil and Political Rights
ICESCR	International Covenant on Economic, Social and Cultural Rights

ICRC	International Committee of the Red Cross
IHL	International Humanitarian Law
ISO	Inter-Services Organization
JAG	Judge Advocate General
JCO	Junior Commissioned Officer
MML	Manual of Military Law
MS	Military Secretary
NHRC	National Human Rights Commission
NCO	Non Commissioned Officer
OR	Other ranks
para	Paragraph
PHRA	Protection of Human Rights Act, 1993
PC Act	The Prevention of Corruption Act, 1988
PIO	Public Information Officer
POCSO	Protection of Children from Sexual Offences
POW	Prisoner of War
RA	Regulations for the Army, 1987
RTI	Right to Information
Sec./s.	Section
SCM	Summary Court Martial
SGCM	Summary General Court Martial
SOFA	Status of Forces Agreement
UN	United Nations
Vol	Volume
WO	Warrant Officer

CHAPTER 1

MILITARY LAW: INTRODUCTION

I. Introduction

Military law in India is contained in the Army Act of 1950. It was passed by the Parliament on 22 May 1950 and came into force on 22 July 1950. The main objects of the Act were (i) to make it self-sufficient by incorporating the relevant provisions of certain other related enactments; (ii) to adapt the existing provisions to suit the new constitutional set-up and present-day requirements; and (iii) on the one hand, to bridge the gap between army and civil laws as far as possible in the matter of punishments and, on the other, to eliminate the disparity between the corresponding provisions of the law governing the Army and the Air Force. This Act, while following the Indian Army Act of 1911 closely, also incorporated the provisions of the Indian Army (Suspension of Sentence) Act, 1920. Certain provisions of the Act were amended in 1955, 1975, and 1992.

The Army Act consists of 15 chapters. Chapter I is preliminary, Chapter II deals with special provisions for the application of the Act, and Chapter III relates to commission, appointments and enrolment. The conditions of service are described in Chapter IV, while Chapter V lists out service privileges. Chapter VI sets out the various offences and Chapter VII the punishments. Chapter VIII deals with penal deductions and Chapter IX describes arrests and related proceedings before trial. Chapters X, XI and XII deal with the court-martial, its procedure, and confirmation and revision of sentence respectively. Chapter XIII relates to execution of sentences, Chapter XIV pardons, remissions and suspensions, while Chapter XV, deals with rule-making powers.

II. Subordinate Legislations

The Army Rules, 1954 made under Section 191 of the Army Act are in the nature of procedural laws, somewhat like the Code of Criminal Procedure.

The Army Rules were last amended in 1993. The Regulations for the Army, 1987 have been issued under the authority of the Government of India. Certain provisions of the Regulations, especially procedures relating to statutory complaints contained in para 364 were amended in 1997.

The Manual of Indian Military Law (MIML) was compiled by the Judge Advocate General of the Army in India in 1912. It was amended and updated in 1937, and was reprinted in 1961. In 1983, the Government of India issued an updated and revised bilingual Manual of Military Law (MML) in three volumes:

- Volume I: It consists of eight chapters dealing with a brief history of military law in India (Chapter I), an outline of the Army Act (Chapter II), arrests and investigations of charges (Chapter III), courts-martial (Chapter IV), evidence (Chapter V), civil offences (Chapter VI), duties in aid of civil power (Chapter VII) and service privileges (Chapter VIII).

- Volume II: It contains the Army Act, 1950, and the Army Rules, 1954, with explanatory notes, forms and appendices.

- Volume III: It contains certain enactments which are referred to in earlier parts of the Manual. This volume also contains Gazette Notifications issued under the Army Act by the Government of India and forms of warrants.

The MML has been revised in 2011. MML Vol. III now contains statutes such as the Right to Information Act, 2005 and the Armed Forces Special Powers Act (AFSPA).

III. Important Definitions

1. Active Service

The term 'active service', as applied to a person subject to the Army Act, means the time during which such person:

(a) Is attached to, or forms part of, a force which is engaged in operations against an enemy, or

(b) Is engaged in military operations in, or is on the line of march to, a country or place wholly or partly occupied by an enemy, or

(c) Is attached to or forms part of a force which is in military occupation of a foreign country. [AA s. 3 (i)].

Where there is any doubt as to whether or not troops are under active service for the purpose of this clause, a declaration should be made under AA s. 9.

2. Civil Offence

The term 'civil offence' means an offence which is triable by a criminal court. [AA s. 3 (ii)].

3. Commanding Officer

The term 'commanding officer', when used in any provision of the Army Act, with reference to any separate portion of the regular Army or to any department thereof, means the officer whose duty it is under the regulations of the regular Army, or in the absence of any such regulations, by the custom of the service, to discharge with respect to that portion of the regular Army or that department, the functions of a commanding officer (CO) in regard to matters of the description referred to in that provision. [AA s.3 (v)].

Regulations for the Army, para 9 provides that except where otherwise expressly provided in the Regulations, the CO of a person subject to the Army Act is either:

(a) the officer who has been appointed by higher authority to be a CO to exercise his power as such, or

(b) where no appointment has been made, the officer who is, for the time being, in immediate command of (i) the unit to which the person belongs or is attached to, or (ii) any detachment or a distinct sizeable separate portion of a unit with which the person is for the time being serving,

and in respect of which it is the duty of such officer, under the Regulations or by the custom of the service, to discharge the functions of a CO.

Command during Temporary Absence of Permanent Commander

When formation commanders are temporarily absent from their commands for periods which do not involve vacation of command, officiating incumbents will be appointed and such appointments notified in the formation orders concerned. In such cases, legal powers subject to the terms of the court-martial warrants held, will be exercised by the officer who is in actual command at the time. In similar circumstances, in the case of a unit commander who is absent, the appointment of the officer on whom the command devolves, will be published in unit orders. His legal powers, subject to the limitations of the Army Act, will be the same as those of the unit commanders. [RA para 53].

When an officer commanding (OC) unit becomes sick or is temporarily absent, the conduct of his duties devolves on the second-in-command whose appointment as officiating OC will be published in unit orders. His legal powers subject to the limitations of the Army Act, will be the same as those of the unit commanders. [RA para 54].

Mutual Power of Command in the Three Services

Officers of the regular Army and the Navy are empowered to exercise command over persons subject to the Air Force Act, 1950, when such persons are attached to or are serving in (i) Army Units or Naval Ships or Establishments; or (ii) Air Force Units commanded by such officers. Members of the regular Army and the Air Force are empowered to exercise command over members of the Indian Navy under certain conditions. These conditions are set out in Ministry of Defence Notification No. SRO 80 dated 24 February, 1961. Officers of the Air Force and the Navy are empowered to exercise command over persons subject to Army Act, 1950, in the circumstances set out in Army Rule, 188, and when such persons are attached to or are serving in (i) Air Force Units or Naval Ships or Establishments; or (ii) Army Units commanded by such officers. [RA para 323].

4. Enemy

The term 'enemy' includes all armed mutineers, armed rebels, armed rioters, pirates and any person in arms against whom it is the duty of any person subject to military law to act. The term 'enemy' includes a soldier running amok. [AA s. 3 (x), notes to s. 3 and RA para 351]. An armed rioter would constitute the "enemy" for purpose of this section. A person subject to AA called out to suppress a riot, who throws away his weapon and runs away from the rioters, could be court martialled for misbehaviour before the enemy.

5. Junior Commissioned Officer

Junior commissioned officer (JCO) means a person commissioned, gazetted or in pay as a junior commissioned officer in the regular Army or the Indian Reserve Forces, and includes a person holding a junior commission in the Territorial Army, who is for the time being subject to the Army Act. [AA s. 3 (xii)].

6. Military Custody

The term 'military custody' means the arrest or confinement of a person according to the usages of the service and includes naval or air force custody. The term 'confinement' includes confinement in the unit quarter-guard or detention in barracks while undergoing sentence of imprisonment under AA s. 80. [AA s. 3 (xiii) and notes].

7. Military Reward

Military reward includes any gratuity or annuity for long service or good conduct, good service pay or pension, and any other military pecuniary reward. A war gratuity is a military reward but a medal or decoration is not. [AA s. 3 (xiv)].

8. Non-commissioned Officer

Non-commissioned officer (NCO) means a person holding a non-commissioned rank or an acting non-commissioned rank in the regular Army or the Indian Reserve Forces, and includes a non-commissioned officer or acting non-commissioned officer of the Territorial Army (TA), who is for the time being subject to the Army Act. An acting NCO is legally a NCO. [AA s. 3 (xv)].

9. Officer

The term 'officer' means a person commissioned, gazetted or in pay as an officer in the regular Army, and includes:

(a) An officer of the Indian Reserve Forces;

(b) An officer holding a commission in the Territorial Army granted by the President with designation of rank corresponding to that of an officer of the regular Army who is for the time being subject to the Army Act;

(c) An officer of the Indian Regular Reserve of Officers who is for the time being subject to the Army Act;

(d) In relation to a person subject to this Act when serving under such conditions as may be prescribed, an officer of the Navy or Air Force;

but does not include a JCO, WO, petty officer or NCO. [AA s. 3 (xviii)].

10. Post

The term 'post' [with reference to AA s. 34 (a)] includes any point or position, whether fortified or not, which a detachment may be ordered to hold. The abandonment of a post would also include the abandonment of a siege if there were no circumstances to warrant such a measure. When used with respect to an individual as in AA s. 34 (h) and (k), the term 'post' means the position or place in which it may be the duty of a person subject to the Army Act to be, especially under arms. [AA s. 34 and notes].

11. Regular Army

Regular Army means officers, JCOs, WOs, NCOs and other enrolled persons who, by their commission, warrant, terms of enrolment or otherwise, are liable to warrant, terms of enrolment or otherwise, are liable to Union in any part of the world, including persons belonging to the Reserve Forces and the Territorial Army when called out on permanent service. [AA s.3 (xxi)].

12. Superior Officer

The term 'superior officer', when used in relation to a person subject to the Army Act, includes a JCO, WO and a NCO, and, as regards persons placed under his orders, an officer, WO, petty officer and NCO of the Navy or Air Force. [AA s. 3 (xxiii)].

IV. Persons subject to Army Act

The Army Act is a special law. It has extra-territorial jurisdiction and a person subject to it continues to be so subject at all times irrespective of the place where he is serving—whether in India or otherwise. The following persons are subject to the Army Act wherever they may be:

(a) Officers, JCOs and WOs of the regular Army;

(b) Persons enrolled under this Act;

(c) Persons belonging to the Indian Reserve Forces;

(d) Officers, JCOs and enrolled persons of the Territorial Army, when doing duty as such or called out or embodied or attached to any regular forces;

(e) Officers appointed to the Indian Regular Reserve of Officers, when ordered on any duty or service for which they are liable as members of such reserve forces;

(f) Persons not otherwise subject to military law who, on active service, in camp, on the march or at any frontier post specified by the Central Government by notification in this behalf, are employed by, or are in the service of, or are followers of, or accompany any portion of, the regular Army.

Every person subject to the AA shall remain so until duly retired, discharged, released, removed, dismissed or cashiered from the service. [AA s. 2].

Application of the AA to certain Forces under Central Government

The Central Government may, by notification, apply all or any of the provisions of the AA to any Force raised and maintained in India under the authority of that Government and suspend the operation of any other enactment for the time being applicable to the said Force. The provisions of the AA so applied shall have effect in respect of persons belonging to the said Force as they have effect in respect of persons subject to the AA holding in the regular Army the same or equivalent rank as the aforesaid persons hold for the time being in the said Force. The provisions of the AA so applied shall also have effect in respect of persons who are employed by or are in the service of or are followers of or accompany any portion of the said Force as they have effect in respect of persons subject to the AA under s 2 (i). While any of the provisions of the AA apply to the said Force, the Central Government may, by notification, direct by what authority any jurisdiction, powers or duties incident to the operation of these provisions shall be exercised or performed in respect of the said Force. [AA s. 4]

The word 'Force' is not defined anywhere in the AA, but the Act clearly contemplates that 'force' referred to in s. 4 must be a force organized on similar lines as the army with rank structure. For instance, the General Reserve Engineering Force (GREF) is a 'Force' organized on army pattern with units and sub-units and rank structure. In exercise of the power conferred by AA s. 4 (1) and (4), the Central Government has applied all the provisions of the AA to the Rastriya Rifles, being a Force maintained in India under the authority of the Central Government. The Central Government has directed that Sector Commander of the Rastriya Rifles shall exercise the jurisdiction, powers and duties of an officer commanding a Brigade in respect of the members of the Force under his command.

Liability of offender who ceases to be subject to AA

Where an offence under the AA has been committed by any person while subject to the AA, and he has ceased to be subject to the Act, he may be taken into and kept in military custody, and tried and punished for such offence as if he continued to be subject to the Act. No such person shall be tried for an offence, unless his trial commences within a period of three years after he had ceased to be subject to the Act.

In computing the period of three years the following period shall be excluded: (i) the time during which such person has avoided arrest by absconding or concealing himself; or (ii) where the institution of the proceeding in respect of the offence has been stayed by an injunction/ order, the period of the continuance of the injunction/order, the day on which it was issued or made, and the on which it was withdrawn. However, the period of three years shall not apply to the trial of any such person for an offence of desertion or fraudulent enrolment or for any of the offences mentioned in AA s. 37; nor shall it affect the jurisdiction of a criminal court to try any offence triable by such court as well as by a court martial.

When a person subject to the AA is sentenced by a court martial to imprisonment for life or imprisonment, the AA shall apply to him during the term of his sentence, though he is cashiered or dismissed from the regular Army, or has otherwise ceased to be subject to the AA, and he may be kept, removed, imprisoned and punished as if he continued to be subject to the Army Act.

When a person subject to the AA is sentenced by a court martial to death, the AA shall apply to him till the sentence is carried out. [AA s. 123]

Commission, Appointment and Enrolment

The President may grant, to such person as he thinks fit, a commission as an officer, or as a junior commissioned officer or appoint any person as warrant officer of the regular Army. [AA s.10]. The following persons, under AA s. 11, can be enrolled:

(a) A citizen of India;

(b) A subject of Nepal;

(c) An alien, with the written consent of the Central Government.

Resignation of Commission by an Officer

An officer has no right to resign his commission but he may submit an application to the Central Government to resign his commission. He shall not be relieved of his duties until the Central Government has accepted his resignation. An officer whose resignation has been accepted may, before he is relieved of his duties may apply to the Central Government for withdrawal of the same. The Central Government may at its discretion, grant the request. [AR 16C].

Procedure before Enrolling Officer

Upon the appearance before the enrolling officer of any person desirous of being enrolled, the enrolling officer shall read and explain to him, the conditions of service for which he is to be enrolled and shall put to him the questions set forth in the prescribed enrolment form. The enrolling officer shall caution the person that if he makes a false answer to any question he will be liable to punishment under the Army Act. Thereafter, the enrolling officer shall record or cause to be recorded the answer to each such question. A false answer to any question set forth in the prescribed form of enrolment is punishable under AA s. 44. [AA s. 13].

Mode of Enrolment and Validity

If, after complying with the above provisions (AA s. 13), the enrolling officer is satisfied that the person desirous of being enrolled fully understands the questions put to him and consents to the conditions of service, and if such officer perceives no impediment, he shall sign and shall also cause such person to sign the enrolment paper, and such person shall thereupon be deemed to be enrolled. [AA s. 14]. Every person who has for the period of three months been in receipt of pay as a person enrolled under the Army Act and been borne on the rolls of any corps or department shall be deemed to have been duly enrolled. He shall not be entitled to claim his discharge on the ground of any irregularity or illegality in his enrolment. [AA s. 15].

Enrolment Paper

On the trial of a person subject to AA for making a false answer on enrolment or for fraudulent enrolment, the answer made or the fact of enrolment can be proved by production of his enrolment paper. [AA s. 141].

Attestation

The following persons are to be attested: (i) all persons enrolled as combatants; (ii) all persons selected to hold a non-commissioned or acting non-commissioned rank; and (iii) all other persons subject to the Army Act as may be prescribed by the Central Government. [AA s. 16].

When a person who is to be attested is reported fit for duty, or has completed the prescribed period of probation, an oath or affirmation shall be administered to him in the prescribed form [AR 9(1)] by his CO in front of his corps or such portion thereof or such members of his department as may be present. The form of oath or affirmation contains a promise that the person to be attested will bear true allegiance to the Constitution of India as by law established, and that he will serve in the regular Army and go wherever he is ordered by land, sea or air, and that he will obey all commands of any officer set over him, even to the peril of his life. The fact of an enrolled person having taken the oath or affirmation directed by AA s. 17 shall be entered on his enrolment paper, and authenticated by the signature of the officer administering the oath or affirmation. [AA s. 17].

V. Restrictions of Fundamental Rights

The Part III of the Indian Constitution guarantees certain Fundamental Rights to every citizen of India. These rights have been abrogated (under Article 33 of the Constitution) in respect of Army personnel because of the maintenance of discipline and the nature of duties performed by them. AA s. 21 provides for the restrictions of certain fundamental rights, which have been elaborated in ARs 19 to 21. Under the said rules, the rights to form associations or unions; communication with the press; and freedom of speech, expression and assembly are abrogated.

VI. Responsibilities in the Army

1. Responsibility of every person subject to Army Act

Obligation to bring Dishonesty to Notice: It is the obligatory duty of every person in military employ to bring at once to the notice of his immediate superior, or the next superior where the immediate superior officer is involved, any case of dishonesty, fraud or infringement of orders that may come to his knowledge. [RA para 317].

Official Documents: Official reports or correspondence, or copies thereof, are not be furnished to any person not officially entitled to receive them, without the special sanction of superior military authority. The publication of official documents, or communicating their contents by any means or using them for any private purpose without due authority, is a breach of the Official Secrets Act, 1923. [RA para 319].

Acquaintance with Regulations and Orders: Officers are to acquaint themselves with Regulations and Orders. Ignorance of published orders will not be admitted as an excuse for their non-observance. JCOs, WOs and OR will be held personally responsible for making themselves acquainted with such orders as are published in accordance with RA para 37(k) and

584, and details of duties as are posted in quarters, as directed by RA para 1155. [RA para 324].

Treatment of Subordinates: Officers, JCOs, WOs and NCOs are to adopt towards subordinates or equal and junior ranks such methods of command and treatment which will not only ensure respect for authority, but also foster the feelings of self-respect and personal honour essential to military efficiency. They will avoid intemperate language or an offensive manner. [RA para 326].

Praising and Censuring of Superiors: Deliberations or discussions by officer, JCOs, WOs and OR with the object of conveying praise, censure, or any mark of approbation towards their superiors or any other in the government service is prohibited. The publication of laudatory orders regarding an officer quitting a station or relinquishing an appointment is forbidden. [RA para 329].

Observance of Religions Customs: Religious customs and prejudices are to be respected by all ranks. [RA para 332].

Private Tuitions in Military subject: All ranks are forbidden, except with the prior sanction of Army Headquarters to assist private tutors or tutorial establishments in preparing candidates for examination in military subjects.[RA para 336].

Borrowing and Lending Money: The officers, JCOs, WOs or ORs are not to lend or borrow money to or from any person belonging to the armed forces or any regimental institutions run by civilian contractors or engage in any transaction whereby they become a debtor or a creditor to any person. However, in exceptional cases where the borrowing or lending takes place between real blood relations or between spouses it may be permitted with the prior sanction of Army Commander in respect of officers and Div Commander in respect of others. Sanction in respect of Officers, JCOs, WOs and OR not serving under an Army Commander will be granted by Adjutant General, Army Headquarters. [RA para 337].

Gambling: Gambling is strictly prohibited in garrisons, camps or cantonments. There is no objection to tambola being organized in units/officers messes on profit basis provided it is confined entirely to members of the units/mess and the stakes are nominal. [RA para 338].

Acceptance of gifts and presents by Army Personnel: The persons subject to the Army Act are not to accept any gift, gratuity or reward for any act performed in their official capacity, directly or indirectly, without the consent of the Government. They will also not accept any gift, gratuity or reward from any person, to whom they can, directly or indirectly, show favour or disfavour in the exercise of their official functions, or in circumstances where such acceptance might place them in an embarrassing position or affect the proper discharge of their duties. For further details on the subject refer RA para 344.

2. Responsibilities of an Officer

Good order and Discipline: An officer is at all times responsible for ensuring that good order and discipline of the service are maintained and the rules and instructions are complied with. He will afford the utmost aid and support to his CO and immediate superior officer in this regard. It is his duty to notice, repress, and instantly report any negligence or impropriety of conduct on the part of junior officers, JCOs, WOs and OR including personnel of paramilitary forces placed under command of army and camp followers [becoming subject to AA under s. 2 (l) (i)] whether on or off duty, and whether the offenders do or do not belong to his own unit. [RA para 316].

Unauthorized Punishments: An officer will not introduce or adopt any system of punishment that is in any respect at variance with the Army Act and Army Rules or the Regulations for the Army. [RA para 353].

Observance of Religions Customs: Officers will take special care that none of their acts, or of their subordinates, wounds the religious feelings of a person or violates the sanctity of any place held sacred. [RA para 332].

Lieutenant Sameul Kamalesan, a Christian officer, had been dismissed from the Indian Army for refusing to participate in the religious ceremonies of his regiment. In June 2017, during one religious parade, the Commandant directed him to enter the sanctum and take part in the puja. When he refused, citing his faith, disciplinary proceedings followed. On November 25, 2025, the Supreme Court upheld his dismissal for refusing to enter a regiment's temple/gurdwara sanctum for religious ceremonies. The Court ruled his refusal was "gross indiscipline" and "insubordination", not a matter of religious freedom.

3. Responsibilities of a Commanding Officer

Security: A general or other officer commanding is responsible for ensuring that all persons under his command are acquainted and comply with the provisions of the Official Secrets Act, 1923, together with the paragraphs of the Regulations for the Army bearing on the same subject, and with the instructions issued by the Government or Army Headquarters for the security of military establishments, offices and official documents, and for regulating admission to national defence establishment and other prohibited places, as required by the above Act and Regulations. [RA para 318].

Prevention of Crime: A commanding officer will use every effort to prevent crime and to suppress any tendency to screen its existence. For first offences, not of an aggravated character, admonition is the most suitable treatment. Other punishment should be resorted to only when admonition has failed to have effect. Quantum of punishment must be commensurate with the crime committed. [RA para 325].

Protection of Women from Sexual Harassment: The commanding officers must ensure that women employees serving in the Army formations and units are treated with respect and dignity. They should create an environment to ensure that the women employees feel safe and secure in the unit's and formations while serving with their male counterparts. Whenever any case of sexual harassment is reported, instructions contained in AO/1/2006/DV must be complied with.

Assistance to Civil Authorities in Criminal Cases: A commanding officer will afford the civil authorities assistance in the execution of criminal proceedings against any person under his command. [RA para 357].

Acquaintance with Orders: The officer commanding a unit is to ensure that all ranks under his command are acquainted with the purport of the Army Act; Sections 18 to 20, 22, 23, 26, 28 to 32, 34 to 78, 80 to 82, 89 and 91; inclusive and paragraphs 333 and 354 of the Regulations for the Army. The provisions of these sections are to be explained to JCOs, WOs and OR and NCs (E) at three successive roll calls at least every three months. They will also be explained to recruits on first joining so as to preclude the possibility of ignorance on their part of the additional offences and punishments to which a person renders himself liable by becoming subject to military law. [RA para 331].

In regard to any matter not specifically provided for in the Army Act or Army Rules, it shall be lawful for the competent authority to do such thing or take such action as appears to it to be just and proper. [AR 6].

VII. Rights and Service Privileges

The persons subject to the Army Act enjoy certain privileges in their relation to civil courts and the law administered by these courts [AA s. 25-32]. In addition, certain other privileges have been conferred upon these persons by the Acts of Parliament [AA s.33]. The important rights and privileges are as follows.

- **Right to pay without deductions**

  The pay of a person subject to the Army Act is to be paid without any deduction other than the deductions authorized Army Act or any other Act. The term pay means rate of pay with increases for the length of service to which a person is entitled by reasons of rank, appointment and includes qualification pay and various forms of additional pay. It is illegal to make deductions which are not authorized and the unlawful detention of pay is an offence under AA s. 61. The authorized deductions are included under AA ss. 90 and 91 and AR 205. Similarly deductions can also be made under the Income Tax Act. [AA s. 25].

- **Immunity from attachment**

  The military equipment and other necessaries of a person subject to the Army Act, used by him for the discharge of his duty are immune from seizure under any decree or order of any civil or revenue court. Similarly the pay and allowances of such a person are immune from attachment in the execution of such a decree or order [AA s. 28; Proviso (j) to section 60 of CPC, 1908]. The words 'civil or revenue court' does not include a criminal court. An authorized deduction can be made from the pay of the officers and other ranks based on a criminal court's warrant under AA s. 90 (f) or 91 (h).

- **Immunity from arrest for debt**

A person subject to the Army Act is not liable to be arrested for debt under any process issued by, or by the authority of any civil or revenue court [AA s. 29].

- **Immunity from arrest for persons attending court martial**

  A person subject to the Army Act while proceeding to, attending or returning from a court martial is not liable to arrest under civil or revenue process. The immunity is also extended to civilian, including legal practitioner or witness while acting in obedience to summon to attend a court martial. If any such person is arrested under any such process, he may be discharged by the order of the court martial [AA s. 30].

- **Priority in respect of hearing of Suit**

  The civil courts are to give priority to hearing any civil suit or proceedings in which person subject to the Army Act are parties so that they may return to their duties on the expiry of leave granted to them for the purpose of attending such suits or proceedings. An individual proceeding on leave to attend the hearing must carry a certificate from the proper military authority. The certificate shall state the first and last day of the leave and a description of the case with respect to which the leave was granted. No fee is payable to the Court in respect of the presentation of any such certificate, or of any application by or on behalf of any such person, for priority for the hearing of his case. Where the Court is unable to arrange for the hearing and final disposal of the suit or other proceedings within the period of such leave, it shall record reasons for its inability to do so, and shall provide a copy thereof to such person without any payment. [AA s. 32 and notes].

- **Postponement of Suits**

  The Indian Soldiers (Litigation) Act, 1925 provides for the postponement in certain circumstances of civil and revenue proceedings in which an unrepresented person subject to the Army Act is a party.

- **Privileged Will**

  Sections 65 and 66 of the Indian Succession Act, 1925 provide that a person subject to the Army Act has a right to make a "privileged will" which may be made either by word of mouth or by writing without complying with the formalities and signatures and attestation which are required in the case of "will" made by ordinary persons, if he is employed in an expedition or engaged in actual warfare.

- **Exemption from Tolls when on duty**

Under section 3 of the Tolls (Army and Air Force) Act, 1901, persons subject to the Army Act while moving under orders of military authorities are together with the members of their families and belongings exempted from payment of any tolls.

- **Appointment of an attorney**

Under order XXVIII, Rule 1 of the Civil Procedure Code, 1908, a person subject to the Army Act, who cannot obtain leave, may authorize any person to sue or defend a suit or proceedings on his behalf.

- **Exemption from Court Fee**

Section 19 (i) of the Court Fees Act, 1870 exempts from court fees in a power of attorney to institute or defend a suit, executed by a person subject to the Army Act, who is not in civil employment.

- **Receipt of Pay**

As per Schedule I (Article 53) of the Indian Stamp Act, 1899, receipt for pay and allowances of NCOs or Sepoy when serving in such capacity need not be paid.

- **Pension protected**

All government pension (including military pensions) are protected from attachment in the execution of the decrees of Civil Courts (Pension Act, 1871, section 11 and Proviso (g) to section 60 of CPC, 1908).

- **Arms Act**

Commanding officer (CO) of a unit of Army is exempted from the operation of Section 3 and 4 of the Arms Act 1959, for such arms and ammunition, as provided for sporting purposes, provided such persons are in possession of a pass granted and signed by their CO to that effect. Similarly the uniform swords, dirks and khukaries supplied to the members of the Army for wearing as a part of their uniform are exempted from the operation of Section 4 of the Arms Act.

Section 45 of the Arms Act provides that nothing contained in the Act shall apply to acquisition, possession or carrying the arms and ammunition by or under the orders of the Central Government. The Government of India vide Ministry of Home Affairs letter No. 9/88/49-police(i) dated 04 July 1950 has specified that all Commissioned Officers are authorized for one pistol each, as personal issue so long they are on active list. They can also keep in addition, one privately owned revolver/pistol. The JCOs are authorized for one pistol, revolver, or stengun each.

- **Redress of Grievance**

Service privileges relating to redress of grievance as contained in AA ss. 26 and 27 are discussed in chapter 6.

CHAPTER 2

OFFENCES AND PUNISHMENTS

The term offence has been defined as 'an act or omission punishable under the Army Act and includes a civil offence'. The term 'civil offence' has also been defined under the Army Act as 'an offence which is triable by a criminal court'. The offences provided under the Indian Penal Code (IPC) or other laws are deemed to be civil offences under section 69 of the Army Act. Chapter VI of the AA (ss. 34-70) contains a list of offences punishable under the Act. These are as follows:

(a) Offences in relation to the enemy and punishable with death (s. 34)

(b) Offences in relation to the enemy and not punishable with death (s. 35)

(c) Offences punishable more severely on active service than at other times (s. 36)

(d) Mutiny, desertion and absence without leave (s. 37 to 39)

(e) Striking or threatening superior officers, disobedience to superior officer, and insubordination and obstruction (ss. 40 to 42)

(f) Fraudulent enrolment and false answers on enrolment (ss. 43 and 44)

(g) Unbecoming and disgraceful conduct, ill-treating a subordinate and intoxication (ss. 45 to 48)

(h) Escape from custody and irregularity in connection with arrest or confinement (ss. 49 to 51)

(i) Offences in respect of property, extortion and corruption, making away with equipment and injury to property (ss. 52 to 55)

(j) False accusations, falsifying official documents and false declaration, signing in blank and failure to report (ss. 56 to 58)

(k) Offences relating to courts martial and false evidence (ss. 59 and 60)

(l) Unlawful detention of pay (s. 61)

(m) Offences in relation to aircraft and flying (s. 62)

(n) Violation of good order and discipline, and miscellaneous offences (ss. 63 and 64)

(o) Attempt to commit any of the above offences and abetment of these offences (ss. 65 to 68)

(p) Jurisdiction of court-martial to try civil offences (ss. 69 and 70)

Offences Relating to Misbehaviour before Enemy

The offences under this category are considered 'most serious' and the maximum punishment for them is death. The offences under AA s. 34 include acts such as:

(a) Shamefully abandoning or delivering to the enemy any garrison or post, which it was one's duty to defend, or compelling or inducing any commanding officer to commit such acts.

(b) Intentionally using any means to compel or induce any person subject to military law to abstain from acting against the enemy, or to discourage such person from acting against the enemy.

(c) In the presence of the enemy, showing cowardice by shamefully casting away arms, ammunition or equipment.

(d) Treacherously holding correspondence or communicating intelligence to the enemy.

(e) Directly or indirectly assisting the enemy with money, arms, ammunition, stores or supplies.

(f) Treacherously or through cowardice sending a flag of truce to the enemy.

(g) In time of war or during any military operation, intentionally raising a false alarm, spreading reports calculated to create alarm or despondency.

(h) While in action, leaving one's commanding officer or post without being regularly relieved or without leave.

(i) Having been made a prisoner of war, voluntarily serving with or aiding the enemy;

(j) Knowingly harbouring or protecting an enemy.

(k) Being a sentry in time of war, sleeping on post or being intoxicated.

(l) Knowingly acting in a way that imperils the success of the military.

There are other categories of offences (AA s. 35) which also relate to misbehaviour before the enemy but are not punishable with death. A military person who is taken prisoner by the enemy owing to want of due precaution or through disobedience of orders, or who has been taken prisoner and fails to rejoin service when able to do so will be charged under this category of offences. Everyone connected with the armed forces needs to recognize the grave danger of assisting the enemy by gossip, whether verbal or written, as to plans, prospects, operations, etc. Therefore, a military person who, without due authority, holds correspondence with the enemy or sends a flag of truce to the enemy could be charged and the punishment under AA s. 35 may extend up to 14 years of imprisonment.

For the purpose of these offences, the term 'enemy' includes all armed mutineers, armed rebels, armed rioters, pirates and any person in arms against whom it is the duty of any person subject to military law to act.

Offences on Active Service

The armed forces are on active service during military operations or before being deployed against an enemy. Military law provides (AA s.36) that in such situations, a military person may be considered guilty of an offence if he (i) uses criminal force against a sentry; (ii) breaks into any house or other place in search of plunder; (iii) being a sentry, sleeps upon his post or is intoxicated; (iv) without orders from his superior officer, leaves his guard or post; or (v) intentionally or negligently raises a false alarm or spreads reports to create unnecessary alarm or despondency. The use of force against a sentry does not necessarily mean the use of physical force. Passing the sentry when warned by his superior officer not to do so, would amount to an offence.

Mutiny

Mutiny implies collective insubordination, or a combination of two or more persons to resist, or to induce others to resist a lawful military authority. It is considered a serious offence in the militaries the world over, and a person could be held accused of the offence of mutiny, if he is present at any such mutiny and does not do his utmost to suppress the same. A military person who has knowledge of a mutiny or has reason to believe in the existence of any mutiny, any intention to mutiny or any such conspiracy, could also be held as an accused of the offence of mutiny, if he does not give information to his commanding or other superior officer. Collective petitions and representations, or the submission of a petition through the medium of any association in respect of military matters are forbidden on this ground. [AA s. 37].

Unauthorized Absence and Desertion

Absence without leave (AWL) is culpable. A military person who remains absent from duty or overstays the leave granted to him without sufficient cause would be committing an offence of AWL (AA s.39). In case a military person, who is on leave of absence and receives information from the proper authority that the corps or unit to which he belongs has been ordered on active service, fails to rejoin without delay, he would also be considered to have committed the offence of AWL. Similarly, the charge of AWL would be brought against any person who (i) without sufficient cause fails to appear at the parade or duty at the time fixed, or (ii) when on parade or on the line of march, without sufficient cause or without leave from his superior officer, quits the parade or line of march. Absence without leave does not include involuntary absence, e.g., due to illness or admission in a civil or military hospital. The offence relates to AWL and not merely absence. The leave of absence must first be granted, then notified to the applicant. A person who has applied for leave and departs from the unit before it is actually granted commits the offence of being AWL, even though the leave has been granted but not notified to him.

Desertion and AWL: Desertion differs from AWL, in that desertion or attempt to desert the service implies an intention on the part of the accused either (i) never to return to the service, or (ii) to avoid some important military duty (commonly called constructive desertion), for example, in a forward area. A person charged with desertion may be found guilty of an attempt to desert or of AWL. A military person who harbours a deserter can be charged for aiding desertion. Similarly, a military person who, being cognizant of any desertion or attempt at desertion, does not inform his superior officer, or does not take any steps to apprehend the deserter can also be charged for aiding desertion. [AA s. 38].

When a person subject to AA remains absent from duty without authorization for a period of more than 30 days, assembly of a court of inquiry is mandatory (AA s. 106). If the person declared absent does not afterwards surrenders or is not apprehended, he is deemed to be deserter. For more details see chapter 7 of the book.

Contempt towards Officers and Insubordination

In the armed forces, the officers have the right to command and the soldiers are bound to obey, as long as the command is lawful. Assaulting a superior officer or using criminal force or threatening language to a superior officer is a grave offence. (AA s. 40). An assault is something less than the use of criminal force, the force being cut short before the blow actually falls. A military person, who shows a wilful defiance of authority, disobeying any lawful command given personally by his superior officer in the execution of his office, would be considered to have committed a serious offence in the armed forces. An individual accused of such offences is punished more severely if he commits the offence while on active service, than otherwise.

To be legally enforceable, an order must be a positive command or a communication delivered orally or in writing, or by a signal which tells the military person receiving the order what to do or not to do. The command must be specific to an individual, i.e., it must be capable of individual execution by the person to whom it is addressed, and justified by military as well as by civil law and usage. The disobedience must be wilful and deliberate. In the armed forces, the term 'superior officer', does not mean only a commissioned officer; it is a relative term and when used in relation to a person subject to military laws, includes a junior commissioned officer, warrant officer and non-commissioned officer, or its equivalent in all the three services. The expression 'superior officer' means not only a superior in rank, but also a senior in the same grade, where that seniority gives power of command according to the usages of the service. [AA s. 41].

A military person charged with an offence may be taken into custody by orders of a superior officer. An officer may order into military custody any officer, though he may be of a higher rank, if he has been engaged in a quarrel, affray or disorder. An officer who has been involved in a quarrel, affray, or disorder is bound to obey the order of arrest given by another officer, and if he refuses the order of arrest or uses criminal force or assaults such officer, he would be committing an offence under the military laws. Similarly, while in custody, if a military person uses criminal force, assaults any person, resists an escort, or disobeys any order, he would be committing an offence under the military law [AA s. 42].

The officers and staff of the military police, exercising power under the command of the provost-marshal, have special powers of apprehension and custody of military offenders. A military person who impedes the provost-marshal or any person lawfully acting on his behalf, or refuses to assist a provost-marshal or any person lawfully acting on his behalf would be breaching the military law and can be tried by a military court for such breaches [AA s. 42 (f)].

Offences Relating to Enrolment

When a person who wants to be enrolled appears before the prescribed enrolling officer (a designated commissioned officer), the conditions of service and other questions set forth in the prescribed form of enrolment are explained to him. The person is cautioned that if he gives a false answer to any question, he shall be liable to punishment under the military law. If subsequently it is discovered that the enrolled person has given a false answer to any question in the form of enrolment, he can be charged and punished accordingly. Similarly, if an individual enrols himself in the armed forces fraudulently, without obtaining a regular discharge from another corps or service, he can be tried for the offence of fraudulent enrolment. [AA ss. 43 and 44].

Disgraceful, Unbecoming Conduct and Ill-treatment

Being members of a disciplined force, armed forces personnel are required to maintain certain standards of conduct and behaviour, whether on duty or otherwise. Any deviation in conduct is considered unlawful. AA s. 45 provides:

> Any officer, junior commissioned officer or warrant officer who behaves in a manner unbecoming his position and the character expected of him shall, on conviction by court-martial, if he is an officer, be liable to be cashiered or to suffer such less punishment as is in this Act mentioned; and, if he is a junior commissioned officer or a warrant officer, be liable to be dismissed or to suffer such less punishment as mentioned in the AA.

The behaviour expected of an officer would include readiness to do one's duty under all circumstances, with mental robustness and strength of will, compatible with the ethics of courageous fighting men of the armed forces. For behaviour to be blameworthy, it must be unbecoming both of the accused's position and the character expected of him as an officer or junior commissioned officer. It should offend the accepted rules of social behaviour and be unsuitable in terms of character from a moral point of view. In serious cases of unbecoming conduct, instead of taking disciplinary action against the offenders, the armed forces in India have preferred administrative dismissal or removal from service. Similarly an officer, JCO, WO or NCO who uses criminal force against or ill treats his subordinate in rank or position would also be committing an offence under the military law. [AA s. 47].

A charge of "disgraceful conduct" could be brought against a military person if he acts in a cruel, indecent or unnatural manner; or malingers, or feigns or produces disease or infirmity in himself, or intentionally delays his cure or aggravates his disease or infirmity; or with an intention to render himself or any other person unfit for service, voluntarily causes hurt to himself or another person. [AA s. 46]. Feigning disease means not merely that the person concerned reports himself sick when he is not sick, but that he does so when he knows that he is not sick, pretending to feel, symptoms which do not exist. Malingering goes further, in that it implies some act committed with the object of producing the appearance of disease or infirmity.

A person subject to the AA if found in a state of intoxication, whether on duty or not could be punished under AA s. 48. A person suspected of being intoxicated cannot be put through any drill or tests for the purpose of ascertaining his condition. [RA para 393 (b)]. Mere abusive and violent language used by an intoxicated person, as the result of being taken into custody, should not be used as the ground for framing a charge of using threatening language to a superior officer under AA s. 40 (b) or (c). A care therefore must be taken to avoid bringing intoxicated person in contact with their superiors. The offence of intoxication cannot be tried jointly.

Offences Relating to Illegal Arrests and Confinements

A military person who is accused of committing an offence may be arrested. The superior officers have an absolute right to arrest a military offender. There are two different types of arrest: 'open' and 'closed'. Open arrest is similar to being on bail, subject to certain conditions and restrictions which may be ordered by the commanding officer, with the individual still having the liberty to move around. When the accused is under closed arrest, he is deprived of the freedom of movement and may be detained in a guard room or place of safe custody. Irregularities in connection with arrest and confinement are offences under military law. In the armed forces, it is the duty of the commanding officer to take care that a person under his command, when charged with an offence, is not detained in custody for more than 48 hours without the charge being investigated. In order to detain a person for more than 48 hours, sanction from the higher military authorities is required. A military commander who unnecessarily detains a person in arrest or confinement without bringing him to trial, or an officer who having the custody of an offender, fails to deliver him for trial could be held liable under military law.

Similarly, if a guard commander (i) releases any person committed to his charge without proper authority, or (ii) refuses to receive any prisoner or person so committed, or (iii) wilfully or without reasonable excuse allows any person committed to his charge to escape would be committing an offence. Duty is also imposed upon a military person under lawful custody. If he escapes or attempts to escape, he would commit an offence under military law. A prisoner is said to 'escape' when he unlawfully goes out of sight, beyond the control of the person in whose custody he is placed. The attempt to escape is itself a substantive offence. [AA s. 49-51].

Extortion, Corruption and Offences relating to Property

A military person who commits extortion or without proper authority exacts from any person money, provisions or service would be held liable under military law. In the armed forces, committing theft of government or private property, dishonest misappropriations, criminal breach of trust, or defraud are considered serious breaches of military discipline and are punishable offences. Stealing from a person subject to military law is regarded as a particularly disgraceful military offence, considering that in the daily routine of military life, persons must constantly leave exposed their arms, uniform and equipment, as well as their private property, such as money, trusting into the honour of their comrades. In a number of cases, the pay of offenders has been withheld due to theft of property. A mere error or irregularity in accounts or a mistaken mis-application of property does not constitute an offence under the law. There must be an intention to defraud on the part of the accused, either for his own benefit or the benefit of some other person.

The government issues property like arms, ammunition, equipment and clothing to military persons for their use. If they lose, sell, pawn, destroy or run away with such property, they will be held liable under military law. Wilful destruction of military property or destruction of property belonging to any other military force or institution is a serious military offence. Military persons are also expected to take care of animals entrusted to their care. In case they are found guilty of killing, injuring or ill treating such animals, they would be prosecuted under military law. [AA ss. 52-55].

False accusations

Making a false accusation against a comrade or making a statement affecting the character of another military person is an offence under the military legal system. Making a false report, declaration or certificate with the intention of defrauding or obtaining for oneself any allowance or other advantage or privilege is a serious military offence. Similarly, when signing any document relating to pay, arms, ammunition, equipment, supplies or stores, or any property of the Government fraudulently leaving in blank any material part for which his signature is a voucher is a military offence. [AA ss. 56-58].

Offences relating to Court Martial

Courts martial are *ad hoc* military courts. A court martial is, in fact, not a part of the judiciary and is not included among the courts established under the Constitution. The military law provides that a military person would be held liable if he commits the following offences in relation to a court martial:

(a) Being duly summoned or ordered to attend as a witness before a court martial, failing to attend wilfully or without reasonable excuse.

(b) Refusing to take an oath or make an affirmation legally required by a court-martial to be taken or made.

(c) Refusing to produce or deliver any document in one's power or control legally required by a court-martial to be produced or delivered by one.

(d) Refusing when a witness to answer any question which one is by law bound to answer.

(e) Being guilty of contempt of court-martial by using insulting or threatening language, or by causing any interruption or disturbance in the proceedings of such court.

A military person can also be convicted for giving false evidence, i.e., if he has been duly sworn or affirmed before any court-martial and makes any statement which is false, and which he either knows or believes to be false or does not believe to be true. [AA ss. 59 and 60].

A person subject to AA, who wilfully gave a false evidence before a court martial, the court may bring his conduct to the notice of the proper military authority, and may also order him to be placed in military custody with a view to his punishment by an officer exercising authority under AA s. 80, 83, 84 and 85, or to his trial by a court-martial [AR 150(1) and (2)].

Good Order and Discipline

Observance of good order and discipline is expected from all military persons, be they on duty or otherwise. It is also the duty of all ranks in the armed forces to uphold the good reputation of the service. AA s. 63, which deals with "violation of good order and discipline", provides: "Any person subject to this Act who is guilty of any act or omission which, though not specified in this Act, is prejudicial to good order and military discipline shall, on conviction by court-martial, be liable to suffer imprisonment for a term which may extend to seven years or such less punishment as is in this Act mentioned." The following are few instances of violation of good order and discipline in the Army: improperly using or obtaining railway warrants, causing disturbance in the lines, sending an anonymous letter to authorities, improperly using government transport for private use, using criminal force to a comrade, stating falsehood to a superior officer, and using unfair means in departmental examinations. [AA s. 63].

Miscellaneous Offences

AA s. 64 lists few additional offences which can be committed by a person subject to Act:

(a) When in command failing to provide due reparations,

(b) Defiling a place of worship, or insulting the religious feelings,

(c) Attempting to commit suicide,

(d) An NCO or Sepoy carrying a rifle, sword or other offensive weapon in civil area when off duty,

(e) Directly or indirectly accepting or obtaining any gratification,

(f) Committing an offence against the property or person, while serving out side the country.

Attempt

Attempt to commit the offences specified in AA ss. 34 to 64 are, except where such attempts are specifically provided for (for example, at attempt to desert) triable under AA s. 65. Attempt to commit civil offences are not triable under this section but are triable under AA s. 69 read with IPC s. 511.

Abetment of offences

Abetment is an instigation to a person to do an act in a certain way or aid some other person in doing an act which in an offence. Abetment can be committed only when there is positive evidence of either instigation or conspiracy or intentional aid. Essentials of abetment are: (i) An abettor, (ii) He must abet, and (iii) The abetment must be an offence. Abettor is a person who abets either the commission of an offence, or the commission of an act which would be an offence, if committed by a person capable by law of committing an offence with the same intention or knowledge as that of the abettor. For example, A instigates B to murder C. B refuses to do so. A is guilty of abetting B to commit murder.

An abetment to any of the offences specified in AA sections 34 to 64, if the offfence abetted has been committed in consequence of the abetment, is triable under AA s. 66. An abetment to an offence, if that offence has not been committed in consequence of the abetment, is punishable under AA ss. 67 and 68.

Civil offences

AA s. 69 provides that a person subject to AA who commits any civil offence (subject to AA s. 70) shall be deemed to be guilty of an offence under the Act, and can be tried by a court martial. AA s.70 prohibits trial of a person subject to AA by a court martial, for three serious civil offences: (i) murder against a person not subject the military, naval or air force law; or (ii) culpable homicide not amounting to murder against such a person, or (iii) rape in relation to such a person However, a person subject to AA can be tried by a court martial for these civil offences, if the said offence was committed:

(a) while on active service, or

(b) at any place outside India, or

(c) at a frontier post specified by the Central Government by notification.

Scale of Punishments

Under AA s. 71, punishments may be inflicted in respect of offences committed by persons subject to the Army Act and convicted by courts-martial, according to the following scale:

(a) Death.

(b) Transportation for life or for any period not less than seven years.

(c) Imprisonment, either rigorous or simple, for any period not exceeding fourteen years.

(d) Cashiering, in the case of officers.

(e) Dismissal from the service.

(f) Reduction to the ranks or to a lower rank or grade or place in the list of their rank, in the case of warrant officers; and reduction to the ranks or to a lower rank or grade, in the case of non-commissioned officers: provided that a warrant officer reduced to the ranks shall not be required to serve in the ranks as a sepoy.

(g) Forfeiture of seniority of rank, in the case of officers, junior commissioned officers, warrant officers and non-commissioned officers; and forfeiture of all or any part of their service for the purpose of promotion, in the case of any of them whose promotion depends upon length of service.

(h) Forfeiture of service for the purpose of increased pay, pension or any other prescribed purpose.

(i) Severe reprimand or reprimand, in the case of officers, junior commissioned officers, warrant officers and non-commissioned officers.

(j) Forfeiture of pay and allowances for a period not exceeding three months for an offence committed on active service.

(k) Forfeiture, in the case of a person sentenced to cashiering or dismissal from the service, of all arrears of pay and allowances and other public money due to him at the time of such cashiering or dismissal.

(l) Stoppage of pay and allowances until any proved loss or damage occasioned by the offence of which he is convicted is made good.

Within the maximum punishment prescribed by AA ss. 34 to 69, the court-martial has discretion to apportion punishment according to the degree of guilt of the person convicted. A sentence of death can only be passed by a GCM with the concurrence of at least two-third of the members; or by a SGCM with the concurrence of all the members. [AA s. 132 (2) and (3)]. A person who is sentenced by a court martial to death continues to be subject to AA till the sentence is executed. [AA s. 123 (4)]. An officer is to be sentenced to be cashiered before he is awarded any of the punishments specified in (a) to (c). [AA s. 74].

Combination of Punishment

The following combined sentences are legal under AA s. 73:

(a) Cashiering, imprisonment, stoppage and forfeiture of pay and allowances in the case of an officer.

(b) Imprisonment, dismissal, reduction (WO and NCO), stoppage and forfeiture.

(c) Dismissal, reduction (NCO), stoppage and forfeiture.

(d) Forfeiture of seniority of rank, forfeiture of service for promotion, severe reprimand and, forfeiture and stoppages in case of an officer, JCO, WO or NCO.

Award of Fine by Court martial

In case of charges under AA s. 69, a court martial can also award any punishment, assigned for the offence under any law in force in India. For example, a fine is not specified as a punishment in AA s. 71, but a court martial exercising jurisdiction under AA s. 69 can award a fine and such fine is recoverable under AA ss. 90 (f), 91 (h) or 174, if the civil offence in question is punishable with a fine under the law in force in India.

Penal Deductions

The pay of a person subject to the AA is protected as provided in AA s. 25. A person subject to the AA is entitled to receive his pay without any deductions other than such deductions as may be authorized by proper authority. A penal deduction is, in principle, a deduction made as a penalty for an offence of which the accused has been convicted and constitutes part or the whole of his punishment. The term has, however, acquired a somewhat specialized meaning and every deduction that is authorized in AA s. 90 and 91 must be understood to be penal irrespective of the common use of that word. AA s. 95 allows penal deductions to be made also from any public money due to a person subject to the AA, other than a pension. Other deductions, which are not penal, may be made from the pay and allowances of a person subject to the AA to meet regimental claims or compulsory contributions to any provident fund or other fund approved by the Central Government. [MML, Vol. I, Ch I, para 16].

How penal deductions to be made: After the finalization of the court of inquiry where the individual has been blamed, a charge sheet to be raised and the particulars of charge must state those facts and the sum of the loss or damage as required vide AR 30 (6). An example of such charge-sheets is given in MML Vol. II (2011 ed.) at page 266-267, see Charge-Sheet No. 87 to 89. The court martial or the officer exercising authority under AA s. 80, 83, 84 and 85, having regard to the gravity of offence and the quantum and magnitude of loss as proved in evidence, should consider the desirability of awarding the punishment of stoppage of pay applying yardstick of proportionality, accountability and responsibility.

The court martial acting under AA s. 71 (l), or officers exercising authority under AA s. 83, 84 or 85 will sentence the offender to stoppage of pay. Similarly during trial under AA s. 80, the accused to be awarded penal deduction under s. 80(i). The recovery, which is mandatory and effected by CDA/PAO on receiving intimation of award will take place under the provisions of AA s. 90 (d), 91 (e) or (g) as applicable. The provisions of AA s 94 and 95 will apply for the implementation of award. In this connection, you must also refer to RA para 435, which is reproduced here:

> **Responsibility for damage by Fire**: An officer, JCO, WO, OR or any other person in military employ will be liable to make good damage done to Government property by a fire which is the result of his own neglect, but in view of the large sum to which liability may extend in such cases, the amount to be recovered usually will be limited to a sum not exceeding one week's pay of the individual who is held responsible.

Collective Fine

The AA s 89 authorizes the imposition of a collective fine on a company or similar unit for the purpose of enforcing collective responsibility. It states, "Whenever any weapon or part of a weapon forming part of the equipment of a half squardon, battery, company or other similar unit is lost or stolen, the officer commanding the army, army corps, division or independent brigade to which such units belongs may, after obtaining the report of a court of inquiry impose a collective fine upon the JCOs, WOs, NCOs and men of such unit, or upon so many of them as in his judgement, should be held responsible for such loss or theft. Such fine shall be assessed as a percentage on the pay of the individuals on whom it falls."

The provision of collective fine as contained in s. 89 is an exception to the general scheme of AA, under which individual responsibility is the basis for punishment or for penal deduction. The powers granted under this provision are of an administrative and not judicial character. The imposition of a collective fine upon persons of a unit is not a bar to trial by court-martial of any person of that unit, whose individual act or omission may have contributed to the loss. The amount of the fine to be imposed is regulated by AR 186 and the fine must be assessed as a percentage on the pay of the individuals on whom it falls. Fine cannot be imposed in respect of weapons or parts of weapons not enumerated in AR 186. A collective fine cannot be imposed upon officers. [AA s. 89 and notes]

Penal deductions under AA s. 89 and 90 could be categorised as 'mandatory' and 'submissive'. The penal deductions under the mandatory clause are those which can be legally affected on receipt of the intimation from the concerned authority. For instance deductions under AA s. 90(a) are mandatory vide Rule 526(a) of P&A Regs and CDA can legally effect them on receipt of intimation about the absence. Deductions under AA s. 90(b) are permissive in nature and may be made under special orders by the Central Government vide Rule 13 and 528(a) of P&A Regs (Officers) Army. Similarly penal deductions under AA s. 91(a), (b) and (c) have been made mandatory, whereas under AA s. 91(d) are permissive and may be made under the orders of the Central Government or other specified officer. For more details on Penal Deductions see AO 7/2003/DV.

Difference between Cashiering and Dismissal

Cashiering can only be awarded to an officer, as a court martial sentence. Whereas dismissal can be awarded to every person subject to the AA, as a court-martial punishment (AA s. 71) or by way of an administrative action under the AR 19. Cashiering is the more ignominious form of dismissal.

Cashiering must precede the sentence of imprisonment and above to an officer; whereas no such stipulation applies to persons below officer rank. Normally an officer who has been cashiered cannot hold an appointment under the government. [AA s. 71 and 74. Also see note 9 to AA s. 71].

Dismissal: Effective Date

A sentence of dismissal awarded by a court-martial shall take effect from the date on which the sentence is promulgated to the person under sentence, or except in the case of an officer, from such subsequent date as may be specified by the CO at the time of such promulgation. When the dismissal is combined with imprisonment which is to be carried out in a military prison or military custody, the dismissal shall not take place until the date on which the prisoner is released from a military prison or from military custody. When dismissal is combined with imprisonment which is to be carried out in a civil prison, the dismissal shall not take effect until the date on which the prisoner is received into a civil prison. [AR 168].

Period of custody to be set off against the imprisonment

When a person subject to the AA is sentenced by a court-martial to a term of imprisonment (not being an imprisonment in default of payment of fine), the period spent by him in civil or military custody during investigation, inquiry or trial, shall be set off against the term of imprisonment imposed upon him. The liability of such person to undergo imprisonment on such order of sentence shall be restricted to the remainder term of imprisonment imposed upon him. [AA s. 169A].

Pardon and Remission

A person subject to the AA, when convicted by a court-martial of any offence, the Central Government or the COAS or, in the case of a sentence, which he could have confirmed or which did not, require confirmation, the officer commanding the army, army corps, division or independent brigade in which such person at the time of conviction was serving, or the prescribed officer may:

(a) either with or without conditions which the person sentenced accepts, pardon the person or remit the whole or any part of the punishment awarded ; or

(b) mitigate the punishment awarded ; or

(c) commute such punishment for any less punishment or punishments mentioned in the AA;

(d) either with or without conditions which the person sentenced accepts, release the person on parole. [AA s. 179].

Suspension of Sentence

A person subject to AA if sentenced by a court-martial to imprisonment, his sentence may be suspended by the Central Government, the COAS, or any officer empowered to convene a GCM or SGCM. For suspending a sentence, it is immaterial whether the offender has already been committed to prison or to military custody. Where a sentence is suspended, the offender is to be released from custody. The authority suspending the sentence may order that the offender be committed to undergo the unexpired portion of the sentence, or the sentence be remitted. [AA ss. 182, 184 and 186]. A periodical review of the suspension of sentence, at intervals of not more than four months must be carried out by the competent authority. He may keep a sentence further suspended. [AA s.187].

In the case of a sentence of dismissal combined with imprisonment has been awarded by a court-martial, and sentence of imprisonment is suspended, then, such dismissal shall not take effect until so ordered by the competent authority under AA s. 182. [AA s. 190].

Where the sentence of imprisonment has been imposed by a court-martial other than a SCM, the confirming officer may, when confirming the sentence, direct that the offender be not committed to prison or to military custody until the orders of the authority authorized to issue suspension have been obtained. Where a sentence of imprisonment is imposed by a SCM, the officer holding the trial or the officer authorized to approve of the sentence may issue similar direction. [AA s. 183].

Suspension of sentences is primarily applicable to offences of a military nature only, although in special cases it may be applied to offences of a civil character. In all cases special attention should be directed to the following points: (i) the age and previous character of the offender, (ii) whether the offence is a first one, (iii) whether the offence was premeditated, (iv) whether the offender was at the time subjected to any special stress, fatigue, disability or temptation, and (v) whether the offender was influenced by others older or of worse character than himself.

Unsatisfactory conduct subsequent to suspension will justify an order to put a suspended sentence into execution, whilst a mere negative abstention from crime would point to the advisability of directing a reconsideration of the sentence at a later date. A person under a suspended sentence is to be regarded entirely as a free man, and is to be placed under no disability whatever excepting only the liability of having his suspended sentence put into execution if he misbehaves. [MML Vol I, Ch. IV, para 119].

Pardon and condonation of Punishment

The accused, at the time of his general plea of "Guilty" or "Not Guilty" to a charge for an offence, may offer a plea in bar of trial on the ground that the offence has been pardoned or condoned by competent military authority [AR 53 (1) (b)]. It has long been recognized as a custom of the service that a military offence can be condoned. For the purpose of barring a trial condonation means such conduct on the part of a competent authority i.e., an authority having power to determine that the charge should not be proceeded with—as is inconsistent with subsequently trying the offender, and as would make it inequitable to do so; it must be a deliberate and intentional act, done with full knowledge of all material facts. If, with full knowledge of the facts, competent authority removes an officer, or allows him to resign, he should not afterwards be tried by court-martial for his offence. The fact that after trial, but before confirmation, the accused has been employed in active operations does not effect the legal validity of the sentence, but affords ground for pardon. Pardon or condonation by competent authority, if proved, operates as a bar to the trial of offender. [Notes to AR 53].

Considerations Affecting Sentence

The court martial, when passing sentence will have regard not only to nature and degree of offence and the previous character of the accused, but also to the consequences of punishment awarded.

Sentences must vary according to the requirements of discipline, but in ordinary circumstances, and for the first offence, a sentence should be light. Care must be taken to discriminate between offences due to youth, temper, sudden temptation, grave and sudden provocation or unaccustomed surroundings, and those due to premeditated misconduct. Persons, who are convicted by court martial of an offence under AA s. 52 or 69, should ordinarily be sentenced to imprisonment and should undergo their sentence in a civil prison. When an offender is convicted on two or more charges, the sentence should be that which is considered adequate for the gravest of the offences, with some addition for each of the other charges.

When a soldier has been convicted by court martial of theft, misappropriation or receiving with guilty knowledge, AA s. 151 provides for the restitution of the stolen property in certain cases. If the soldier has been sentenced 'to be placed under stoppages in respect of the property stolen or unlawfully obtained', and any sum of money that may have been found on him has been appropriated to the above use, he should be placed under stoppages for the balance only of the stoppage awarded by the court.

A court martial in framing sentences will observe the following rules; (i) terms of imprisonment for one or more years to be recorded exactly, (ii) for one month or upwards be recorded in months; and (iii) sentences consisting partly of months and partly of days should be recorded in months and days.

A copy of RA para 468 is to be kept in every Court Martial Box.[For more details see RA para 468].

A court martial awarding punishment should take into consideration the following points:

(a) **The maintenance of discipline**: The proper amount of punishment to be inflicted is the least amount by which discipline can effectively be maintained.

(b) **Degrees of criminality**: A NCO should be dealt with more severally than a sepoy; where several offenders are found guilty of the same offence it may be proper to award different amounts of punishment.

(c) **Premeditation**: An accused who has clearly made long preparation to commit some crime should be more severely punished than one who has acted on the spur of the moment.

(d) **Provocation**: While provocation is no defence, the court must take this into consideration.

(e) **Previous convictions**: An habitual offender deserves more punishment than an infrequent offender, and a first offender, if possible, be treated leniently.

(f) **Prevalence of offence**: When there is a general prevalence of offences or of offence of a particular kind, an example may be necessary, and therefore a severe punishment may properly be awarded, in respect of an offence which would otherwise receive a more lenient punishment.

The court must award such punishment as the members consider just and proper and must not presume that the convening authority, in sending the case for trial, took a more serious view of the facts. [MML Vol I, Ch. IV, para 84].

Execution of Sentence of Imprisonment

The sentence of imprisonment awarded to a person subject to the AA, other than an officer, JCO or a NCO will be dealt as follows:

(a) A sentence of imprisonment not exceeding 3 month will, unless accompanied by dismissal, be carried out by confinement in military custody.

(b) A sentence of imprisonment exceeding 3 months whether accompanied by dismissal or not will be carried out by confinement in a civil prison.

[RA para 494]

CHAPTER 3

ACTION AGAINST MILITARY OFFENDER

Arrest and Custody

The Army Act provides that a military person who is charged with an offence may be taken into military custody. The provisions relating to arrest are as follows:

(a) A military person may be ordered into military custody be any superior officer;

(b) An officer may order into military custody any officer, though he may be of a higher rank, engaged in a quarrel, affray or disorder; [AA s. 101 (2) and (3)].

(c) A provost marshal, his deputies and assistants may arrest and detain any person subject to military law; [AA s. 107(3)].

(d) A police officer or magistrate may arrest within his jurisdiction a military person who is accused of an offence or who is a deserter, on a written request of the commanding officer of such person; [AA ss. 104 and 105(1)].

(e) A police officer may arrest without warrant a person reasonably believed to be a military person and a deserter or travelling without authority. [AA s. 105(2)]. [MML Vol. I, Ch. III, para 1]

For arrest no warrant is required. Basically military custody includes two types of arrests—the "open arrest" and the "closed arrest". The restraint imposed under each type is according to the usages of the service and the regulations. Under closed arrest, a person is usually confined to a room or barracks and remains under the escort of a person of equal rank. Under open arrest, he remains under a moral restraint not to go beyond a certain area, usually the camp.

Arrest when necessary

It is not necessary that every person charged with an offence, must be put under close arrest. If the offence is not serious it may be investigated and disposed of without placing the offender under arrest. The following factors may be considered before placing an individual under close arrest.

(a) Availability of the individual for trial

(b) Individual may not abscond

(c) Individual may not harm to himself

(d) Individual may not temper with evidence or influence prosecution witnesses

(e) In case the offence is serious like murder, mutiny or the ends of discipline require an immediate arrest to set an example. [RA Para 392 and MML Vol I Ch III, para1].

Escorts

An officer, JCO, WO or NCO under close arrest will be placed under the charge of an escort consisting of another officer, JCO, WO or NCO of the same rank, if possible and will not leave his quarters or tent except to take such exercise, under supervision, as the medical officer considers necessary. An officer, JCO, WO or NCO may, however, if circumstances so require, be placed for custody under the charge of a guard, piquet, patrol, sentry or provost-marshal. An officer, JCO or WO under arrest will not wear sash, sword, belt or spurs. [RA para 394 (b) and (c), and 395 (a)].

A sepoy under close arrest, will be placed in confinement under charge of a guard, piquet, patrol, sentry or provost-marshal and will be searched and deprived of knives or other weapons. The accommodation usually available in barracks for the temporary confinement of sepoys under close arrest is the guard detention room attached to a guard room, and similar smaller rooms for the confinement of those who are to be kept apart. [RA para 395 (b)].

Escorts for Women Officers

A women officer under closed arrest shall all the time remain under an escort of another women officer. Under no circumstances a women officer will be kept under a male escort. Where another women officer is not available in the unit, a women officer from other unit/stations will be made available under station arrangements. During her visit to other places for purposes of investigation, recording of summary of evidence, attending her trial etc., she shall be escorted by another woman officer who may be assisted by another male officer. [AG Branch letter No. A/56102/AG/DV-1, dated 26 June 1996].

Arrest in cases of Intoxication

An OR who is intoxicated will be placed under close arrest alone, if possible, in a guard detention room. He may be deprived of his bedding and boots, except when the weather is cold and he is likely to suffer in consequence. He will be visited, and his condition ascertained, at least every two hours by a NCO of the guard and, an escort. In case any symptoms of serious illness are observed, a medical officer to be approached immediately. A person suspected of being intoxicated will not be put through any drill or test for the purpose of ascertaining his condition. A person charged with intoxication will not be brought before an officer for investigation of the charge until he is sober. For this purpose 24 hours should usually be allowed to elapse before the investigation. [RA para 393].

Release from arrest

The release of an officer placed under arrest may be ordered either by the officer who imposed the arrest or by an officer superior to him. Once an arrest has been ordered and the matter has been reported to superior authority, it would not be proper to order the release of person without the sanction of such superior authority. An officer could be released from arrest without prejudice to re-arrest. In such a case, where such re-arrest is considered justified or necessary, it will always be affected by the person ordering the release or by some higher authority. Normally when an officer is released unconditionally, he will not be again arrested on the same charge unless circumstances had changed and some new conditions arose which justified the action. The general rules applicable to the arrest of officers apply to JCOs, WOs and other ranks also. These are contained in AA s. 101-105; and RA paras 391-397, 401 and 402.

Restrictions under Open Arrest

An officer, JCO or WO under open arrest may take exercise at stated periods and within stated limits, which will usually be the precincts of the barracks or camp of his unit. These limits could be enlarged at the discretion of the CO. An arrested person will not appear in any place of amusement or entertainment, or at public assemblies. He will also not appear outside his quarters or tent dressed otherwise than in uniform. [RA para 394(d)].

The COAS or prescribed officer may direct withholding of the whole or any part of pay and allowances of a person subject to AA while he is in custody or under suspension from duty on a charge for an offence, in order to give effect to the provision of clause (b) of AA ss. 90 and 91. The underlying principle in withholding pay and allowances in such case is that a person, while under arrest or suspension, does not perform any military duty and, therefore, his pay and allowances must be restricted. [AA ss. 93 and 94].

Identification Parade

When circumstances render identification of an alleged offender necessary, the identification should be carried out in the presence of an officer. It is essential that identification parade is conducted in such a manner as to be fair to both the suspect and the witness. Parades for the identification of a person subject to AA by a witness is divided into two categories:

(a) Where there is reason to believe that the military person against whom a witness is prepared to give evidence belongs to a particular unit or sub-unit, and other evidence on the charge under investigation has not yet permitted the singling out of any particular person.

(b) Where the evidence permits of a definite person being singled out, but where it is desired to determine whether a certain witness is, or is not, able to recognize the suspect.

As regard parade of the first category, all personnel of the unit or sub-unit be assembled. The following instructions are to be observed in all parades of the second category. Clauses (i) and (v), (vi) and (vii) will also be observed for parades of the first category:

(i) Parade should take place as soon as possible after the offence has been discovered.

(ii) The witness or witnesses must not see the suspect under escort or in custody before the parade.

(iii) Ten or twelve military personnel of similar physique, appearance and turn out will be paraded. Personnel should not be paraded bare-headed. It is up to witness to ask a particular person in the parade to uncover his head.

(iv) The suspect should be permitted to choose his own position in the rank of the parade. No communication which will facilitate identification must be made to any witness who is waiting his/her turn to identify.

(v) The witness should be instructed to walk round the ranks, and if he/she is prepared definitely to identify a particular person, to touch him on the shoulder without speaking. If the witness cannot make any identification, he/she is to be told that he/she can report any suspicions that he/she may have to the officer in charge of the parade.

(vi) When walking round the ranks, the witness should not be followed too closely nor should he/she be spoken to.

(vii) When there is more than one witness, each witness will walk round the ranks separately. No witness shall be allowed to observe the parade or the actions of any other witness till his/her turn comes.

(viii) The suspect will be permitted to change his position in the ranks after the departure of each witness and before the arrival of the next. A witness who has completed identification must not be permitted to communicate with one who is awaiting his/her turn to identify.

When the person has been identified, his/her demeanour, and any statement made by him at the time of identification, should be carefully noted. The report of the officer in charge of the identification will include the place, date and hour of the parade, the number of persons on parade, the name of each witness and the name of person(s) identified. [RA para 406].

Investigation and Disposal of Charge

Duty of Commanding Officer: Under AA s. 50 (b), it is the duty of a person subject to the Army Act, who commits any person into military custody to deliver at the time or within 48 hours thereafter to the officer or other person into whose custody the offender is committed, an account in writing signed by himself of the offence with which the person so committed is charged. If such person fails to do so, he could be charged under AA s. 50 (b). In case a charge report is not received within 48 hours, or other evidence sufficient to justify the continued arrest is not forthcoming, the commanding officer will, at the expiration of seventy-two hours from the time of committal, will order the release of the person in custody (without prejudice to his re-arrest).

The commander of the guard will, on the request of any person received into custody, inform him of the rank and name of the person preferring charges against him or ordering his arrest, and give to him a copy of the charge report as soon as he himself receives it. [RA para 401].

Delay reports

In every case where a person subject to the Army Act, who is not on active service, is in military custody for a period longer than eight days without a court-martial for his trial having been ordered to assemble, or without a punishment having been awarded him under AA s. 80, the CO shall make a report [in the form specified in AR Appendix III] to the officer empowered to convene a general or a district court-martial for the trial of such person. Such report shall be made to at intervals of every eight days until a court-martial is ordered to assemble, or a punishment is awarded under s. 80, or such person is released from custody as the case may be.

A copy of every such report made on or after the forty-eighth day of such custody shall be sent by the CO direct to the Deputy JAG of the command in which such person is held in custody. Detention in custody beyond two months of a person who is not on active service and in whose case a court-martial is not ordered to assemble requires the sanction of the COAS. Such detention beyond three months requires the sanction of the Central Government. [AR 27].

Unnecessary Detention

If necessary an accused person may be released from arrest without prejudice to his re-arrest, if trial cannot be convened within 2 or 3 months. If his detention beyond a period of two or three months is considered necessary, steps should be taken to obtain the sanction well in advance. An accused person should not be kept in such detention in anticipation of a sanction. Detaining an accused in custody beyond two or three months without a sanction, makes such detention illegal and a post-facto sanction obtained would not render such detention legal. Under AR 33(6) an accused has a right to address a petition to the DJAG or AJAG of the command concerned if he is kept in custody longer than 48 days without being brought to trial or is not given full liberty for preparing his defence. Unnecessary detention of an accused without bringing him to trial amounts to an offence under AA s. 50 (a). [AR 27].

Investigation of Charge

The investigation of charges is to be carried out as prescribed in the AR 22. Every charge, whether against a JCO, WO or OR, should be investigated in the first instance by the company commander, at his company orderly room which will be held at such an hour as will allow of an offender remanded for disposal by the CO being ready to go before him at the appointed time. [RA para 402]. For more details on investigation of charge see next chapter.

Charge-sheet

A charge means an accusation contained in a charge-sheet that a person subject to the AA has been guilty of an offence. [AR 28 (2)]. Each charge shall state one offence only, and in no case shall an offence be described in the alternative in the same charge. Each charge shall be divided into two parts:

(a) statement of the offence; and

(b) statement of the particulars of the act neglect or omission constituting the offence. [AR 30].

Statement of offence

The statement of offence must be in the words of the section of the AA, which creates the offence. If different words are used, it is likely that an error may be made and an altogether new offence which is not declared as an offence by the law may come to be averred. It may result in charge being bad at a later stage. For example: AA s. 56 (a) declares the "making of a false accusation against any person subject to that Act knowing or having reason to believe such accusation to be false" an offence. If in the statement of the offence it is stated instead "making a false statement against any person" the statement of offence does not amount to the offence contemplated by s. 56 (a) and as such, the charge would be bad in law. Please refer AR Appendix II, Part III for statement of offences.

Preparation of Charge-sheet

The charge-sheet is usually prepared by the CO or adjutant of the accused's unit. However, in the case of a trial by GCM or DCM; AR 37 makes the convening officer equally responsible for its correctness. It must be signed by the officer in actual command of the unit to which the accused belongs. If the accused is attached to another unit, the charge-sheet must be signed by the CO of the unit to which he is so attached. The order for the trial must be endorsed at the foot of the charge-sheet and signed by the convening officer or by a staff officer "for" him. Charge-sheet cannot be endorsed for trial by a staff officer as such.

The charge-sheet should contain the place and date of signature. If for reasons of security it is inadvisable to disclose the place of signature, it may be shown as "field". The date of signature is of assistance in ascertaining whether or not provisions of AR 34 regarding warning of the accused for trial, have been complied with. [AR 28-31].

The RA provides that in all cases for trial by GCM, and all cases of indecency, fraud, theft (except ordinary theft) and civil offences except simple assaults under the AA, the charge-sheet and summary of evidence, and all the exhibits will be referred by the convening officer to the deputy JAG of the command or deputy/assistant JAG of the Corps, before trial is ordered. The convening officer can also seek advice from the Assistant/ Deputy JAD in other cases of doubt or difficulty. [RA para 459]

Golden Rules for Framing a Charge-sheet

The framing of charge-sheet is not difficult, if following 'golden rules' are kept in mind:

1. Before determining what act, omission or neglect the individual has committed, refer to (i) relevant AA section and its notes, and (ii) in case of civil offence, related section of the BNS.
2. A single charge disclosing two separate offences should be avoided.
3. An alternate charge should not be preferred, where a special finding is possible under AA s. 139.
4. The statement of the particulars must be stated briefly in ordinary language and should support the statement of offence.
5. The exact or approximate date and time of offence should be averted in the particulars.
6. The charge-sheet should contain the place (or 'Field') and date of signature.
7. It must be signed by the officer in actual command of the unit to which accused belongs. [AR Appendix II (Parts I, II, III and IV); and para 403, 405 and 459 of the RA].

Alternative charges

A court martial has no power to find a person guilty of offence other than that with which he has is charged in the statement of offence. Therefore, alternative charges may be preferred in a charge-sheet when a doubt exists as to under which section of the AA the offence has been committed. Where the officer framing charge is doubtful whether the offence so capable of being proved by legal evidence is more accurately described by one word or expression, or by another, he may frame two or more alternative charges, each charge containing, one of the word or expressions which appear to the officer to be applicable to the facts as capable of proof. An alternative charge is not required where a special finding under AA s. 139

is permissible. An example of alternative charge given in MML Vol. II (2011 ed.) at page 261, see Charge-Sheet No. 60. [AA s. 139, note 1 and 2; AR 28 note 6]

Summary of Evidence

A summary of evidence is a written record of evidence for the prosecution and the defence, made by the commanding officer or by another officer on his orders, in relation to a charge against a person subject to the Army Act. It enables the commanding officer to determine whether or not, a prima facie case exists on the alleged charge, and whether the charge be proceeded with or dismissed.

The term 'summary' is sometimes misleading, because a summary of evidence is expected to be as far as possible a complete record of whatever relevant evidence that is available in respect of the charge(s) against the accused. In military law, when a disciplinary case develops into a court martial trial, the only previous record of the evidence that could be used, though to a very limited extent, at the trial is the summary of evidence. A summary of evidence must be in conformity with the rules of evidence.

Recording

Summary of evidence is recorded in every case where it is intended to remand the accused for trial by a GCM or DCM; or where the accused is an officer, JCO or WO, for summary disposal of charge under AA s. 83, 84 or 85. In case of SCM, a summary of evidence need not be made, if it is intended to try the accused forthwith without reference to superior authority. In such cases the CO must record sufficient evidence at the trial vide AR 118 to enable him to determine the sentence and the reviewing officer to know all the circumstances connected with the case.

The summary of evidence can be recorded by the CO himself or by an officer detailed by him for that purpose. [AR 23 (1)].

Procedure for Recording

The recording of the summary should preferably commence on the same day, on which the charges were heard and concluded as early as possible. The officer recording a summary of evidence has two separate duties to perform: (i) conduct a preliminary investigation into the case with a view to collect all available evidence; and (ii) recording of evidence. He must follow the following procedure:

1. The evidence of every witness who gave evidence before the CO must be taken down in narrative form as nearly as possible in his own words. The evidence of witnesses who did not appear before the CO may also be taken for either prosecution or defence, so long as it appears to be relevant.

2. In reducing the evidence to writing immaterial statements may be omitted and all hearsay and irrelevant matter should be excluded. However, if the accused insists that certain piece of evidence is material in his defence, the same should be recorded.

3. The accused must be allowed to put any reasonable question to a witness, and especially to put questions respecting any variance between the evidence taken down and that given before the CO. If the accused declines to cross-examine any witness the fact should accordingly be stated.

4. After the evidence against the accused has been recorded in the summary of evidence, the accused will be asked: "Do you wish to make any statement? Your are not obliged to say anything unless you wish to do so, but whatever you say will be taken down in writing and may be given in evidence." Any statement there upon made by the accused shall be taken down and read to him, but he will not be cross-examined upon it. The accused may also call his witnesses, including if he so desires, any witnesses as to character. The statement of accused recorded without formal caution shall be invalid. [AR 23 (3)].

5. If it is necessary to take additional summary, the accused must again be formally cautioned before he makes any further statement.

6. The fact that the accused was duly cautioned should be recorded in the summary. It is necessary to have an independent witness present when the accused is cautioned and when he makes the statement. Such independent witness apart from the officer recording the summary, would also be competent to prove the statement of the accused at the trial subsequently, if necessary.

7. The officer recording summary should act impartially, without favour or affection and make a faithful record of evidence. He must know that (i) summary of evidence cannot be taken on oath or affirmation, and (ii) the accused cannot claim to be represented by counsel at the taking of summary of evidence. The accused has the right to correspondence with his legal advisor.

Suspension of rules on the ground of military exigencies or the necessities of discipline

Where it appears to the officer convening a court-martial, or to the senior officer on the spot, that military exigencies, or the necessities of discipline render it impossible or inexpedient to observe the provisions of the Army Rules 23, 24 or 25 he may, by order under his hand, make declaration to that effect specifying the nature of such exigencies or necessities. Thereafter the trial or other proceedings shall be valid as if the rule mentioned in such declaration had not been contained herein. However, it is necessary that the accused is given full opportunity of making his defence. The power conferred by AR 96 to the convening officer should rarely be exercised except on active service and then only if absolutely necessary. If AR 23 is suspended, the accused must be informed before hand, the nature of the charge, the names of the witnesses and the effect of their evidence. The court must take care that the accused is not prejudiced by reason of the suspension, by not having received a summary of evidence.

Attendance of Witnesses

Any witness who is not subject to military law may be summoned to attend by order under the hand of the CO of the accused. [AR 23 (6)]. Summon is to be sent through the Magistrate under whose jurisdiction witness resides. When a witness is required to produce any particular document or any other thing in his possession or power, the same should be stated in the summons. [AA s. 135 (4) and note 7 to AR 137]. Appropriate Air Force or Naval authority should be approached for the attendance of witnesses subject to the Air Force Act and the Navy Act.

Importance of summary of evidence

The summary of evidence is a basic document for initiation of disciplinary proceedings against an accused. A properly recoded summary of evidence enables the CO and the convening authority to decide whether charge against the individual is to be proceeded with or dismissed. It help the officers of JAG branch to examine the case and advice the convening authority accordingly. It informs the prosecutor of the nature of the evidence sought to be produced at the trial. A summary of evidence assists the court in deciding whether they should accept a plea of guilty if offered; and if accepted, in determining the appropriate sentence. A badly recorded summary of evidence discloses faulty investigation, which may delay the administration of justice and also defeat the purpose for which it is recorded.

Difference between court of Inquiry and summary of evidence

A court of inquiry is a fact finding mission which merely collects evidence on orders of certain authority for a certain purpose. In a summary of evidence the evidence is collected against the accused, while in a court of inquiry there is no accused. Even if a court of inquiry finds blame against any individual for certain lapses, is does not from the basis for bringing him to trial by court martial.

Options available after completion of Summary of Evidence

After completion of summary of evidence, if the evidence discloses offence(s) other than the offence which was the subject of the investigation, the commanding officer may frame suitable charge(s) on the basis of the evidence so taken [AR 22(4)].

After completion of a summary of evidence, the CO has following options:-

(a) he may remand the accused for trial by a SCM, or

(b) he may apply for trial by GCM, DCM or SGCM; or

(c) he may refer the case to proper superior military authority for summary disposal, if he has no power; or

(d) If he thinks it is desirable, re-hear the case and either dismiss the charge or dispose it of summarily. [AR 24].

Administrative Action

In military law, a CO occupies an important position. Unlike a superior in a civilian government organization, a CO exercises discretion in deciding whether an offence should be charged and how an offender should be punished. He has a number of options for the resolution of disciplinary problems. The CO may choose to take no action. The circumstances surrounding an event may warrant that no adverse action be taken. The preliminary inquiry might indicate that the accused is innocent, that the only evidence is inadmissible, or the CO may decide that other valid reasons exist for not prosecuting the alleged accused. The CO has a number of options for the resolution of disciplinary problems. He may: (i) initiate administrative action against a military offender, (ii) dispose of the offence summarily with a minor punishment, or (iii) dispose of the case with the help of a court-martial. He may choose from four potential levels of court-martial: summary, district, summary-general, or general. These courts-martial differ in the procedures, rights, and possible punishment that can be adjudged.

Administrative action is meant to be corrective and rehabilitative. It is not punitive in character. Administrative actions include measures ranging from reproof or reprimand to dismissal from the service. The factors which need be considered in deciding whether it is appropriate to take administrative action in a particular case are as follows.

(a) The context in which the incident occurred and its impact on operational effectiveness

(b) The likelihood and extent of adverse impact on the individual, unit or service

(c) The rank of the individual or level of responsibility

(d) The age and maturity of the individual

(e) The individual's previous conduct and warnings given to him earlier

(f) Any relevant personal circumstances or mitigating factors

(g) The individual's response following the discovery of the incident

In the Army, administrative action implies any of the following actions against persons subject to the Army Act.

A. Award of Censure

Joint Armed Forces Order No 01/2023 dated 30 October 2023 issued by MoD/Dept of Mil Affairs provides a comprehensive framework on award of censure to officers of the Armed Forces. As per this policy, the Central Government holds the authority to award censure with a permanent effect, while senior commanders like the COAS, CNS, and CAS can impose censure for specified periods, ranging from one to five years, depending on the severity and level at which it is awarded. The operational period of censure affects its implications on promotion and selection; once considered by a Selection or Promotion Board, it ceases to be operative for future considerations. Notably, all awarded censures will be retained in an officer's administrative record, influencing sensitive appointments, re-employment, and selection for career courses, although it does not outright bar promotion. Additionally, the policy allows for redressal against awarded censure, enabling superior authorities to mitigate or cancel censure based on findings of illegality or excessiveness. However, censures awarded earlier will be operative for the period as per original award and the provisions of this instant policy will come into effect from the date of issue of the Censure Policy by MoD/DMA. The said policy is as follows:

Joint Armed Forces Order No. 01/2023
Award of Censure to Officers of the Armed Forces

1. Introduction

The customs of service in the Armed Forces demand highest standards of personal conduct and respect for military law The selection of officers for various career and professional aspects requires the past disciplinary/ administrative record to be placed before the Selection Boards/ Promotion Boards. The award of Censure requires distinct consideration consistent with the service conditions, promotion prospects and other policies on the subject.

2. Background

Censure is awarded for an act, conduct, omission or offences of minor nature. An act/omission where there is an absence of criminal intent can be dealt with by award of Censure. Censure can be awarded to officers,

including MNS officers and re-employed officers. It takes the form of Reproof/ Warning. Displeasure/ Letter of Displeasure, Severe Displeasure/ Letter of Severe Displeasure.

3. In the Indian Army and Indian Air Force, the award of censure is an administrative action, in keeping with the customs of the service. However, in the Navy, the award of censure to an officer is a minor punishment imposed under the Navy Act, 1957, section 81(1)(n).

4. Awarding Authority and Operability of Censure of Reproof/ Warning

The authorities to award Reproof/ Warning, manner administering the same and the application of mind to the case before award Reproof/ Warning' will continue to be governed by respective Service Regulations and customs of service.

5. Severe Displeasure/ Letter of Severe Displeasure and Displeasure/ Letter Displeasure is given below:

The authority to award Censure and its operative duration are as follows:

Sl. No.	Authority Who can Award Censure	Type of Censure that can be awarded	Operative Duration
(a)	Central Governmen	(i) Severe Displeasure /Letter of Severe Displeasure (ii) Displeasure / Letter of Displeasure	Operative permanently from date of award
(b)	COAS/CNS/CAS	(i) Severe Displeasure/Letter of Displeasure Severe	Operative as specified by awarding authority up to a maximum of 5 years from date of award. During the operative period, if a Censure has been considered once as a part of a Selection Board Promotion Board, it will cease to be operative thereafter.

		(ii) Displeasure / Letter of Displeasure	Operative as specified by awarding authority up to a maximum of 3 years from date of award. During the operative period, if a Censure has been considered once as a part of a Selection Board or Promotion Board, it will cease to be operative thereafter
(c),	GOC-in-C Command, Adm Authority (IN). AOC-in-C, C-in-C Andaman & Nicobar Command, C-in-C Strategic Forces Command & Equivalent Rank Officers of Army, Navy and Air Force	(i) Severe Displeasure/ Letter of Severe Displeasure	Operative as specified by awarding authority up to a maximum of 3 years from date of award. During the operative period, if a Censure has been considered once as a part of a Selection Board or Promotion Board, it will cease to be operative thereafter
		(ii) Displeasure/ Letter of Displeasure	Operative as specified by awarding authority upto a maximum of 2 years from date of award. During the operative period, if a Censure has been considered once as a part of a Selection Board or Promotion Board, it will cease to be operative thereafter

(d)	GOC Corp, GOC Commandant Category Establishment Area, A (Commanded by Lt Gen & Equivalent Rank Officers), DG Assam Rifles, DG Border Roads, DG NCC, DG Assurance, Quality Dy C-in-C, Strategic Forces Command (Not below rank of Lt Gen/ Vice Admiral/ Air Marshal	(i) Severe Displeasure/ Letter of Severe Displeasure	Operative as specified by awarding authority up to a maximum of 2 years from date of award. During the operative period, if a Censure has been considered once as a part of a Selection Board or Promotion Board, it will cease to be operative thereafter.
		(ii) Displeasure/ Letter of Displeasure	Operative as specified by awarding authority up to a maximum of 1 year from date of award. During the operative period, if a Censure has been considered once as a part of a Selection Board or Promotion Board, it will cease to be operative thereafter.
(e)	GOC Division, GOC Sub Area & Equivalent Officers AFSOD	(i) Severe Displeasure/ Letter of Severe Displeasure	Operative up to a maximum of 2 years from date of award as specified by awarding authority. During the operative period, if a Censure has been considered once as a part of a Selection Board or Promotion Board, it will cease to be operative thereafter.
		(ii) Displeasure/ Letter of Displeasure	Operative up to a maximum of 1 year from date of award as specified by awarding authority. During the operative period, if a Censure has been considered once as a part of Selection Board or Promotion Board, it will cease to be operative thereafter

Note:

1. Quantum of award should not to be less than six months and further in multiples of six months.

2. Paragraph 5 (d) & 5 (e) have been specifically included for Indian Army, due to its longer chain of command and may be adopted by IAF and IN, as suited to their functional requirements.

3. Post the operative period, the record of Censure will be retained in Disciplinary/ Administrative Record of the Officer.

6. Any authority in the Chain of Command may recommend the award of a censure by authority superior to him, if in his opinion, an award of censure by the said authority will not be adequate. In such cases, the relevant documents along with the recommendations of that authority should be forwarded to the superior authority for examining the case on its merits and taking an appropriate action thereupon.

XXXXXX

12. Reporting of Award of Censures

Once a censure has been awarded, the awarding authority will inform the next higher Commander in chain of the same. In addition, a copy of the censure, duly signed by the affected officer will also be forwarded to respective Service Headquarters (AG's Branch & MS Branch or equivalent) for the purpose of record keeping.

13. Recording of Censures

All censures awarded to an officer will remain part of the officer's administrative record in accordance with respective Service Regulations However, the operability of such censures shall continue to be governed by the period as specified in Paragraph 5 above. Procedure for record keeping of such administrative action will be evolved under the respective service arrangements. For the purpose of Selection/ Promotion Boards to be shared with Central Government, it would be sufficient to place the record of past 10 years instead of the overall records.

14. Redressal Against Award of Censures

Redressal against award censure may be submitted and processed as per the respective service regulation. An authority superior to the authority who awarded the censure may cancel the award, remit a portion of whole of it, or condone, on the opinion of that authority, the censure is illegal, unjust or excessive. Any representation seeking redressal of censure should be finalised within two years from the date of receipt. Condonation of delay beyond the given timelines may be granted, depending upon merits of the case by the authority superior to the one who initiated/ finalised such administrative action but not below the level of GOC in-C/ Equivalent Officer. While granting redress by mitigating, cancelling, remitting or commuting the award, the competent authority must invariably mention the date from which the said order is to be operative and also inform the immediate superior authority of the same.

15. Review/ Revocation of Censures

The case of award of Censure to an officer should not be ordinarily reopened unless in exceptional cases where it suffers from lack of jurisdiction, or non-application of mind or a malafide exercise of power. etc. In the aforesaid cases and in cases where an Administrative Action has been initiated/ finalised for acts involving Moral Turpitude, Fraud, Theft, Dishonesty, or Financial Irregularity/ Impropriety and Misappropriation, the authority superior to the one who initiated/ finalised such administrative action and not below the rank of GOC-in-C/ FOC-in-C/AOC-in-C shall be competent to invoke its inherent power suo-moto and revoke/ set aside such actions/ directions and pass appropriate direction thereupon.

16. Implementation of Service Specific Orders

For the purpose of carrying into effect the provisions of the policy, detailed procedure/ modalities on the aspects incidental to or connected with the award of Censure, considering the unique service conditions of Army/ Navy/ Air Force, as the case may be, will be issued by the respective Service HQs within 60 days of the date of issue of this policy letter. Such service specific orders must be in consonance with provisions of this policy. However, censures awarded earlier will be operative for the period as per original award and the provisions of the instant policy will come into effect from the date of issue of the Censure Policy by MoD/DMA.

Subsequently all the three Service HQs issued their respective new policy based on the Joint Armed Forces Order dated 30 October 2023. The Army HQ issued its directions vide policy letter dated 22 April 2024. It reinforces that censure is an administrative action reflecting the customs of service, applicable to minor infractions rather than serious misconduct involving moral turpitude, fraud, or dishonesty. Furthermore;

the procedures for awarding censure, reporting, and redressal are detailed, ensuring consistency across the services. Censure remains a significant part of an officer's record, influencing career aspects while also providing a mechanism for review and redressal within specified timelines. It specified that the censure while being operative may be taken in consideration for an officer's career in various ways, including their posting to sensitive appointments, re-employment, deputation or secondment, and selection for career courses, UN missions, or foreign postings and the duration for which it will be applicable would be same as specified in Para 13 of the order dated 30 October 2023, Joint Armed Forces Order No 01/2023 dated 30 October 2023.

Policy on Award of Censure to Officers of the Armed Forces in Pursuance of Joint Armed Forces Order No. 01/2023 dated 30 October 2023

1. This policy letter must be read in conjunction with Joint Armed Forces Order No 01/2023 w.r.t. award of Censure to officers of the Armed Forces which has been issued by Govt of India (Ministry of Defence) vide letter No 560/US (P)/D (N-11) 2022 dt 30 Oct 2023. In case of any conflict or doubt, the Joint Armed Forces order No 01/2023 shall have overriding effect.

2. This policy letter is being issued under Para 16 of the Joint Armed Forces No 01/2023 in order to bring into effect the procedure to be adopted on effect of award of censure taking into consideration unique service conditions of the Army. The Joint Armed Forces Order No 01/2023 provides for laying down the detailed procedure! modalities for the purpose of carrying its provisions into effect, on the aspects, mentioned specifically thereat as also incidental to or connected with the award of Censure, considering the unique service conditions of the respective Service etc. In pursuance thereof, this policy is hereby issued and it should be read in conjunction with the said Joint Armed Forces Order.

3. Applicability

The award of Censure is an administrative action, in keeping with the customs of the service which can take the form of 'Reproof", 'Displeasure' or "Severe Displeasure of the Authority/ Officer awarding the Censure. This policy is applicable to Officers, including MNS officers and re-

employed Officers. Censure except Reproof (in terms of Para 327 of Regulations for the Army (Revised Edition), 1987) is not awardable to Warrant Officers and Other Ranks. The award of Censure to JCOs shall continue to be governed by the existing policy on the subject.

4. Censure is awarded for an act, conduct, omission or offence of a minor nature and NOT in cases involving moral turpitude, fraud, dishonesty, financial irregularity and misappropriation. The latter are to be tried by a Court Martial or by a prosecution in a civil court in accordance with Para 432 of the Regulations for the Army (Revised Edition), 1987. An act/ omission where there is an absence of criminal intent can be dealt with by award of censure. An offence will not be disposed-off prematurely by award of censure, without reference to a superior authority who may consider disciplinary action under the Army Act 1950.

5. Presiding Officer/ Members of Board of Officers/ Court of Inquiry/ Summary of Evidence/ Court-Martial will not be subjected to administrative action with regard to lapse concerning a bonafide formulation of an opinion. However, there is no legal embargo to initiate action against such Presiding Officer/ members as aforesaid for any proved misconduct in performance of such duties. Care will be taken by the authorities not to initiate action which may convey an impression of interference or exerting command influence over the officer assigned to undertake statutory functions.

6. Cases though not of minor nature but still do not involve question of moral turpitude, fraud, theft, dishonesty, financial irregularity or misappropriation, and where trial by a Court Martial is not practicable being time-barred or is inexpedient due to other reasons, may if found appropriate, be forwarded to Integrated Headquarters of Ministry of Defence (Army). Adjutant General's Branch, D&V Directorate at the discretion of the GOC-in-C for consideration of the award of censure by the COAS/ Central Government.

Competent Authority to award Censures

7. Reproof

The authorities to award Reproof, manner of administering the same, its effect and the application of mind to the case before award of Reproof has been laid down in Para 327, Regulations of the Army (Revised Edition), 1987.

8. Displeasure and Severe Displeasure

The newly promulgated Joint Armed Forces Order No 01/2023 on Award of Censure to Officers of the Armed Forces dt 30 Oct 2023 gives out the authority competent to award a Censure, along with the operative period and role of chain of command in Para 5 & 6 of the policy. The effect of censure on the career prospects of the Officer has been given in Para 18 below.

9. Procedure for the Award of Displeasure/ Severe Displeasure

Broad procedure for the award of Censure has been covered in para 7-10 of the Joint Armed Forces Order No 01/2023 dt 30 Oct 2023. Certain explanatory provisions are reiterated in the succeeding paras.

12. Para 10 of the Joint Armed Forces Order No 01/2023 states that in case the recipient Officer brings out any new facts in his reply to the SCN, these should first be investigated by the Competent authority before taking any further action, if considered appropriate. The term "if considered appropriate" would mean that the Competent Authority would investigate those fresh facts stated in the reply to SCN, only if they are not only verifiable but relevant and prima facie having a direct bearing on the act, conduct, omission or offence in question, necessitating any kind of investigation.

13. Award of Censure to Navy/ Air Force Personnel

Army authorities shall be empowered to award censure to Navy/ Air Force personnel serving in or attached to the Inter-Services Organisation (ISO), duly notified in accordance with Inter- Services Organisation (Command, Control and Discipline) Act, 2023. However, such Navy/ Air Force personnel when serving in or attached to an organisation not duly notified as ISO, the Army authorities will not award Censure and if such a step is necessitated in the interest of discipline, the details of the case along with connected documents will be forwarded to the Integrated Headquarters of Ministry of Defence (Army), Adjutant General's Branch, D&V Dte through staff channel.

Reporting of Award of Censure

16. Once a decision has been taken to award a censure, the concerned authority through the Command Headquarters will inform this fact by the fastest means with full particulars of the officer to the following authorities at Integrated Headquarters of Ministry of Defence (Army): (a) Adjutant General's Branch, D&V Directorate. (b) MS Branch (MS-4 CR/ MS-X for Brigadiers and above). (c) Concerned controlling group of the MS Branch.

17. Once a censure has been awarded, the awarding authority will inform the next higher Commander in chain of the same. In addition, a copy of the censure, viz, Severe Displeasure or Displeasure, duly received by the affected officer, will also be forwarded to Army Headquarters (AG's Branch/ DV Dte and MS Branch/ MS-4) for the purpose of record keeping. In case of Brigadiers and above, the same will be endorsed to MS (X) instead of MS-4(CR).

18. Recording of Censure

Aspects related to recording of Censure have been given in para 13 of the Joint Armed Forces Order No 01/2023 on Award of Censure to Officers of the Armed Forces dt 30 Oct 2023. The record of all discipline/ administrative action is being maintained centrally under the aegis of Adjutant General's Branch, D&V Directorate/ DV-2 (Records).

Effect of Censure on Career Prospects

19. The award of a censure does not debar an officer from being considered for promotion and other career aspects and censure, by itself, may not affect his promotion/selection. However, while it is operative, it is taken cognizance of as part of the officer's overall record of service in assessing the officer as per relevant policies governing such promotion/selection. As per Para 5 of the Joint Armed Forces Order No 01/2023, during the operative period of censure, it shall be considered by the Selection/ Promotion Board only once and it shall cease to be operative thereafter for the purpose of Selection/Promotion Board.

20. The censure order, while it is operative, may be taken into consideration for the purpose of: (a) Posting an Officer to sensitive appointment; b) Re-employment; (c) Deputation/ Secondment; (d) Nomination/Selection for Career Courses; (e) Selection for UN Mission/ Foreign posting; or (f)

For any other purpose as laid down from time to time by the MS Branch policies on the subject including the aforesaid aspects

Redressal of Grievances

21. Redressal against the award of censure may be submitted and processed in terms of Para 304 of the Regulations for the Army (Revised Edition) 1997. Details on the subject are covered in Para 14 & 15 of the Joint Armed Forces Order No 01/2023 dated 30 Oct 2023.

22. ADG DV/ DV-1 (P) policy on the subject "Award of Censure in Officers promulgated vide letter No 32008/ AG/ DV-1 (P) dt 11 Aug 2017" is hereby superseded. However, it shall continue to apply in all the cases where Censure has been awarded under the aforesaid policy dt 11 Aug 2017.

23. Nothing contained in this Policy shall render invalid any action taken or acts performed, immediately after the promulgation of Joint Armed Forces Order No 01/2023 and prior to the issuance of this policy.

B. Dismissal or Removal from Service at the Pleasure of the President of India

AA s. 18, dealing with tenure of service provides, "Every person subject to this Act shall hold office during the pleasure of the President." This provision is analogous to Article 310 (1) of the Constitution. The principle that the employees of a State hold office during the pleasure of the head of the State is known as the 'doctrine of pleasure'. The power conferred by AA s. 18 is supreme and unfettered. Thus, for termination of service under s.18, it is not mandatory to hold any enquiry. The pleasure of the President is not required to be exercised by him personally; he may act according to advice tendered by his Council of Ministers.

In the Army, occasions may arise when it is considered risky to retain a person in service. The doctrine of pleasure is invoked when the risk apprehended may be too great. While it is unfair to condemn a person unheard, it may be undesirable to retain him in service because of possible injury to the state. In such cases, it would be prudent to terminate the service of the person without making such termination punitive.

C. Termination of Service by the Central Government

AA s. 19, states "Subject to the provisions of this Act and the rules and regulations made thereunder, the Central Government may dismiss or remove from the service any person subject to this Act." Dismissal or removal under Section 19 could be for reasons of serious misconduct, failure to qualify at an examination, inefficiency or physical disability.

When an officer does not appear at, or having appeared fails to qualify for, the retention examination or promotion examination or any other basic course or examination within the time or extended time specified in respect of that examination or course, the Chief of the Army Staff (COAS) or Military Secretary (MS) shall call upon the officer to show cause as to why he should not be compulsorily retired or removed from the service. If the COAS deems the explanation unsatisfactory, the matter may be submitted to the Central Government for orders, together with the officer's explanation and the recommendations of the COAS as to whether the officer should be (i) called upon to retire; or (ii) called upon to resign. The Central Government, after considering the officer's explanation, if any, and the recommendations of the COAS, may call upon the officer to retire or resign. If the officer refuses to do so, he may be compulsorily retired or removed from the service on pension or gratuity, if any, admissible to him.

The procedure for termination of service is contained in ARs 13-A, 14, 15 and 15-A. These Rules are applicable to officers only.

D. Dismissal, Removal or Reduction by the Chief of the Army Staff in Respect of a Person Other than an Officer

AA s. 20 provides that the COAS may dismiss or remove from the service any person subject to the Army Act other than an officer. The COAS is also empowered to reduce to a lower grade or rank or the ranks any warrant officer or any non-commissioned officer. A brigade commander or equivalent commander or any prescribed officer may dismiss or remove from the service any person serving under his command, other than an officer or a junior commissioned officer. These officers may also reduce to a lower grade or rank or the ranks any warrant officer or non-commissioned officer under their command. The commanding officer of an acting non-commissioned officer may order him to revert to his permanent grade as a non-commissioned officer, or if he has no permanent grade above the ranks, to the ranks. There are certain limitations under AA s.20. A warrant officer reduced to the ranks shall not be required to serve in the ranks as a sepoy.

The procedure for dismissal or removal is contained in AR 17. The rule of natural justice requires that no person should be condemned without having been given an opportunity to put across his point of view. Rule 17 provides that before dismissal or removal under AA s. 20, the affected person is to be informed of the particulars of the cause of action against him and be allowed reasonable time to state in writing any reasons he may have to urge against his dismissal or removal from the service.

Rule 17 further provides that if in the opinion of the officer competent to order the dismissal or removal, it is not expedient or reasonably practicable to comply with the above provision, he may after certifying to that effect, order the dismissal or removal without complying with the prescribed procedure set out in the Rule. All cases of dismissal or removal where the prescribed procedure has not been complied with shall be reported to the Central Government. However, in cases of misconduct leading to conviction by a criminal court or a court martial, the procedure contained in Rule 17 is not required to be followed before dismissal or removal from the service.

Conduct Sheet Entries

A conduct sheet (IAFF 3013) is prepared and maintained for every person subject to AA. The conduct sheets of officers, JCOs and WOs are maintained as confidential documents, while those of ORs are kept with other service documents. Entries are made in the conduct sheets of officers in respect of all convictions by court-martial or criminal court or summary punishments awarded under AAs 83 or 84. The following entries are made in the conduct sheets of JCOs, WOs and ORs as red-ink entries:

(a) Forfeiture of seniority of rank (JCOs and WOs only)

(b) Conviction by court martial

(c) Conviction by a civil court, except when a fine was the only punishment

(d) Reduction of an NCO to a lower grade or to the ranks for an offence but not for inefficiency

(e) Deprivation of an appointment or of lance or acting rank, for an offence but not for inefficiency

(f) Severe reprimand

(g) Imprisonment

(h) Detention

(i) Confinement to the lines exceeding 14 days

(j) Forfeiture of good-service or good-conduct pay

Black-ink entries are made in the conduct sheets of JCOs, WOs and ORs in respect of all punishments not included in the list of red-ink entries. These include convictions by civil courts, which in the CO's opinion do not merit a red-ink entry. When the record of a court-martial or summary award is ordered to be removed, the entry must be erased and the authority quoted. [RA para 386-388].

Administrative Action: Redress of Grievance

An officer, JCO, WO or OR who deems himself wronged by an administrative action may seek redress by submitting a statutory complaint under AA ss. 26 and 27. The procedure for submission and processing of petitions is contained in the RA para 364.

The Armed Forces Tribunal, as provided in sub-section 3 (o) (iv) (i), (ii) and (iii) of the AFT Act, shall not have any jurisdiction in (i) dismissal or removal from service at the pleasure of the President under Section 18 of the Army Act, 1950. As far as other administrative actions like reproof, displeasure, severe displeasure, dismissal, termination, removal and reduction are concerned, only two terms, 'termination of service' and 'reversion', are included in the definition of the term 'service matters' under sub-section 3 (o) (ii) of the Act.

The military chain of command must use its powers appropriately in keeping with the context of the offence/misconduct and the operational circumstances. The existence of an administrative action regime does not prevent a commander from proceeding directly to disciplinary action where it is more appropriate. Also, good management practice may require that certain professional failings be dealt with without recourse to either regime. Such minor transgressions may be corrected more informally and immediately.

CHAPTER 4

SUMMARY PUNISHMENTS

Disciplinary action can be taken against a person subject to the Army Act accused of an offence under the Act. The disciplinary action can be by way of (i) a summary punishment by the designated officers or (ii) a court-martial. A CO or a designated senior commander can deal with Army personnel up to the rank of Major in the case of minor offences and award a punishment summarily under Sections 80, 83, 84 and 85 of the Army Act. The officer disposing of the case summarily under these sections is not a 'court' and the BSA, does not apply to such proceedings. Further, unlike a trial by court-martial, the accused has no right to be represented by a counsel/defending officer or even be assisted by a 'friend' of the accused. The accused is, however, authorized to cross-examine those who give evidence against him. The whole essence of summary justice is that it must be very swift in order to be effective.

Hearing of Charge

A charge against a person subject to the AA must be heard by the CO in the presence of the accused. The accused must have full liberty to cross-examine any witness against him, and call witnesses and make a statement in his defence. This is a mandatory requirement. However, where the charge against the accused arises as a result of investigation by a court of inquiry, wherein the provisions of the AR 180 have been complied with in respect of that accused, the CO may dispense with calling and hearing of witnesses. Even in such cases, the CO must read out and explain the charges to the accused and pass an appropriate order on conclusion of the hearing.

In case of any doubt regarding non-compliance of AR 180 in letter and spirit, the CO shall not dispense with the procedure prescribed in AR 22(1). The charge at this stage is a "Tentative" charge which may be modified after the Hearing or during the procedure described in AR 22(3) or during examination after completion of the procedure under the said sub-rule, depending on the evidence adduced, under AR 22(4). As a matter of abundant caution, hearing of charge should be conducted in the presence of two Independent Witnesses. It must, however, be ensured that the said Independent Witnesses are not listed as Prosecution Witnesses [AR 22 and AO 03/2018/DV].

Options after Hearing a Charge

The CO has following options after hearing a charge:

(a) He can dismiss a charge if, in his opinion, the evidence does not show that an offence under the Act has been committed. However, he shall not dismiss a charge which he is debarred to try it under AA s. 120 (2), without reference to superior authority.

(b) If he is of the opinion that the charge ought to be proceeded with, he can:

(i) dispose of the case under AA s. 80 by awarding punishment, which he is authorized to award.

(ii) refer the case to proper superior military authority for trial under AA ss. 83, 84 or 85; or

(iii) adjourn the case for the purpose of having the evidence reduced to writing; or

(iv) order trial by SCM, if the accused is below the rank of warrant officer. [AR 22 (2) and (3)].

However, the CO is not no to order trial by SCM without a reference to the officer empowered to convene a DCM or on active service a SGCM for the trial of the alleged offender unless (i) the offence is one which he can try by a SCM without any reference to that officer, or (ii) he considers that there is grave reason for immediate action and such reference cannot be made without detriment to discipline. [Proviso to AR 22 (3)]. No particular time is fixed within which a CO must dispose of a charge, so that he can always carefully consider a difficult case, but as a rule he should decide immediately, and should never delay for more than a day, unless further evidence is required.

Offences which cannot be disposed Summarily

AA s. 120 (2) provides that a CO should not dispose of summarily, offences which he cannot dispose of by SCM. These are: (i) very serious offences punishable with death under section 34, (ii) mutiny under section 37, (iii) civil offences under section 69, and (iv) an offence against himself. In case of grave reasons for immediate action, where reference can be detrimental to discipline, the CO can try these offences without reference. The CO is the best judge in deciding which case should be tried by him without reference and sanction. If subsequently it appears to superior authority that his actions were not justified, this may be viewed as a grave irregularity for which the CO may be held responsible, but it does not affect the legality of the finding and sentence warded by the CO.

Trial by Commanding Officer: Under AA s. 80, the Chief of the Army Staff with the consent of the Central Government, has prescribed certain officers who may exercise the powers of punishment under AA s. 80 [see RA para 443], and may proceed against a non-commissioned officer or sepoy, charged with an offence under the Act, and award one or more of the following punishments:

(a) Imprisonment in military custody up to twenty-eight days;

(b) Detention up to twenty-eight days;

(c) Confinement to the lines up to twenty-eight days;

(d) Extra guards or duties ;

(e) Deprivation of position of the nature of an appointment or of corps or working pay, and in the case of non-commissioned officers, also deprivation of acting rank or reduction to a lower grade of pay;

(f) Forfeiture of good service and good conduct pay;

(g) Severe reprimand or reprimand;

(h) Fine up to fourteen days' pay in any one month; and

(i) Penal deductions under clause (g) of AA s. 91.

A CO can dispose of a case summarily by awarding the punishment(s) specified above, subject to certain limitations on the award of these punishments. In the case of an award of two or more of the punishments specified in clauses (a), (b), (c) and (d) above, the punishment specified in clause (c) or clause (d) shall take effect only at the end of the punishment specified in clause (a) or clause (b). When two or more of the punishments specified in clauses (a), (b) and (c) are awarded to a person conjointly, or when the person is already undergoing one or more of the said punishments, the whole extent of the punishments shall not exceed an aggregate of forty-two days. The punishments specified in clauses (a), (b) and (c) shall not be awarded to any person who is of the rank of non-commissioned officer or was, at the time of committing the offence for which he is punished, of such rank. The punishment specified in clause (g) shall not be awarded to any person below the rank of a non- commissioned officer. [AA s. 81].

The punishments which can be awarded to a Sepoy under AA s. 80

(a) Imprisonment in military custody up to 28 days.

(b) Detention up to 28 days.

(c) Confinement to the lines up to 28 days.

(d) Extra guards or duties.

(e) Fine up to 14 days pay in one month.

(f) Penal seductions under section 91 (g), Army Act.

Punishment awardable to NCOs

(a) Extra guards or duties

(b) Deprivation of a position of the nature of an appointment or of corps or working pay, deprivation of acting rank or reduction to a lower grade of pay

(c) forfeiture of good service and good conduct pay

(d) severe reprimand or reprimand

(e) fine up to fourteen days' pay in any one month

(f) penal deductions under clause (g) of Section 91 of the Act

The term NCO, as defined in AA s. 3 (xv) includes an acting NCO.

Limit of punishments under AA s. 80.

In the case of an award of two or more of the punishments specified in s. 80 (a), (b), (c) and (d), the punishment specified in s. 80(c) or (d) shall take effect only at the end of the punishment specified in s. 80(a) or (b). When two or more of the punishments specified in s. 80 (a), (b) and (c) are awarded to a person conjointly, or when already undergoing one or more of the said punishments, the whole extent of the punishments shall not exceed in the aggregate 42 days. The punishments specified in s. 80(a), (b) and (c) shall not be awarded to any person who is of the rank of non-commissioned officer or was, at the time of committing the offence for which he is punished, or such rank. The punishment specified in s. 80 (g) shall not be awarded to any person below the rank of a non-commissioned officer.

A term of imprisonment or detention awarded by a CO should be awarded in days and will commence to run from the day of award. In law there is no division of a day, and therefore, however late in the day a prisoner is committed, his term of imprisonment or detention is considered to have commenced at the first minute of that day that is, the first minute after midnight. The sentence will therefore, begin on the first minute of the day of award, and end at sunset of the day it expires. The award is considered final when the accused has been removed from the presence of the CO. The CO can at any time diminish the punishment before its completion, though he cannot add to it.

A JCO commanding a detachment, not being an officer within the meaning of AA s. 3 (xviii), cannot award any of the punishments under AA s. 80.

Other Punishments

Under the provisions of AA s. 82, the COAS, with the consent of the Central Government, has specified the following "other punishments" which may be awarded under AA s. 80: (i) Extra drill for two hours a day up to fifteen days; and (ii) Reduction to a lower class of pay for period up to 28 days. [RA para 443 (b)].

Adjutant of a unit, if authorized by the CO, can award punishment of (i) confinement to lines for a period up to five days and (ii) extra drill for two to Regimental boys. Adjutant of a depot is authorized to award only the first punishment. [RA para 443 (a) (xiii), and column IV of Table].

Summary of Evidence

A summary of evidence must to be recorded in cases where it is intended to remand the accused for trial by GCM, DCM, SGCM or SCM or where the accused is an officer, JCO or WO, for summary disposal of the charge under AA ss. 83 to 85. For details on recording of summary of evidence please refer chapter 3.

Action by Superior Officer

A superior officer to whom a case has been referred may deal with it as follows:

(a) He may refer the case to superior officer, or

(b) He may direct the disposal of case summarily or by SCM, or

(c) He may convene a GCM or DCM, is he has power to do so, or

(d) In the case of an officer, JCO or WO he may dispose of the charge summarily under AA s. 83, 84 or 85. [RA para 449].

Summary Punishments: Officer, JCOs and WOs

Summary punishments listed under AA ss. 83, 84 and 85, may be inflicted by senior commanders in respect of offences committed by persons subject to the Act without the intervention of a court-martial. [AA s. 79]. The following officers can deal summarily under the AA.

A. Brigade Commander or Equivalent Commander

Under Section 83 of the Army Act, a brigade commander or equivalent commander or an officer specified by the Chief of the Army Staff (COAS) may with the consent of the Central Government, proceed in the prescribed manner [ARs 22 and 26; and RA para 444 - Appendix Q], against an officer below the field rank (up to the rank of Captain), JCO or a WO who has committed an offence, and may award one or more of the following punishments:

(a) severe reprimand or reprimand; and

(b) stoppage of pay and allowances until any proved loss or damage occasioned by the offence of which the accused is convicted is made good.

B. Area Commander

Under AA s. 84, an area commander or an equivalent commander or an officer empowered to convene a general court-martial or such other officer may, with the consent of the Central Government [specified by the COAS], proceed against an officer below the rank of lieutenant colonel, a JCO or a WO, and award one or more of the following punishments:

(a) forfeiture of seniority, or in the case of any of them whose promotion depends upon length of service, forfeiture of service for the purpose of promotion for a period not exceeding twelve months, but subject to the right of the accused previous to the award to elect to be tried by a court-martial;

(b) severe reprimand or reprimand; and

(c) stoppage of pay and allowances until any proved loss or damage occasioned by the offence of which the accused is convicted is made good.

An officiating area or equivalent commander or other officer specified in this section irrespective of his rank can exercise the power under this section. A person subject to Army Act as no right to elect to be tried by court-martial, except as provided in section 84 (a) of the Act. If the authority dealing summarily with the case proposes to award 'forfeiture of seniority of rank or service', he shall ask the accused "Do you elect to be tried by court-martial or will you accept my award?" Option can be exercised before the award of punishment.

C. Commanding officer

Under AA s. 85, a CO may proceed against a junior commissioned officer and award one or more of the following punishments:

(i) severe reprimand or reprimand; and

(ii) stoppage of pay and allowances until any proved loss or damage occasioned by the offence of which the accused is convicted is made good.

The punishment specified in clause (i) shall not be awarded if the commanding officer or such other officer is below the rank of Colonel.

D. The following officers can also deal with the cases summarily:-

(a) Chief of Staff HQ Corps and Command: The COAS, with the consent of the Central Government has specified the Chiefs of Staff at Command and Corps Headquarters as officers who can exercise powers under AA s. 84 in respect of personnel of those Headquarters and the units which are directly under the command of those Headquarters. [Army HQ letter No. 41776/PS dated 23 May 1977].

(b) Deputy GOC at Divisional HQ: The COAS, with the consent of the Central Government has specified the Deputy General Officers Commanding at Divisional HQs as officers who can exercise powers under AAs. 83 in respect of personnel of the Divisional HQ and Divisional Troops Units. [Army HQ letter No. 41776/AG/DV-1 dated 17 June 1988].

Rights to appeal against Punishment awarded under AA ss. 80, 83, 84 and 85

Once an offender has been punished or the CO has disposed the charged, he cannot be tried by court-martial for the same offence. Similarly, he cannot be subjected to a minor punishment, for any offence of which he has been acquitted or convicted by a court-martial or a criminal court. There is no right to appeal against the punishment awarded under ss. 80, 83, 84 and 85.

However, any officer superior in command to the officer who awarded the punishment may review punishment awarded under s. 80, and if such punishment appears to be illegal, unjust or excessive. Such officer may cancel, vary or remit the punishment and make such direction as may be appropriate in the case. Where the punishment awarded is wholly illegal or in excess of the authorized punishment, it may be cancelled or varied by an Officer-in-Charge records also. [RA para 442].

If any punishment awarded under sections 83, 84 or 85 appears to a superior military authority to be illegal, unjust or excessive, such authority may cancel, vary or remit the punishment and make such other directions as may be appropriate in the case. [AA ss. 87 and 88]. In case a person considers himself wronged by the award under AA ss.80, 83, 84 or 85, he may make a Statutory Complaint under paragraph 364 of the Regulations for the Army.

Under AA s. 88 (b), the COAS has specified the GOC-in-C of a Command as the superior military authority for the purpose of review of punishments awarded to Officers, JCOs and WOs under ss. 83 and 84 of the Act. Powers conferred under AA s. 87 shall normally be exercised within a period of two years from the date of award of the punishment. [RA para 442].

Illegal, Unjust and Excessive Punishment

A punishment is 'wholly illegal' if (i) the finding of guilty cannot be upheld; or (ii) the only punishment awarded is of a kind which cannot be awarded for the offence charged; or (iii) where the punishment awarded is of a kind which the authority dealing with the case is not authorized to award. In case of award of an illegal punishment, it must be cancelled and appropriate directions must be made by the superior military authority.

A punishment is treated as 'excessive' when it is in excess of the punishment authorized by law for the offence, i.e., where it is of a kind which the authority dealing with the case is authorized to award for the offence charged but is greater in amount than he is authorized to award. For example, where the amount of loss averred in the particulars of charge is Rs 1000/- but the authority dealing summarily with the case under the Army Act awards stoppage of Rs 1500/-, it will amount to excessive punishment. A superior officer may vary the punishment by reducing the amount of punishment to an amount which is authorized by law.

Where the punishment though not in excess of the punishment authorized by law, appears to be 'unjust' or severe, the superior military authority has the power to remit the whole or part of the punishment. [AA s. 87 notes].

Trial of Army personnel by Naval or Air Force Officers

A medical officer including Naval or Air Force officer commanding a hospital or other medical unit shall be a CO for the purpose of AA s. 80 of a person subject to the Army Act, not belonging to the medical personnel, who is a patient in or is employed in that hospital or medical unit. He may either himself dispose of a charge against such person or refer it for disposal, if the person has left the hospital or medical unit to the commanding officer of the unit or detachment to which such person belongs or is attached. But the medical officer-in-charge of regimental establishment shall not, unless the establishment is detached, be a CO for the purpose of the establishment or any person who is a patient in or is employed in that establishment.[RA para 443 (d)]

Appeal to the Armed Forces Tribunal

An individual can invoke the 'original jurisdiction' of the tribunal only in cases of 'summary disposals and trial' where the punishment of 'dismissal' is awarded. The term 'summary disposals and trials' has been further clarified in sub-section 3 (p) of the AFT Act, to signify, "summary disposals and trials held under the Army Act, 1950, the Navy Act, 1957 and the Air Force Act, 1950". Under the Army Act, the punishment of dismissal is not awarded summarily; therefore, there is no right to appeal to the Armed Forces Tribunal against punishments awarded under AA ss. 80, 83, 84 and 85. The Principal Bench of the Armed Forces Tribunal at Delhi in the case of *Sub Satyavir Singh v. Union of India* [WP (C) No. 4778 of 2002, T.A. No. 748 of 2009] refused to grant relief to the petitioner who was charged under AA s. 63 and was awarded the punishment of severe reprimand by the competent authority. Summary punishments have a grave effect on the career of Army personnel. Since the tribunal does not exercise jurisdiction in 'summary punishment', an individual may approach the higher courts through the writ jurisdiction.

CHAPTER 5

COURT MARTIAL

Military discipline requires the quick disposal of offences relating to armed forces personnel. To achieve this, justice is dispensed through various types of temporary tribunals (court martial) vested with varying powers. Under the Army Act, the constitution of a court martial depends upon the nature and gravity of the offence and the rank of the accused. A court martial is a criminal court as per the definitions in the Code of Criminal Procedure, 1973. It has no civil jurisdiction and cannot enforce a contract or award damages in favour of an individual. The proceedings of a court martial are judicial in nature and the rules of natural justice need to be observed. [AAs 152]. Only a court martial that is properly convened and composed is capable of rendering valid judgments.

Kinds of Court Martial

The Army Act provide for four types of courts martial: general court martial (GCM), district court martial (DCM), and summary general court martial (SGCM), and summary court martial (SCM). [AA s. 108].

Power of Punishment

(a) A **GCM** is the highest court martial in military law. It has the power to try any person subject to the Army Act for any offence punishable therein and award a sentence up to death.

(b) A **DCM** has the power to try any person subject to the Army Act other than an officer or a junior commissioned officer, for any offence made punishable therein; and to pass any sentence authorized by the Act, other than the sentences of death, transportation or imprisonment for a term exceeding two years.

(c) A **SGCM** has the same power as a GCM. It can try any person subject to the Army Act for any offence punishable therein, and award any sentence authorized thereby. However, the sentence of death cannot be passed a by SGCM without the concurrence of all the members.

(d) A **SCM** may try any person subject to the Army Act and under the command of the officer holding the court, except an officer, JCO or a warrant officer. A SCM may pass any sentence under the Army Act except the sentence of death or imprisonment for a term exceeding one year in case the officer holding the trial is of or higher than the rank of Lieutenant Colonel, and three months, if the officer is below that rank.

A chart containing composition, power, persons who could be tried, power of punishment and confirming authorities in relation to various courts martial is given on succeeding pages. The procedure for holding GCM and DCM are contained in ARs 37-105. The procedure for holding SCM and SGCM are contained in ARs 106-133 and ARs 151-165 respectively. The instructions for award of punishment by SCM are contained in RA para 448. For issues relating to witnesses, evidence and preservation of proceedings of a court martial, ARs 143-150 are to be referred.

Reference to the Judge Advocate General's Department

In all cases for trial by GCM, and other cases under the AA relating to indecency, fraud, theft (except ordinary theft), and civil offences except simple assaults, the charge sheet and summary of evidence, and all the exhibits are to be referred by the convening officer to the deputy JAG of the command or deputy/assistant JAG of the Corps, before trial is ordered. The convening officer should also refer for advice any other cases of doubt or difficulty. [RA para 459].

Type of Court-Martial (AA s. 108)	Power to convene	Composition	Who can be tried	Powers of Punishment	Confirming Authority	Misc Points
1. General Court martial [GCM]	1. Central Government, or 2. The COAS, or 3. By an officer empowered by warrant of the COAS [AA s. 109]	1. Minimum Number of five officers. 2. The officers must have held a commission for not less than three years. 3. Four of the members must be of the rank of Capt or higher rank. [AA s. 113] 4. They must not belong exclusively to the corps or departments to which accused belongs [AR 40 (1) and 187 (3)]. 5. For trial of a commanding officer see RA Para 460.	All persons subject to the AA. [AA s. 118]	1. All sentences authorized by s. 71 of the AA. [AA s. 118]. 2. Sentence of death cannot be passed by GCM without concurrence of at least two-third of members of the court. [AA s. 132 (2)]. 2. Also see RA para 472 for confirmation based on rank of the accused and gravity of the sentence. 3. Finding and sentence can be sent back for revision once to the court martial. [AA s. 160 and AR 68].	1. Central Government or by any officer empowered in this behalf by warrant of the Central Government. [AA s. 154].	1. Must be attended by a Judge Advocate, senior in rank to the accused. [AA s. 129]. In case such an officer is not available due to the exigencies of service, the convening officer has to append a certificate. 2. For trial of a field officer all members shall be of a rank, not below that of the officer. [AR 40 (3)] 3. GCM is to give brief reasoned order. [AR 62 (1)].

Type of Court-Martial (AA s. 108)	**Power to convene**	**Composition**	**Who can be tried**	**Powers of Punishment**	**Confirming Authority**	**Misc Points**
2. District Court martial [DCM]	1. Officer empowered to convene a GCM 2. Officer empowered in this behalf by warrant of an officer empowered to convene a GCM. [AA s.110]	1. Minimum number of three officers. 2. Officers must have held a commission for not less than two whole years. [AA s. 114]. 3. The presiding officer should be of field rank. [RA para 460(c)].	All persons subject to AA other than officers and Junior Commissioned Officers. [AA s. 119].	1. All sentences authorized under the AA, other than a sentence of death, imprisonment exceeding two years. 2. It has no powers to award imprisonment to a warrant officer. [AA s. 119].	1. Officer empowered to convene GCM; or 2. Officer empowered in this behalf by warrant of officer empowered to convene GCM. [AA s. 155]. 3. Finding and sentence can be sent back for revision once to the court martial. [AA s. 160 and AR 6].	1. May be attended by a Judge Advocate. [AA s. 129] 2. DCM is to give brief reasoned order. [AR 62 (1)].

Type of Court-Martial (AA s. 108)	Power to convene	Composition	Who can be tried	Powers of Punishment	Confirming Authority	Misc Points
3. Summary General Court Martial [SGCM]	1.Officer empowered to convene by orders of (a) Central Government, or (b) COAS 2. On active service: (a) officer commanding the forces in field; or (b) any officer empowered by him in this behalf; or (c) Officer commanding detachment of the regular Army on active service, when in his opinion it is not practicable to try the offence by GCM having due regard to the exigencies of service and to discipline. [AA s. 112]	1. Minimum number of three officers. [AA s. 115]. 2. No qualification prescribed in the AA. AR prescribes one year's minimum commissioned service for members of SGCM. However, it would be preferential to have officers with minimum three years of service. [AR 151 (2)].	All persons subject to AA. [AA s.118].	1. All sentences authorized by the AA s. 71. [AA s. 118] 2. SGCM and GCM, both can award death sentence. However, a SGCM can not award the sentence of death, without the concurrence of all the members. [AA s.132 (3)]	1. Convening officer; or 2. Authority superior to the convening officer, if latter so desires. (AA s. 157 and notes). 3. Finding and sentence can be sent back for revision once to the court martial. [AA s. 160 and AR 68].	1. May be attended by a Judge Advocate. [AA s. 129]. 2. In case accused is an officer or JCO; and in complicated cases, a Judge Advocate must be appointed in the SGCM. Army HQ latter dated 17 November 1962. 3. SGCM is to give brief reasoned order. [AR 62 (1)].

Type of Court-Martial (AA s. 108)	Power to convene	Composition	Who can be tried	Powers of Punishment	Confirming Authority	Misc Points
4. Summary Court Martial [SCM]	1. Held by the commanding officer of any corps, department, or detachment of the regular Army. [AA s. 116]. 2. The commanding officer to make reference to the officer empowered to convene a DCM, in respect of offences under sections 34, 37, 69 or any offence against him. [AA s.120 (2)].	Commanding officer alone constitutes the court. Two officers, or JCOs, or one of the either must attend throughout the trial. [AA s. 116].	All persons subject to AA under the command of the commanding officer, except officers, JCOs and Warrant Officers. [AA s. 120 (3)].	All sentences authorized by the AA other than a sentence of death, imprisonment exceeding one year (when CO is of the rank of Lt Col or above). In case commanding officer is below the rank of Lt Col, imprisonment cannot exceed three months. [AA s. 120 (5)].	1. Confirmation not required. [AA s. 161]. 2. In case, the commanding officer is of less than five years service and is not on active service, the sentence must be approved by an officer commanding not less than a Brigade. [AA s. 161 (2)]. 3. Proceedings to be forwarded to officer commanding division or brigade. [AA s. 163].	1. Proceedings are reviewed by officer commanding div or brigade to whom proceedings are forwarded. 2. The procedure for trial is given in Army Rules 106 to 133. 3. Accused allowed services of a person of his choice as 'friend' to help him defend the case. [AR 129].

Whether a GCM or DCM

In deciding whether an accused should be tried by GCM or DCM, the convening authority must consider the following factors:

(a) The nature of the offence;

(b) The prevalence of the particular offence charged;

(c) The general state of discipline in his command;

(d) The character of the accused; and

(e) The maximum punishment that can be imposed having regard to any sentence which the accused may be already serving. [MML Vol. I, Chapter IV, para 24].

The Role of Convening Authority

The convening officer, when he receives an application for trial by court martial from the CO, must satisfy himself that (i) the charge or charges against the accused constitute an offence under the AA and are framed in conformity with the Army Rules, (ii) the summary of evidence discloses sufficient admissible evidence for trial by court-martial, and (iii) the case is a proper one to be tried by the kind of court martial which the CO proposes to convene. [AR 37]. If the convening officer is not satisfied with the charge or evidence he can order the release of the accused or direct further recording of the summary, called 'additional summary of evidence'. The Judge Advocate of the concerned command gives necessary pre-trial advice to the convening officer. [RA para 459].

Convening Order

Once it is decided that an accused will be tried by court martial, an order for the assembly of the court, known as the convening order, will be issued. This order is to be signed by the convening officer or by a staff officer on his behalf. The convening order contains the details of officers to form the court. [AR 37 and MML, Vol. I, Ch. IV, para 26].

Composition of Court Martial

In addition to the restrictions in the rank of officers appointed to serve on courts martial which are prescribed by the AA and the AR, the following to be observed:

- Whenever an officer of the rank of colonel or above is available to sit as presiding officer of a GCM, an officer of inferior rank will not be appointed. Whenever a GCM may have to be so detailed that an officer below the rank of a colonel will be the senior member and consequently its presiding officer, the convening officer must obtain the prior sanction of his next superior authority and state in the order convening the court that such sanction has been obtained. When the CO of a corps is to be tried, as many members as possible will be officers who have held or are holding commands equivalent to that held by the accused.
- In the case of a GCM, when a trial is likely to be prolonged, it will be expedient to form the court of a larger number than the legal minimum, and two or four additional members should be detailed. Waiting members should also be detailed to meet reduction by challenge.
- The presiding officer of a DCM should, if possible, be of field rank. For a DCM the legal minimum will ordinarily be sufficient; but, if necessary a larger number may be detailed, and waiting members provided. For the trial of doubtful or complicated cases, a DCM should, when possible, consist of five officers. When the minimum number is detailed, not more than one member should be a subaltern.
- Each officer serving as a member of a Court Martial will render the following certificate which will be attached by the Presiding Officer to the proceedings of the court-martial.

Certificate of Commissioned Service

> I, No. ….., Rank ….., Name …….., Unit, ……., hereby certify that I have on the …… day of …… held a commission for …… years. I understand that any service as a JCO or any period of ante-date of commission does not count towards the commissioned service mentioned above, and I have excluded all such periods from the reckoning.
>
> [RA para 460]

The Army Act provides that every GCM shall, and every DCM or SGCM may be attended by a judge advocate who either belongs to the department of the Judge Advocate General (JAG) or in his absence, an officer approved by the JAG or his deputies. The judge advocate is not required to be present at a SCM.

Persons disqualified to serve as members of court martial

(a) An officer not subject to the AA.

(b) An officer not having minimum period of commissioned service.

(c) An officer who has convened the court

(d) An officer who is the prosecutor or witness for prosecution

(e) An officer who has investigated the charges or took down summary of evidence.

(f) An officer was a member of a court of inquiry respecting the matters on which the charges against the accused are founded

(g) CO of the accused.

(h) The provost-marshal or his deputies.

(i) An officer having personal interest in the case. [AR 39 and 40]

Suspension of rules on the ground of military exigencies/ discipline

Where it appears to the officer convening a court-martial, that military exigencies or the necessities of discipline render it impossible or inexpedient to observe any of the AR 23, 24, 33, 34, and 95 (2), he may, by an order, make declaration to that effect specifying the nature of such exigencies or necessities. The court martial trial thereafter shall be as valid as if the rule mentioned in such declaration had not been contained herein. However, it is necessary that the accused is afforded full opportunity of making his defence, having due regard to the said exigencies or necessities. The power conferred by this rule should rarely be exercised except on active service and then only if absolutely necessary. [AR 36].

Prohibition of second Trial

A court martial cannot try or punish a person for any offence of which he has been already acquitted or convicted by a court martial or by a competent civil court or where the charge against him has been dismissed, or he has been dealt with summarily. The prohibition does not apply where there has been no valid trial, resulting in an acquittal or conviction, or where the finding and sentence which require confirmation, have not been confirmed. In such cases the offender can be tried afresh. Such fresh trial should be ordered only in exceptional circumstances. Pardon or condonation by competent military authority, operates as a bar to the trial of an offender. [AA s. 117 (4), 121 and 153; AR 53 (1) (a) and (b)].].

Warning of Accused

The accused before he is arraigned shall be informed by an officer of every charge for which he is to be tried. The accused is to be provided with a copy of the charge-sheet and a copy of the summary of evidence to prepare his defence. Necessary reasonable steps must also be taken to procure witnesses to whom the accused desires to call in his defence. The interval between his being so informed and his arraignment shall not be less than 96 hours or on active service 24 hours. The Supreme Court in the case of *Union of India v A K Pandey* [Civil Appeal No. 1681 of 2002, decided on 16 Sep 2009] held that the provision in Army Rule 34—the interval between the accused being informed of charge for which he is to be tried and his arraignment shall not be less than 96 hours—is mandatory.

An accused person shall have the right to interview any witnesses whom he may wish to call in his defence. The provisions of AR 137 shall apply to procuring the attendance of such witnesses. The accused is also given a list of officers who are to form the court. On the morning before the trial, the accused is medically examined with a view to ascertain whether he is fit to stand the trial by court martial and a medical certificate is obtained in respect of the accused and this is repeated on each morning of the trial until the trial concludes. [RA para 462].

Preparation of Defence

As soon as trial has been ordered, the accused must be afforded a proper opportunity to prepare his defence. He must be permitted to have free communication with any witnesses whom he may desire to call. At any GCM or DCM, an accused may be represented by any officer subject to the AA who is called "the defending officer" or assisted by any person whose services he may be able to procure and who shall be called "the friend of the accused". Every effort should be made to secure the services of a competent officer as a defending officer, and he should be allowed time and opportunity for properly preparing the defence of the accused.

In every GCM and DCM, counsel shall be allowed to appear on behalf of the accused. The counsel shall have the right to call, and orally examine, cross-examine, and re-examine witnesses, to make an objection or statement, to address the court, to put in any plea, and to inspect the proceedings. [AR 95-101].

In a SCM, accused may be assisted by a 'friend'; but such 'friend' whether a legal adviser or not, may only assist the accused by suggesting questions and preparing the defence. He is not allowed to examine or cross-examine witnesses, personally address the court, or take any part in the proceedings. [AR 129].

Defence of accused charged with offence punishable with death

When a person subject to the AA is tried by a court martial for an offence punishable with death and such person is unable to engage a counsel for his defence owing to lack of pecuniary resources and the convening officer is satisfied about his inability, a counsel for the defence of the accused may be engaged by the convening officer at government expenses in consultation with the Dy JAG concerned. The counsel is entitled to TA and DA as admissible to an officer for appearance at court martial. [RA Para 479].

Procedure: Trial by Court-Martial

On the date and time appointed for the trial, the members, the waiting members, and the judge-advocate, if any, assemble in closed court. The senior member takes over as the presiding officer. The members comprising the court then satisfy themselves that (i) the court is legally constituted, (ii) the court consists of a number of officers not less than the minimum required by the law, (iii) each of the officers is eligible for serving on that court martial; (iv) the judge advocate (in cases of GCM and DCM) has been duly appointed and is not disqualified for sitting on that court martial; (v) the accused is amenable to military law and to the jurisdiction of the court; and (vi) each charge discloses an offence under the Army Act. [AR 41 and 42].

If the court is satisfied as to its legal constitution, then the court is opened and the prosecutor and the defending officer or counsel as well as the accused enter the court room taking their respective places.[AR 43]. The accused is introduced in the court duly escorted. The convening order is then read to the accused who is asked whether he objects to be tried by any officer sitting in the court. [AA s. 130; this right is not available in SCM]. Requirement of asking an accused whether he objects to any officer is mandatory. If the accused objects to any of the officers, his objection and any evidence in support are recorded. The remaining officers of the court, in the absence of the challenged one, then vote on the objection. The objection is allowed if one half or more of the officers entitled to vote support it. The member objected to retires immediately and the vacancy thus created is filled in by the senior-most of the waiting officers, subject to the right of the accused to object to him as well. [AR 44].

Swearing or Affirmation of Court

Once the court is duly constituted, the members and the judge-advocate are administered the prescribed oath. If there is any interpreter and a short-hand writer, they are administered the oath prescribed for them. It is followed by the arraignment of the accused. [AR 45].

Arraignment of accused

It is conducted by the judge advocate or by the presiding officer. The important steps are following.

(a) It consists of calling upon the accused by his number, rank, name and description as given in the charge sheet.

(b) Reading each charge separately and if necessary charges are translated and explained to him.

(c) Calling upon the accused to state whether he is guilty or not guilty to each charge separately as it is read out.

(d) When two or more persons are jointly charged and tried for same offence each is separately arraigned. [AR 48].

Accused may object to a charge on the ground that it does not constitute offence under the Act or is not in accordance with the Army Rules. [AR 49]. He may also offer a special plea on the general jurisdiction of the court.

Special Plea to the jurisdiction

An accused, before pleading to any charge may offer a special plea to the jurisdiction of the court and give evidence in support of that plea. In special plea to the jurisdiction (the right of the court to try the accused) the accused may plead that court is improperly constituted in respect of the number of the members, or that he is not amenable to the court, either as not being subject to AA or not subject to that description of the court. For example, a JCO being brought for trial before a DCM.

Evidence in support of special plea must be taken on oath or affirmation. The court will decide the question of jurisdiction in the same manner as any other question. If the plea is over-ruled, the court will proceed with the trial. It has been held in the case of *Maj Dimple Singla v. Union of India* 2008 (2) SLR (Punjab and Haryana) (DB) 306 that the decision of the court martial rejecting special plea under AR 51 should be reasoned one so that it could be examined by the appellate court.

If the special plea is allowed the court must record its reasoned decision and report to the convening officer and adjourn. Such decision is not subject to confirmation and the convening authority should either convene another court for the trial of the accused, or order release of the accused. If the court is in doubt as to the validity of the plea, it may refer the matter to the convening authority, and may adjourn for that purpose or may record a special decision with respect to such plea, and proceed with the trial. [AR 51 and MML Vol. I, Ch IV para 46].

General Plea of Guilty or Not Guilty

If no special plea to the general jurisdiction of the court is offered, or if such plea being offered, is overruled; the accused's plea of "Guilty" or "Not Guilty" is recorded on each charge. If an accused pleads "Guilty", that plea shall be recorded as the finding of the court. However, before it is recorded, the presiding officer or judge-advocate, shall ascertain that the accused understands the nature of the charge to which he has pleaded guilty and shall inform him of the general effect of that plea, and in particular of the meaning of the charge to which he has pleaded guilty, and of the difference in procedure which will be made by the plea of guilty. The court shall advise him to withdraw that plea if it appears from the summary of evidence that the accused ought to plead "Not guilty". The court must satisfy itself that the accused understands the charge(s) and the effect of the plea of "guilty". It must make a record of compliance of AR 52 (2). A plea of "Guilty" shall not be accepted in cases where the accused is liable, if convicted to be sentenced to death, and where such plea is offered, a plea of "Not Guilty" shall be recorded and the trial shall proceed accordingly. [AR 52].

Plea in Bar

It is also open to the accused to offer a plea in bar of the trial on the grounds that (i) he has been tried previously for the same offence by a competent court (criminal court or a court martial), or (ii) he has been dealt with summarily, (iii) a charge in respect of the offence in question had been dismissed by the commanding officer during the investigation by him, (iv) the offence has been pardoned or condoned by competent military authority, or (v) the trial is barred by limitation under the AA s. 122. The court considers the plea in bar and if the facts stated by the accused are sufficient to support the plea, it receives evidence offered by the accused or his counsel and the prosecutor in reference to the plea. If the plea in bar is proved, the court records its findings and notifies it to the convening officer and adjourns. If the findings in relations to the plea in bar are not confirmed, the court may be reassembled by the convening officer and proceed as if the plea had been found not proved. If the court finds that the plea in bar is not proved, it proceeds with the trial. [AR 53].

The accused may offer a plea in bar of trial on the ground that the offence has been pardoned or condoned by competent military authority [AR 53 (1) (b)]. It has long been recognized as a custom of the service that a military offence can be condoned. For the purpose of barring a trial, condonation means such conduct on the part of a competent authority i.e., an authority having power to determine that the charge should not be proceeded with—as is inconsistent with subsequently trying the offender, and as would make it inequitable to do so; it must be a deliberate and intentional act, done with full knowledge of all material facts. If, with full knowledge of the facts, competent authority removes an officer, or allows him to resign, he should not afterwards be tried by court martial for his offence. The fact that after trial, but before confirmation, the accused has been employed in active operations does not effect the legal validity of the sentence, but affords ground for pardon. Pardon or condonation by competent authority, if proved, operates as a bar to the trial of offender. [Notes to AR 53].

Procedure: When Accused Pleads Guilty

Where the accused pleads guilty to the first of two or more charges laid in the alternative, the prosecutor may withdraw such alternative charge or charges without requiring the accused to plead to these and a record to this effect is made in the proceedings. Where alternative charges are preferred and the accused pleads 'not guilty' to the charge which alleges the more serious offence and 'guilty' to the other, the court tries him as if he has pleaded 'not guilty' to all the charges. If the accused pleads 'guilty' to some charges and 'not guilty' to other charges on the same charge-sheet, the trial first proceeds with respect to the latter charges, and, after the finding on these charges, proceeds with the charges on which a plea of 'guilty' has been entered.

After recording the plea of 'guilty' on a charge(s), the court receives any statement which the accused desires to make in reference to the charge. The summary of evidence is read in the court by the prosecutor and is annexed to the court proceedings. The accused can then make a statement in mitigation of punishment and may call witnesses to his character. If from the statement of the accused or from the summary, it appears to the court that the accused does not understand the effect of the plea of 'guilty', it may alter the records and enter the plea of 'not guilty' and proceed with the trial. [AR 54].

Procedure: When Accused Pleads "Not Guilty"

When the accused pleads 'not guilty' to a charge(s), the same is recorded and the court asks the accused whether he wishes to apply for an adjournment on the grounds that any of the rules relating to the procedure before trial have not been complied with or on the ground that he has not had sufficient opportunity for preparing his defence and his reply is recorded. If the court is satisfied with the statement of the accused it may grant such adjournment. After such adjournment the prosecutor begins his case by making an opening address stating the substance of the charge against the accused and the nature and the general effect of the evidence which he proposes to adduce. The prosecutor then calls his witnesses, one by one. The witnesses, who are sworn or affirmed in accordance with the prescribed oath or affirmation, are then examined by the prosecutor. The accused, through his counsel or defending officer, may cross-examine each witness. After the cross-examination, the prosecutor may re-examine the witness. The court may also put a question to a witness if it considers it relevant and necessary to elicit the truth. The judge-advocate too may question the witness. After this the statement of the witness is read over in open court and a certificate is appended to this effect at the end of the evidence, the witness withdraws. [AR 56].

The prosecutor is not bound to call all the witnesses who give evidence in the summary. If the prosecutor intends to call a witness whose evidence is not contained in the summary of evidence, notice of such intention is given to the accused a reasonable time before the witness is called, together with an abstract of his proposed evidence. In case such a witness is called without any notice, the accused is entitled to an adjournment. It is the duty of the court to inform the accused of his right to demand such an adjournment. [AR 134 and 135].

Summoning of Civilian Witnesses: The convening officer, the presiding officer of a court-martial, or the judge advocate or the CO of the accused person may, by summons a civilian person to give evidence in a court martial. The summons to be sent to the magistrate within whose jurisdiction he resides, and such magistrate shall give effect to the summons as if the witness were required in the court of such magistrate. When a witness is required to produce any particular document or other thing in his possession or power, the summons shall describe it with reasonable precision. [AA s. 135].

Examination of Witness on Commission: Whenever in the course of a trial by a court-martial, it appears to the court that the examination of a witness is necessary for the ends of justice, and that the attendance of such witness cannot be procured without delay, the court may address the JAG in order that a commission to take evidence of such witness may be issued. The JAG will then issue a commission to the district magistrate within the local limits of whose jurisdiction such witness resides, to take evidence of such witness. The magistrate shall take down the evidence, which will be read in the court and shall form the part of the proceedings of the court-martial. [AA ss. 137 and 138].

Written reply of Government Officials: If at any trial for desertion, absent without leave, overstaying leave, or not rejoining when warned for service, the accused relies in his defence on a sufficient or reasonable excuse and refers in support thereof to any Government Officer, or if it appears that any such officer is likely to through light on the truth or otherwise of such defence, the Court shall address such officer and adjourn the proceedings until his reply is received. The written reply so received, if signed by the said officer, shall be received in evidence and shall have the same effect as if made on oath at the trial. [AA s. 143].

Plea of No Case

At the close of the case for the prosecution, it is also open to the accused to offer a plea of no case, that the evidence given on behalf of the prosecution in respect of the charge(s) has not established a prima facie case against him and he should not be called upon to make his defence to the charge(s). Where the accused takes such a plea, the prosecutor may address the court in answer thereto and the accused may reply. [AR 57]. If the court allows the plea, it records a finding of 'not guilty' in respect of the charge(s). If it rejects the plea of 'no case' it follows the procedure for taking down the statement of the accused and his evidence. The court shall also record brief reasons while arriving at the finding on the plea. The court may, on its own motion, after the close of the case for prosecution, and after hearing the prosecutor find the accused 'not guilty' of the charge(s), and announce the finding in open court as subject to confirmation.[AR 57 (7)].

Defence of the Accused

After the evidence of prosecution is over, the accused is asked whether he wishes to examine any witness in his defence. The accused is not required to give to the prosecutor or the court a list of his witnesses in advance, but it rests with him alone to secure the attendance of his witnesses. [AR 136 and 137]. The accused is then questioned whether he would like to make a statement in respect of the charge(s). Such a statement may be made orally or in writing but no oath is administered to the accused. The court or the judge-advocate may question the accused for explaining him any fact appearing in his statement. [AR 58]. The accused does not render himself liable to punishment for refusing to answer such questions, though the court is free to draw inferences from such refusals. The accused is also a competent witness for the defence and may give evidence on oath or affirmation in disproof of the charges made against him, but (a) he cannot be called as a witness except on his own request in writing; (b) his failure to give evidence cannot be made the subject of any comment by any of the parties or the court; and (c) if he gives evidence on oath or affirmation, he is examined as the first witness for the defence and shall be liable to be cross-examined by the prosecutor and be questioned by the court. [AR 58 (2)].

Summing up

After the examination of the witnesses, the prosecutor sums up the case and the accused, his defending officer or counsel addresses the court in reply. But if any point of law is raised by the accused, the prosecutor may make his submission with regard to that point. [AR 59]. After the address of the prosecutor and defence, the judge-advocate sums up the case in open court. He explains the charges, the provision of law on which they are based and the legal issues and sums up the evidence on each of the issues of fact. [AR 60].

Duties of Prosecutor

The prosecutor is an officer whose duty is to assist the court in the administration of justice. He should behave impartially to bring the whole of the transaction before the court, and not to take any unfair advantage of, or suppress any evidence in favour of the accused. He should therefore put before the court facts which show the true character of the offence, and must be careful to prove affirmatively any facts tending to show the innocence of the accused or extenuate his offence. He must not introduce matters of aggravation into evidence against the accused unless they are relevant to the charge against him. [AR 77 (1) and (2)].

Finding and Sentence

The court is closed after the judge-advocate's summing up for the consideration of the finding in the presence of the judge-advocate. The finding is reached by a majority vote. The finding on every charge is recorded as a finding of guilty or not guilty.[AR 61 (1) and (2)]. After deliberation on the finding is completed, the findings of the court are announced on each charge in open court, subject to confirmation. [AR 62 (10)].

Speaking Order

Under the Army Act, it was not necessary till 1993, to give evidence on the basis of which the conclusion is arrived at. However, now the court is required to give a brief reasoned order, popularly known as a 'speaking order', in support of its finding. [AR 62 (1)].

Special Findings

The court is also empowered to arrive at special findings, i.e., conviction for an offence not charged. Some examples of special findings are: (i) A person charged with desertion may be found guilty of attempting to desert or being absent without leave. (ii) A person charged with using criminal force may be found guilty of assault. (iii) A person charged with using threatening language may be found guilty of using insubordinate language. (iv) A person charged with any offence under the Army Act may be found guilty of having attempted or abetted the commission of that offence, although the attempt or abetment is not separately charged. [AA s. 139].

Conviction/Acquittal of the Accused

If the finding on charge(s) is 'not guilty' the presiding officer and the judge advocate sign the proceedings, which are transmitted for confirmation. [AR 63]. If the finding on the charge(s) is 'guilty', then the court takes evidence of the records and the general character, age, service, rank, distinguished conduct of the accused, previous convictions by a court martial/criminal court, length of the time in the custody and military decorations or awards of the accused. Evidence of these matters is given by witnesses who have the relevant supporting documents in their custody and the accused may cross-examine such witnesses and may lead evidence in rebuttal. The accused is also entitled to address the court in mitigation of the punishment. [AR 64].

Sentence

The sentence is considered in closed court in the presence of the judge-advocate. The court awards a single sentence in respect of all the offences of which the accused is found guilty.[AR 65]. All the members of the court are required to vote in respect of the quantum of sentence, which is entered in the proceedings and authenticated by the presiding officer and the judge advocate. If the court makes a recommendation for mercy, it must cite the reasons for its recommendations. [AR 66]. The sentence and any recommendation for mercy are announced in open court. The sentence is announced subject to confirmation. [AR 67]. The sentence has to suit the offence and the offender. It should not be vindictive, unduly harsh or disproportionate in a way that it amounts to conclusive proof of bias. For more details on sentencing, please refer Chapter 2.

Confirmation of Finding and Sentence

The finding or sentence of a GCM, DCM or SGCM is not valid unless confirmed. [AA s. 153]. The findings are in the nature of recommendations which may or may not be accepted by the authority empowered to confirm the findings and sentence. The findings and sentence of a GCM may be confirmed by the Central Government or by any officer empowered in this behalf by warrant of the Central Government.[AA s.154]. The findings and sentence of a district court martial (DCM) may be confirmed by any officer having power to convene a general court martial or by any officer empowered in this behalf by warrant of such officer. [AA s. 155]. The findings and sentence of a SGCM may be confirmed by the convening officer or, if he so directs, by an authority superior to him. [AA s. 157]. However, in the case of award of the death sentence, it will be confirmed by the Central Government. [RA para 472 (a)].

In the event that a court-martial finds the accused 'not guilty' the power to confirm or non-confirm the proceedings rests with the COAS in cases:

(a) when the offence charged against any officer is punishable with death, and (b) if the accused officer holds or held the rank of Brigadier or above at the time of commission of the offence. In all other cases of 'not guilty' the powers to confirm or non-confirm the proceedings rests with the GOC-in-C. [RA para 472 (d)].

A member of a court martial, or an officer who has acted as a prosecutor at a court martial, is not to confirm the finding or sentence of that court-martial, and where such member or prosecutor becomes confirming officer, he shall refer the finding the sentence of the court-martial to a superior authority competent to confirm the findings and sentences of court martial. [AR 74].

Power of confirming authority over sentences

The following are the powers of the confirming authority with relation to the sentences of court martial:

(a) Mitigation of punishment to a less amount of the same punishment (AA s. 158 and AR 72).

(b) Remission of the whole or part of a sentence (AA s. 158 and AR 72).

(c) Commutation of the punishment to a different form of punishment lower in the scale of punishments authorized in (AA s. 158 and AR 72).

(d) Variation of a sentence informally expressed, or which is in excess as regards its duration of the punishment allowed by law (e.g., three years' imprisonment awarded by a DCM) (AR 73).

(e) Suspension of the execution of the sentence. (AA s. 182 and 183).

(f) In the case of sentences of imprisonment not combined with dismissal the confirming authority may direct that the sentence shall be carried out by confinement in military custody or military prison. Sentences of imprisonment, combined with dismissal should, as a rule, be undergone in civil prison. [MML Vol. I, Ch IV, para 94].

Mitigation, Remission and Commutation of Punishment

Mitigation is awarding a less amount of the same species of punishment. For example, reducing the length of imprisonment to which an offender has been sentenced; and is in effect equivalent to a remission of part of the sentence. The power to mitigate etc., cannot be exercised whilst execution of sentence is suspended. Remission may be remission of whole or part of the sentence, thus a sentence of imprisonment may be remitted altogether, or a portion of the term may be remitted. Commutation is changing the description of punishment by awarding a punishment lower in the scale of punishment in AA s. 71. For example, forfeiture of seniority in lieu of reduction in rank. [AA s. 158 notes].

Revision of Finding and Sentence

If the confirming authority is dissatisfied with the findings of a GCM, DCM or SGCM, and a confirmation is required, the findings and sentence may be once revised by order of the confirming authority. On such revision, the court, if so directed by the confirming authority, may take additional evidence. The court on revision shall consist of the same officers as were present when the original decision was passed. [AA s. 160].

When the finding is sent back for revision, the court re-assembles in open court, the revision order is read and if the court is directed to take fresh evidence, the same is taken in open court. The court then deliberates on its finding in closed court. If it does not adhere to its earlier finding, it revokes the finding and sentence and records the new finding, and if necessary passes a fresh sentence. When the sentence alone is sent for revision the court cannot revise the finding. After revision the proceedings are transmitted for confirmation. [AR 68]. The power of revision can only be exercised once.

The proceedings of the court martial are processed through the judge advocate to the confirming officer for confirmation. The reports of the officers of the JAG department are confidential and are not communicated directly or indirectly to any lower authority to whom they are addressed. When the proceedings are forwarded to lower formations or to units, such reports are removed. [RA para 471].

The confirming officer, on receipt of the proceedings of a court martial, may confirm or refuse confirmation or reserve confirmation for the superior authority. His decision in this regard is entered in and forms a part of the proceedings. [AR 70]. Non-confirmation of the finding of guilty does not amount to acquittal of the accused. The finding or sentence of a court martial, once confirmed by the confirming officer, becomes final.

Convening of Summary Court Martial (SCM)

It is necessary that the provision of SCM should be used sparingly and exceptionally and preferably only in operational areas where resort to a regular trial is not practicable or when summary/administrative action would not meet the requirements of discipline. The Supreme Court in the case of *Union of India v. Vishav Priya Singh* (decided on July 5, 2016) affirmed the view taken by the Delhi High Court that SCM is an exception and it is imperative that a case must be made out for immediacy of action. The reasons to convene an SCM must be followed by well-articulated reasons or the record itself must justify such resort.

Revision of SCM Proceedings

The findings of a SCM cannot be revised and do not require confirmation. The sentence awarded by the SCM may be carried out forthwith. However, If the officer holding the trial is of less than five years service, he shall not, except on active service, carry into effect any sentence until it has received the approval of an officer commanding not less than a brigade. [AA s. 161].

The proceedings of every SCM must be forwarded (through the Dy JAG of the command in which the trial is held) for review to the officer commanding the division or brigade within which the trial is held or to the prescribed officer. The reviewing officer should, if he considers that justice has been done and that proceedings may legally be upheld, countersign the proceedings. The reviewing officer can, for reasons based on the merits of the case, set aside the proceedings or reduce a legal sentence to any other which the court might have passed. If the sentence is illegal it may be treated as a nullity, and if invalid one of the authorities referred to in AA s. 163 can substitute a valid sentence. If he decides to treat it as nullity, he should when countersigning the proceedings, set aside the sentence and direct that the accused be relieved of all consequences of the sentence, though not of the conviction. After review the proceedings to be returned to the corps to which the accused belonged and preserved for three years. [AA s.162 and AR 133 and 146 (2)].

Annulment of proceedings

The Central Government, the COAS or any prescribed officer may annul the proceedings of any court-martial on the ground that they are illegal or unjust. The prescribed officer for the annulment of proceedings are the officer commanding an army, army corps, division or brigade in respect of proceedings confirmed by him or by a person under his command. [AA s. 165 and AR 202].

Promulgation

The charge(s), finding, sentence, recommendations to mercy, if any and confirmation or non-confirmation of the proceedings of a court martial is promulgated in all cases to the accused. In case of officers, the details of the proceedings are read out to the accused by the formation commander in the presence of his CO and such other officers of his staff as he considers necessary. If the accused has been sentenced to cashiering or dismissal, he will be stripped of his badges of rank and all regimental insignia. In the case of JCOs, WOs and NCOs, the details of proceedings are read out to the accused by his CO in the presence of the adjutant and the senior JCOs of the unit. If he has been sentenced to dismissal, or reduced to ranks or to a lower rank or grade he will be stripped of his badges of rank and regimental insignia. The date of promulgation is recoded on the proceedings. Until promulgation the findings and sentence are not held to have been confirmed. [AR 71, RA para 473].

Remedy against Finding or Sentence of Court Martial

(a) **Before Confirmation**. Any person subject to the AA who considers himself aggrieved by any order passed by any court martial may present a petition to the officer or authority empowered to confirm the findings or sentence of such a court martial, and the confirming authority may take such steps as may be considered necessary to satisfy itself as to the correctness, legality or propriety of the order passed or as to the regularity of any proceeding to which the order relates. [AA s. 164 (1)].

(b) **Post-confirmation**. Any person subject to the AA who considers himself aggrieved after the finding or sentence of a court-martial has been confirmed, may present a petition under AA s. 164 (2) to the Central Government, the COAS or any prescribed officer superior in command to the one who confirmed such finding or sentence, and the Central Government, the Chief of the Army Staff or other officer, as the case may be, may pass such order thereon as it or he thinks fit.

Petition may only be addressed by an aggrieved person either personally or through a representative appointed by a power of attorney. [Notes to AA s. 164]. The procedure for submission of petition is contained in RA para 365.

Pardon, Remission and Parole

The Central Government, the COAS, or other prescribed officers are empowered to take following actions on the petition:

(a) Either with or without conditions which the person sentenced accepts, pardon the person or remit the whole or any part of the punishment awarded; or

(b) Mitigate the punishment awarded; or

(c) Commute such punishment for any less punishment or punishments mentioned in the AA; or

(d) Either with or without conditions which the person sentenced accepts, release the person on parole. [AA s. 179].

These provisions are to be explained to every convicted person at the time of promulgation of the finding and sentence of a court martial. [RA Para 365 (l) and (m)].

However, this power must not be exercised by an officer holding a command inferior to that of the authority confirming the sentence. A pardon takes away the conviction, and when a pardon has been grated the record of conviction must be removed from the pardoned person's conduct sheet. It will not be provable against him, if he is tried again by a court martial and convicted of any offence. Release on parole with conditions has no effect on the finding but merely suspends the execution of the sentence. Unconditional release on parole is tantamount to remission of the unexpired portion of the sentence. [AA s. 179 notes].

If a pardon, parole or a remission of punishment has been granted on any condition; and in the event such conditions not being fulfilled, the authority which granted such pardon, parole or remission may cancel it. The sentence of the court is to be carried into effect thereafter as if such pardon, release or remission had not been granted. [AA s. 180].

Recommendation of Mercy

In view of the discretion of the court martial in awarding sentence, a recommendation to mercy is exceptional. However, if the court makes a recommendation to mercy, it shall give its reasons for its recommendation. The number of opinions by which the recommendation of mercy is made under AR 87 (1), or any question relative thereto, is adopted or rejected, may be entered in the proceedings. A recommendation to mercy will be appended to the sentence; it forms part of the proceedings of the court. [AR 66 and notes]

Suspension of Sentence

A person subject to AA if sentenced by a court-martial to imprisonment, his sentence may be suspended by the Central Government, the COAS, or any officer empowered to convene a GCM or SGCM. For suspending a sentence, it is immaterial whether the offender has already been committed to prison or to military custody. Where a sentence is suspended, the offender is to be released from custody. The authority suspending the sentence may order that the offender be committed to undergo the unexpired portion of the sentence, or the sentence be remitted. [AA ss. 182, 184 and 186]. A periodical review of the suspension of sentence, at intervals of not more than four months must be carried out by the competent authority. He may keep a sentence further suspended. [AA s.187].

In the case of a sentence of dismissal combined with imprisonment has been awarded by a court-martial, and sentence of imprisonment is suspended, then, such dismissal shall not take effect until so ordered by the competent authority under AA s. 182. [AA s. 190]. Where the sentence of imprisonment has been imposed by a court-martial other than a SCM, the confirming officer may, when confirming the sentence, direct that the offender be not committed to prison or to military custody until the orders of the authority authorized to issue suspension have been obtained. Where a sentence of imprisonment is imposed by a SCM, the officer holding the trial or the officer authorized to approve of the sentence may issue similar direction. [AA s. 183].

Suspension of sentences is primarily applicable to offences of a military nature only, although in special cases it may be applied to offences of a civil character. In all cases special attention should be directed to the following points: (i) the age and previous character of the offender, (ii) whether the offence is a first one, (iii) whether the offence was premeditated, (iv) whether the offender was at the time subjected to any special stress, fatigue, disability or temptation, and (v) whether the offender was influenced by others older or of worse character than himself.

Unsatisfactory conduct subsequent to suspension will justify an order to put a suspended sentence into execution, whilst a mere negative abstention from crime would point to the advisability of directing a reconsideration of the sentence at a later date. A person under a suspended sentence is to be regarded entirely as a free man, and is to be placed under no disability whatever excepting only the liability of having his suspended sentence put into execution if he misbehaves. [MML Vol I, Ch. IV, para 119].

Limitation for Trial

An offence other than mutiny, desertion or fraudulent enrolment cannot be tried by court-martial, if three years have elapsed since the date of its commission. A person (other than an officer) cannot be tried even for desertion, other than desertion on active service, or for fraudulent enrolment if the said person, has, subsequently to the commission of offence, served continuously in an exemplary manner for not less than three years with any portion of the regular Army. [AA s. 122 (4) and RA para 465 and 466].

Trial of offender who ceases to be subject to Army Act

Where an offence under the AA had been committed by any person while subject to this Act, and he has ceased to be so subject, he may be taken into and kept in military custody, and tried and punished for such offence as if he continued to be so subject. A court-martial can try such a person who has ceased to be subject to the AA provided that the trial for the offence committed by him while so subject, commences within a period of three years of his ceasing to be so subject. [AA s. 123]. The period of limitation of 3 years does not apply to an offence of desertion or fraudulent enrolment or for any of the offences mentioned in AA s. 37.

The period of limitation commences:

(a) On the date of the offence; or

(b) Where the commission of the offence was not known to the person aggrieved by the offence or to the authority competent to initiate action, the first day on which such offence comes to the knowledge of such person or authority; or

(c) Where it is not known by whom the offence was committed, the first on which he identity of the offender is known. [AA s. 122].

Dissolution of Court Martial

A court martial shall dissolve in the following circumstances:

(a) When court martial is reduced below the minimum number of officers required under the AA.

(b) On account of illness of the Judge Advocate or of the accused before the finding, if it is impossible to continue the trial.

(c) If it appears to the officer who convened the court-martial that the exigencies of the service or the necessities of the discipline renders it impossible or inexpedient to continue the said trial. [AA s. 117].

Insanity of Accused

Whenever, in the course of a trial by a court-martial, it appears to the court that the person charged is by reason of unsoundness of mind incapable of making his defence, or that he committed the act alleged but was by reason of unsoundness of mind incapable of knowing the nature of the act or knowing that it was wrong or contrary to law, the court shall record a finding accordingly. This application of unsoundness of mind of accused and his incapability of making defence should be made before arraignment by his defence. The evidence is support must be given. [AA s.145].

If two or more persons visiting the lunatic asylum certify that the accused person detained therein is capable of making his defence then the Officer

Commanding the army, army corps, division or brigade within the area of whose command the accused is detained or the convening officer or any authority superior to him may take steps to have the accused tried by the same or another court-martial for the offence(s) with which he was originally charged or, if the offence is a civil offence, by a criminal court. [AA s. 146 (b) read with AR 199 (2)].

Re-Trial

When any person subject to the AA has been acquitted or convicted of an offence by a court-martial or by a criminal court, or has been dealt with under AA sections 80, 83, 84 or 85, he shall not be liable to be re-tried on the same offence. There is however, an exception to this rule. Where the court is not legally constituted and has no jurisdiction, for example, the court has been convened by an officer not empowered to do so, the number of officers composing the court is below legal minimum, or if unqualified officers constitute to court, or if AR 22 had not been complied with, then it would amount to the accused not having been really tried and may be tried again on the same charge. [AA s. 121 read with Note 2].

Joint trial of Several Accused

Any number of accused persons may be charged jointly and tried together for an offence averred to have been committed by them collectively. Any number of accused persons, although not charged jointly, may be tried together for an offence averred to have been committed by one or more of them and to have been abetted by the other or others. In such cases, notice of the intention to try the accused persons together shall be given to each of the accused at the time of his being informed of the charges.

The accused(s) may claim, that he or some other accused be tried separately on the ground that the evidence of the other accused persons proposed to be tried together with him, will be material to his defence, or that otherwise he would be prejudiced or embarrassed in his defence. The convening authority or court, if satisfied, shall try the accused(s) separately. If two accused persons are charged separately with committing the same offence, they cannot, even at their own request, be tried together, because they have not been charged jointly. [AR 35].

Court Martial to be Public

The place in which court martial is held for the purpose of trying an offence under the AA shall be an open court to which the public generally may have access. However, if the court is satisfied that it is necessary or expedient in the public interest or for the ends of justice, the court may at any stage of the trial order that the public generally or any portion thereof or any particular person shall not have access to it. [AR 80 and 80 A].

Hours of sitting

A court-martial may sit at such times and for such period between the hours of six in the morning and six in the afternoon as may be directed by the proper superior military authority, but court shall not sit for more than six hours in any one day. If the court considers it necessary to continue the trial after six in the noon or to sit for more than six hours in any one day, it may do so but if it does so should record in the proceedings the reason for so doing. In cases requiring an immediate example or when the convening officer certifies that it is expedient for the public service, trials may be held at any hour. When the court sits on a Sunday or a gazetted holiday, the reasons for so doing should also be recorded in the proceedings. [AR 81].

Need for an Independent Appellate Forum

The remedies available 'before confirmation' and 'after confirmation' in AA s. 164 do not afford any right to an affected person. In fact, AA s.164 defines the powers of military authorities in relation to a court-martial proceeding. Articles 136(2) and 227 (4) of the Constitution of India, provide that the Supreme Court and high courts cannot give special leave to appeal against any judgment, determination or sentence of a military court or tribunal. The absence of even one appeal with power to review the findings and sentence of a court-martial has been a lacuna in the Indian military legal system until recently. The Supreme Court in *PPS Bedi v Union of India* (1982) critically evaluated the Indian military justice systems and recommended for setting up of an independent appellate forum where appeals from court martial could be entertained.

Armed Forces Tribunal Act, 2007

The Armed Forces Tribunal Act (AFT Act) was passed by the Parliament in 2007. The Armed Forces Tribunal and its Benches, established since

August 2009, now exercise the jurisdiction against any order, decision, finding or sentence passed by a court-martial. [AFT Act s. 15 (1)]. The term 'court-martial' has been defined under the AFT Act as "court-martial" means a court-martial held under the Army Act, 1950. [AFT Act s. 3 (f)]. For further details on the subject please refer Chapter 8.

Procedure at Court Martial

Table showing procedure being followed at various kinds of courts martial is as shown in Appendix. (refer page 312)

CHAPTER 6

COMPLAINTS AND PETITIONS

Part III of the Indian Constitution contains Fundamental Rights which are available to every citizen. However, Article 33 of the Constitution empowers the Parliament to restrict or abrogate the Fundamental Rights of military personnel for proper discharge of duties and maintenance of discipline. The Army Act restricts and abrogates some of the Fundamental Rights of members of the Army. Under section 21 of the Act, they are denied the right to be members of trade unions or associations, to attend political meetings and to communicate with the Press. The Parliament has, however, bestowed on them the right to make complaints seeking redress of their grievances. This statutory right has been accorded exclusively to armed forces personnel and is not available to the members of the para-military forces.

AA s. 26 provides that any person below the officer rank (PBOR) who deems himself wronged by any superior or other officer may complain to the CO for the redress of his grievance. When the officer complained against is the officer to whom the complaint should be preferred, the aggrieved person may complain to the officer who is next in superiority to that officer. AA s. 27 provides that any officer who deems himself wronged by his CO or any superior officer, and who on due application made to his CO does not receive the redress to which he considers himself entitled, may complain to the Central Government. The detailed procedure for making statutory complaints under the provisions of AA ss. 26 and 27 is contained in RA para 364.

Complaints

RA para 364 provides that the complaints may be of two kinds: statutory and non-statutory.

Statutory Complaints

Statutory complaints may be made under the provisions of AA ss. 26 and 27 by the following:

(a) Any person subject to the AA other than an officer who deems himself wronged by any superior or other officer.

(b) Any officer who deems himself wronged by his CO or any other superior officer.

(c) Any person subject to the AA against the decision of an authority disposing of a case under AA ss. 80, 83, 84 or 85.

(d) An officer or a JCO who deems himself wronged by the award of censure.

A petition against the finding and sentence of a court-martial needs to be submitted under the AA s. 164, read with RA para 365 and not under para 364.

Number and Extent

An officer has the right to complain to the Central Government, while a JCO, WO and OR can complain only to the Chief of the Army Staff (COAS) and not the Central Government. This right can be exercised only once. A second complaint to these authorities will be allowed only if fresh facts and circumstances have come to light necessitating reconsideration of the case.

Procedure for Submission and Channel to be followed

Statutory complaints by officers are to be addressed to the Central Government, and those by JCOs, WOs and OR, will be addressed to the COAS. The following channel is to be followed while forwarding a statutory complaint:

(a) Company commander or other immediate superior

(b) Commanding officer

(c) Brigade commander or the Sub Area Commander

(d) Divisional Commander or Area Commander

(e) GOC Corps, where applicable

(f) GOC-in-Command

(g) COAS

(h) Central Government

In order to make it easier for all intermediary formations and the Army Headquarters to closely monitor the progress of a statutory complaint, the CO of the complainant shall forward an advance copy of the complaint to all the intermediary formation headquarters and the concerned Branches or Directorates and Complaint and Advisory Board (CAB) (in respect of officers only) at the Army Headquarters. Advance copy of complaints on discipline and vigilance ((DV) matters will not be endorsed to the CAB but only to the Army Headquarters.

The complainant must desist from writing directly to Army Headquarters or the Central Government with regard to the progress of the case. However, if the final decision on the statutory complaint, with or without an accusation against any superior officer, is not taken within a period of 12 months or 9 months, respectively, from the date such a complaint is submitted, the complainant will have the right to represent directly to the Army Headquarters or the Central Government. The complainant needs to inform his CO about his action.

Statutory complaints by officers of the Army Medical Corps (AMC) and Army dental Corps (ADC) and by all JCOs, WOs and OR which pertain to matters relating to promotion, posting, release and discharge will be processed through departmental channels. Where no departmental channel exists, the complaints will be processed through the respective staff channel.

Layout of Complaint

The format for the submission of a complaint will be laid down by the Army Headquarter from time to time. Accordingly, all complaints will be submitted in a standard format prescribed by the Army Headquarter. The complainant is to ensure that the complaint is couched in respectful and proper language. A complaint containing a false statement or a false accusation would render the complainant liable for disciplinary action under the AA. If a complaint contains ac accusation, the complainant will render a certificate, which will be annexed to the complaint and will read as follows:

> "I undertake that any false statement or false accusation made by me in this complaint will render me liable for disciplinary action."

If the complaint contains a serious accusation against any superior officer pertaining to moral turpitude, maturity or professional competence, the next superior authority to the one against whom such an accusation has been made will take necessary the steps to conduct an investigation, as considered necessary.

Action by the Intermediary Authorities

The immediate superior authority in chain will offer his detailed paragraph-wise comments on the complaint. He will also ensure that if the conditions mentioned below are not satisfied, he will withhold the complaint to inform the next superior authority and will inform the complainant of the reasons for withholding the complaint:

(a) That the complaint is complete in all respects and is in the correct form.

(b) That the complaint is not couched in discourteous, disrespectful or improper language.

(c) That the complaint does not contain official documents and correspondence, access to which has not been sanctioned by any formal authority.

Where the complaint is withheld on any of the grounds mentioned in sub-paragraphs (a), (b) and (c) above, the date of submission of the complaint will be counted from the date of the revised complaint, if any. An intermediary authority will examine the complaint and may take any of the following actions:

(a) Where the intermediary authorities arrive at a view, after due examination, that only a partial redress will meet the ends of justice, the same may be granted. In such cases, the intermediary authority granting such redress will further call upon the complainant to express whether he desires to withdraw the complaint, in view of the partial redress granted, within 90 days, and if he concurs it will be communicated to all concerned and the complaint proceeds.

(b) Where the intermediary authority decides to grant full redress, the complainant shall be suitably informed. The next higher authority to the authority granting such relief will be kept informed of the redress sought. Such cases will not be forwarded to the authority to whom the complaint is addressed.

(c) Where the redress prayed for is not given at all, the intermediary authority will forward the complaint, along with his comments and recommendations, through the normal channels to the authority to whom the complaint is addressed for final disposal.

Before forwarding the complaint to the next higher authority, the immediate superior authority of the aggrieved individual will endeavour to interview the complainant, if required, and make such investigations as he considers necessary. He will then forward the complaint, along with his detailed paragraph-wise comments and recommendations, to the next superior intermediary authority. While forwarding the statutory complaint to the next higher authority, the concerned formation headquarters will invariably inform the Army Headquarters about the progress of the case and also inform the complainant through his commanding officer. The paragraph-wise comments are not communicated to the complainant.

Time-Frame for Processing of Complaints

All complaints are required to be dealt with expeditiously at all levels. The following time schedule will be strictly followed:

(a) Time taken to reach Army Headquarters (including transaction period) where the complaint does not contain any accusation requiring investigation.

(i) Unit	-	20 days (where paragraph-wise comments are required to be forwarded)
(ii) Brigade or Sub-Area	-	20 days
(iii) Division or Area	-	25 days
(iv) Corps Headquarters	-	30 days
(v) Command Headquarters	-	40 days
Total	-	**135 days**

(b) Time taken to reach Army Headquarters (including transactions period) where the complaint contains an accusation requiring investigations as mentioned above:-

(i) Unit	-	20 days (where paragraph-wise comments are required to be forwarded)
(ii) Brigade or Sub-Area	-	20 days
(iii) Division or Area	-	25 days
(iv) Corps Headquarters	-	30 days
(v) Command Headquarters	-	40 days
(vi) Additional time for investigation to the Formation HQs which order such investigation	-	45 days (extendable to 60 days)
Total	-	**180 days**

With a view to enable all intermediary formations and the Army Headquarters to closely monitor the progress of statutory complaints, all intermediary and higher authorities will be kept informed. All statutory complaints will be accompanied by a delay report, which will be duly filled and initialled, before forwarding the complaint to the next higher authority. The format for the report will be laid down by the Army Headquarters. Whenever a complaint is delayed for any period exceeding the stipulated time-frame, the reasons for the delay will be annexed to the delay report on a separate sheet of paper. The monitoring of statutory complaints through suitable monitoring schedules and standard operating procedures (SOPs) will be strictly enforced at all levels of the chain of command. The delay apprehended will be projected in time to ensure timely processing and finalization of the complaint. The intermediate formations and headquarters will maintain a record and watch the progress of complaints scrupulously. This includes ensuring accountability for delays, and taking action against the defaulting officers.

The orders of the authority disposing of the complaint will be communicated to the complainant through normal channels. However, a copy of the orders will also be endorsed directly to the complainant by the disposing officer. This will be acknowledged by the individual directly to the authority disposing of the complaint. In addition, the formation/unit concerned will also inform the branch concerned at the Army Headquarters, in writing, that a copy of the order has been handed over to the individual. The orders of the authority need not be reasoned.

Procedure at Army Headquarters

Statutory complaints in respect of JCOs, WOs and OR will be put up to the COAS for a final decision by the concerned directorates through the respective PSO dealing with the subject on which the complaint has been made. In case the subject pertains to more than one branch, the view of the PSOs of those branches should be obtained while projecting the case to the COAS. Cases involving disciplinary matters should be routed through the Adjutant General.

The statutory complaints of officers will be put up to the COAS through the CAB (except statutory complaints on DV matters) by the respective directorate/branches at the Army Headquarters. The COAS may grant full redress to the complainant. In cases where the COAS grants partial redress and in cases where no redress has been granted, the complaint will be forwarded to the Central Government with the recommendations of the COAS.

Non-Statutory Complaints

These can be made under the authority of the Army Order on subjects where the complainant considers himself wronged by an authority other his superior officer or commanding officer and is on subjects that are not covered under the AA ss. 26 and 27. Non-statutory complaints will only be addressed to the immediate superior, company commander or commanding officer, as the case may be. Such complaints will not be addressed directly to higher authorities other than those mentioned in this paragraph, nor will copies be endorsed to such authorities. These complaints are also required to be dealt with expeditiously.

Presently non-statutory complaints are only permitted by the officers against CRs gradings and non-empanelment for promotion. These complaints to be submitted within 60 days of the communication of remarks to the officer concerned or result of promotion board. Format of complaint is as prescribed by MS branch [RA para 364(a)(ii),(o),(p) and AO/02/2016/MS, para 156, 157].

Action at Army Headquarter and Ministry of Defence

The Regulations for the Army do not provide any time-frame within which the Army Headquarter and the Central Government are bound to give the final order. In this regard, the Additional Secretary (I), Ministry of Defence vide ID No. 6891/AS/(I) dated 17 October 2005 has conveyed view of the Raksha Mantri for timely disposal of statutory and non-statutory representations. The Ministry of Defence letter states that "from the time the statutory representation is received in the Service Headquarters to the time it is finally decided, the period should not exceed six months." [Additional Directorate General D&V, Adjutant General's Branch letter No. 62736/AG/DV-1 (P) dated 28 October 2005]. Therefore, keeping in view the RA para 364, and the above mentioned Ministry of Defence letter, the time for disposal of a statutory representation could be a minimum of one year (135 to 180 days of transit period in addition to six months at the Army Headquarters/Ministry of Defence). The transitory period is mentioned in para 364 of the Regulations is minimum and wherever a complaint is delayed for any period exceeding the stipulated timeframe, the reasons for the delay could be explained on a separate sheet of paper.

After a statutory complaint has been rejected by the competent authority, a second non-statutory/ statutory complaint on the same subject based on fresh facts, will not be disposed of by the intermediary authority. Such cases will be forwarded to the competent authority for reconsideration of earlier decisions [RA para 364(a)(ii),(o),(p) and AO/02/2016/MS, para 156, 157].

Statutory Complaints: Ex-servicemen

The persons, who have ceased to be subject to the Army Act, on retirement, discharge, dismissal or termination of service under AA ss. 19 or 20, may submit statutory complaints subject to the following conditions.

(a) The complaint should pertain to a military wrong suffered while in service and dating back to the period of 90 days from the date of retirement, discharge, dismissal or termination from the service.

(b) The complaint should be filed within 90 days from the date of retirement, discharge, dismissal or termination from the service.

(c) Under exceptional circumstances, supported with sufficient reasons, a complaint may be submitted after 90 days. However, it will be solely at the discretion of the authority to whom the complaint is addressed, whether to entertain it or not.

There complaints are treated 'statutory', as if filed under section 26 and 27 of the Army Act. [ADGD&V letter No. 62736/AG/DV-1 (P) dated 16 December 1999].

Petitions

Petitions relates to request made to a civil authority seeking redress for wrong or the grant of some official favour. The Regulations for the Army provides for processing of petitions from serving personnel as well as ex-servicemen.

Petitions of Serving Personnel: Petitions addressed to civil authorities from all ranks, which are forwarded regimentally, are to be forwarded by the commanding officer, who will satisfy that the petition does not concern:

(a) the grievances of anyone except the petitioner, his wife or minor children or any near relative who is unable to represent his case;

(b) a case pending before a court, except a request for its expedition; or

(c) the re-opening of a case already decided by a civil or criminal court. [RA para 367].

Petitions by Ex-Soldiers: The procedure to be observed for the submission of petitions to the military authorities by persons who have been but are no longer in military employ (including reservists), or their relative, on matters relating to their military service is as under:

(a) In the first instance the person who wishes to submit a petition should, whenever possible, consult the nearest member of Zila Sainik Board.

(b) When necessary, a petition is to be addressed to the commanding officer the petitioner's last unit or in the case of disbanded units to the authority indicated on the discharge certificate. Wherever possible, the remarks of the member of the Zila Sainik Board concerned are to be endorsed thereon.

(c) Commanding officers, after careful consideration, refer petitions to higher authority, which they are unable to dispose of themselves or on which it is desirable that the orders of higher authority should be passed. Such referred petitions will be accompanied by full particulars and, where possible, a definite recommendation.

(d) Petitions should in no case be sent direct to the Central Government, the Chief of the Army Staff, or to officers at Army Headquarters. Petitions so addressed involve further delay in examining the petitioners request as it is invariably necessary to refer it to the petitioners unit before any reply can be given.

Commanding officers are to ensure that these orders are understood by all persons in military employ at the lime of their transfer to reserve or discharge. [RA para 368].

Disposal

Petitions, especially those submitted by ex-soldiers or their relatives to military formations are to be replied to in clear and sympathetic language. As far as possible, the replies should be in the language in which they are written and also in the language in vogue for correspondence for the benefit of touring officers. In cases where a petitioner's request cannot be granted, the reasons for rejection should be sympathetically explained. Paragraphs of regulations or instructions are not to be quoted, as in the majority of cases they convey no meaning to these petitioners. [RA para 369].

CHAPTER 7

COURT OF INQUIRY

Definition and Composition

A court of inquiry is an assembly of (i) officers, or (ii) junior commissioned officers, or (iii) officers and junior commissioned officers/ warrant officers/ non-commissioned officers directed to collect evidence, and, if so required, to report with regard to any matter which may be referred to them. The court of inquiry should normally consist of three members. However, it may consist of any number of officers of any rank, or of one or more officers together with one or more JCOs or WOs or NCOs. The members of the court may belong to any branch or department of the service, according to the nature of the investigation. [AR 177 (1) and (2)].

Members of Courts of Inquiry

The convening officer is to ensure that a court of inquiry is composed of members whose experience and training best fit them to deal with the matter at issue. The personnel detailed to constitute the court of inquiry should have no personal interest or involvement, direct or indirect, in the subject matter of the investigation.

The officer assembling a court of inquiry is to appoint a presiding officer by name. The senior member has to preside, if such officer has not been appointed. [RA para 517]. When the character or military reputation of an officer is likely to be material issue, the presiding officer of the court of inquiry must be senior in rank and other members at least equivalent in rank to that officer. [RA para 518].

Assembling Authority

A court of inquiry may be assembled by the officer in command of any body of troops, whether belonging to one or more corps. [AR 177 (3)]. A departmental court of inquiry may be assembled by head of an arm or service to enquire into departmental matters like poor quality of work, financial losses in MES, or medical installations. A staff court of inquiry may be assembled by a formation commander to inquire into matters concerning discipline as well as department. [Army Headquarters letter A/004/AG/DV-1 dated 12 April 1991].

Recording

- The court shall be guided by the written instructions of the authority who assembled the court. The instructions must be full and specific and state the general character of the information required. Previous notice of the time and place of the assembly of a court of inquiry, and of all adjournments of the court, must be given to all persons concerned in the inquiry.
- While recording the evidence of witnesses, the court may put such questions to a witness as it thinks desirable for testing the truth or accuracy of any evidence he has given and otherwise for eliciting the truth. The whole of the proceedings of a court of inquiry is to be forwarded by the presiding officer to the officer who assembled the court.
- Evidence must be collected as per the terms of reference.
- Provisions of AR 180, where applicable, must be complied with to avoid miscarriage of justice.
- The court may be re-assembled as often as the officer who assembled the court may direct, for the purpose of examining additional witnesses, or further examining any witness, or recording further information. [AR 179].
- When investigating damages to service equipment, the evidence of a technical officer who is experienced and fully conversant with the technical details of the equipment should be recorded [RA para 518].

Evidence on oath or affirmation

The evidence in a court of inquiry is to be recorded on oath or affirmation when a court of inquiry is assembled:

(a) on a prisoner of war, or

(b) to inquire into illegal absence under AA s. 106, or

(c) in any other case when so directed by officer assembling the court.

The court is to administer the oath or affirmation to witnesses as if the court were a court-martial. The form of oath and affirmation is contained in AR 140. The members of the court are not required to be sworn or affirmed. [AR 181].

Attendance of Civilian Witnesses

A civilian witness may be summoned to attend a court of inquiry. The summons (in the form provided in Appendix III to the AR) can be issued under the hand of the presiding officer or the officer assembling the court. [AA s. 135 (1), AR 179 (5A)]. Civilian witnesses are entitled to conveyance and travelling expenses.

Procedure when Character or Military Reputation is Affected

In a court of inquiry, as soon as it appears to the court, that the character or military reputation of any person subject to the AA is affected by the evidence put forward, the presiding officer must immediately arrange for such person. He may adjourn the court if necessary for the purpose of securing the attendance of the affected person. The affected person must be given full opportunity (i) to be present throughout the inquiry, (ii) to make any statement, and of giving any evidence he may wish to make or give, (iii) to cross-examining any witness whose evidence, in his opinion, affects his character or military reputation, and (iv) to produce any witnesses in defence of his character or military reputation. [AR 180].

Whenever it appears that the character or military reputation of a person subject to the AA is likely to be affected as the result of the court of inquiry, the authority who assembles the court is to take all necessary steps to ensure that provisions contained in AR 180 are observed. The presiding officer of the court shall take such steps to ensure that the person so affected and not previously notified receives notice of and fully understands his rights, under the rule. The ultimate responsibility of ensuring that they are observed in every case rests upon the presiding officer of the court of inquiry.

AR 180 has a statutory force and is mandatory. It incorporates the principles of natural justice which alone can ensure a fair trial to a person whose character or military reputation is in danger. It is now well settled that even in administrative action the principles of natural justice must be observed because the administration is obliged to follow fair play in action when it is dealing with the character and reputation of a person. There is one other reason why the requirements of AR 180 are to be strictly interpreted, the normal protection of fundamental rights as per the provisions of Article 311, available to the civil servants under the Union or a State are not available to military personnel. The procedural safeguards envisaged under the rule are not only fair but also just. It ensures fairness in action and affords equality before law and equal protection of law to a person who is subject to AA and who is brought before the court of inquiry.

The Armed Forces Tribunal (Principal Bench) in *Lt Gen Avadhesh Prakash (Retd) v. Union of India* (OA 66 of 2010) decided on 22 February, 2010 held: "the norms of principles of natural justice are required to be followed in the court of inquiry proceedings. The Army Rule 180 clearly contemplates that the incumbent should get fair opportunity and fair opportunity means that in normal course all the witnesses should have been examined in his presence so that the person, whose reputation is at stake, should get an opportunity to cross-examine the witnesses. This is the normal rule."

It was alleged by the petitioner that he was not given sufficient opportunity before the court of inquiry to defend himself, when his reputation and his character was assassinated, which is in serious violation of AR 180. He was called as 19th witness, when 18 witnesses have been deposed. At the end of his statement cognizance was taken against him and he was asked to cross-examine other witnesses. He was asked to sign a certificate, which stated that he has been given an opportunity to cross examine witnesses or to peruse the statements, which were already recorded in his absence.

The Tribunal had earlier examined the provision in the case of *Lt Gen Surender Kumar Sahni v. Union of India* [TA No. 34 of 2009] and was of the view that AR 180 clearly stipulates that throughout the court of inquiry full opportunity should be given to incumbent including the right to cross-examine or examine any witness. Delhi High Court had also examined the provisions of AR 180 [2008 (3) SLR 39] and was of the view that the requirement under AR 180 would be mandatory.

Proceeding of court of inquiry not admissible in evidence

The proceedings of a court of inquiry, or any confession, statement, or answer to a question, made at a court of inquiry, are not admissible in evidence against a person subject to the AA. The evidence recorded in a court of inquiry cannot be given against any such person except upon the trial of such person for willfully giving false evidence. However, the proceeding can be used by the prosecution or the defence for the purpose of cross-examining any witness. [AR 182].

No Right to Demand a Court of Inquiry

An officer, JCO or WO has no right to claim that a court of inquiry be assembled to inquire into any incident or matter. [RA para 394 (f)].

Right of persons to copies of statements and documents

Any person subject to the AA whose character or military reputation is affected by the evidence before a court of enquiry shall be entitled to copies of such statements and documents as have a bearing on his character or military reputation, unless the COAS for reasons recorded by him in writing, orders otherwise. Any person subject to the AA who is tried by the court-martial shall be entitled to copies of such statements and documents contained in the proceedings of a court of enquiry, as are relevant to his prosecution or defence at his trial. [AR 184].

Court of Inquiry a must in Certain Cases

The following cases must be investigated by a court of inquiry:

- (a) Absence without leave exceeding 30 clear days (AA s. 106).
- (b) Loss of a weapon or its part (AA s. 89).
- (c) Financial irregularities (RA para 519).
- (d) Fatal or grievous injuries (RA para 520).

(e) On prisoner of war (AR 181 and RA para 524).

(f) Loss of secret document (RA para 525).

(g) Explosions and accidents on range (RA para 602).

(h) Outbreak of fire (RA para 1195).

(i) Breaches of discipline: collective insubordination, serious MT accidents, suicide or attempted suicide, murder and rape when committed against a person subject to the Army Act, Navy Act or Air Force Act (RA para 522).

Court of inquiry into Illegal Absence

A court of inquiry as to illegal absence held under AA s. 106, when assembled, requires the attendance of such witnesses as it thinks sufficient to prove the absence. The court shall examine all witnesses who may be desirous of coming forward on behalf of the absentee. The court shall put such questions to them as may be desirable for testing the truth or accuracy of any evidence they have given and otherwise for eliciting the truth, and the court in making its declaration shall give due weight to the evidence of all such witnesses. An oath or affirmation shall be administered to the witnesses as specified in AR 140.

The court shall take down the evidence in writing and at the end of the proceedings shall make declaration that (number, rank, name) illegally absented himself for a period of 30 clear days, excluding the day on which the absence commenced and that on which the court of inquiry assembled. The CO of the absent person shall enter in the court-martial book of the corps or department a record of the declaration of the court, and the original proceedings will be destroyed. When the declaration is to be produced in evidence at a court-martial, a copy will be made on IAFD-918 which is admissible under AA s. 142 (4), and to be produced instead of the court martial book. [AR 183].

AR 183 (4) provides that the court shall examine all witnesses who may be desirous of coming forward on behalf of the absentee, and shall put such questions to them as may be desirable for testing the truth or accuracy of any evidence they have given and otherwise for eliciting the truth, and the court in making its declaration shall give due weight to the evidence of all such witnesses.

Court of inquiry relating to absence without leave and desertion in areas where law and order situation is bad or where terrain is inhospitable should be conducted thoroughly before declaring an individual absentee. There may be occasions where individual might have met with an accident resulting in death while the unit authorities presume him to be a deserter. It is desirable that the circumstances under which the person has absented are examined in greater depth and the unit must ascertain that that there are sufficient reasons to believe that the individual has deserted. If the person concerned has a good service record and there is no apparent motive for him to desert the service the possibility that he has met with some untoward incident or was involved in an accident must be explored and ruled out before he is declared absent without leave.

Court of Inquiry in case of Prisoner of War

The officer who assembled the court shall, when the court is held on a returned prisoner of war or on a prisoner of war who is still absent, direct the court to record its opinion whether (i) the person concerned was taken prisoner through his own willful neglect of duty, or (ii) whether he served with or under, or aided the enemy. The assembling authority shall also direct the court to record its opinion in the case of a returned prisoner of war, whether he returned as soon as possible to the service and in the case of a prisoner of war still absent whether he failed to return to the service when it was possible for him to do so. The officer who assembled the court shall also record his own opinion on these points. [AR 179 (2)].

A court of inquiry on a prisoner of war who is still absent may be assembled in order to assist the authorities in determining what remission of forfeiture of pay and allowances to be ordered and the provision [in terms of AA ss. 98 and 99] to be made for the dependants of such prisoner of war. A second court of inquiry must be assembled as soon as possible after the return of the prisoner of war. [RA para 524].

Declaration by Members on recovered Prisoner of War: When the court of inquiry is on recovered prisoners of war, the members shall make the following declaration: "I do declare upon my honour that I will duly and impartially inquire into and give my opinion as to the circumstances in which ....(name of person) became a prisoner of war, according to the true spirit and meaning of the regulations of the regular Army; and I do further declare, upon my honour that I will not on any account, or at any time disclose or discover my own vote or opinion or that of any particular member of the court, unless required to do so by competent authority". [AR 178].

Court of Inquiry: Loss of Secret Document

Every loss of a Top Secret, Secret or Confidential document or key is brought to the notice of the formation commander concerned, who will convene a court of inquiry. The court should be presided over by a senior officer not belonging to the unit or headquarters where the loss has occurred, and include not less than two other officers, to investigate the matter and to advise what further steps should be taken.

Any individual subject to AA who is implicated in any way in the loss of the document forming the subject of the court of inquiry, will be afforded full opportunity of being present throughout the inquiry, and of making any statement, and of giving any evidence he may wish to make or give, and of cross examining any witness, whose evidence in his opinion affects his character or military reputation, and of producing any witness in defence of his character or military reputation (AR 180).

The court will sit 'in camera'. Every witness will be cautioned that any disclosure by him of any matters forming part of the proceedings of the court may be treated as an offence against the Official Secrets Act, 1923. A copy of the proceedings of the court will be forwarded to Army Headquarters, General Staff Branch, MI Directorate, MI-11 through staff channels. [RA Para 525].

Court of Inquiry: MT Accidents

The cases of MT accident resulting in death or serious injuries must be investigated by a court of inquiry. The following witnesses to be examined in the inquiry:-

(a) Eye witnesses (including civilians, if any) to the accident.

(b) Co-driver/person (s) sitting in on co-driver's seat.

(c) Persons sitting in the body of the vehicle.

(d) Persons who detailed the vehicle.

(e) Persons who inspected the vehicle for roadworthiness before the journey.

(f) Persons who inspected the vehicle after the accident.

(g) Medical officers or doctors, who attended the victims, declared the person dead and carried out post-mortem examination.

(h) Civilians injured in the accident.

(i) Persons who identified the dead body to the medical officer.

(j) Person who took over the dead body after post-mortem examination and performed last rites.

(k) Person who can produce evident regarding damage caused to service vehicle as a result of the incident.

Recording of evidence: The court must record the following evidence:-

(a) Mission of the service vehicle (whether on bonafide duty).

(b) Whether it was roadworthy before commencement of the journey.

(c) Whether the driver was physically fit to undertake the journey and drive the vehicle or had he complained of any illness before proceeding on duty. Experience of driver for driving the vehicle on the highways.

(d) Route on which the vehicle was driven immediately prior to the accident, nature of traffic on the road, road surface, whether conditions, width of the road and with of the road bends, topography of the place of incident, etc.

(e) Circumstances leading to the accident, such as sudden failure of the brakes, appearance of victims, or cattle in front of the vehicle.

(f) How exactly the accident occur? Evidence collected should bring out clear details without any vagueness. The evidence e should give a clear picture so that it may be possible to deduce whether the driver could or could not have avoided the accident.

(g) The exact place where accident took place.

(h) Events after the accident such as evacuation of the victim and injured persons to hospital, reporting of incident to police, post-mortem, cremation/burial of the deceased and treatment of the injured person.

Medical evidence: The medical officer or doctor who first attended the victims after the accident should state the following: (i) General conditions of the victims; (ii) Injuries observed by him; (iii) Treatment given to the victims; (iv) If brought dead or died while giving treatment; date and time of death; (v) Whether he declared the victim dead; and (vi) Probable cause of death of the victim, if possible. In case of victim who were injured, the medical officer or doctor who first attended the victim after the accident should state the following: (i) Nature of the injuries; (ii) Probable cause of injuries; (iii) How long the victim was treated; and (iv) Date of discharge. The doctor who conducted the post-mortem examination of the victim should state the general condition of the victim, extent of external and internal injuries, probable cause of death and the particulars of person who identified the dead body to the doctor?

The following documents relating to the service vehicles are required to be produced through independent witnesses: (i) Traffic accident report (IAF-2022); (ii) Technical inspection report (EO-3); (iii) Extract of car diary; (iv) Civil police 'Panchnama' with English translation; (v) Report from Provost Unit; (vi) Cost of damage to service vehicle as assessed by the Electrical & Mechanical Engineering workshop, if any; and (vi) Copy of FIR.

Court of Arbitration

Courts of arbitration (panchayat) for the settlement of private disputes may be held in units with the consent of the parties concerned. The commanding officer is to ensure that the record contains (i) the substance of the matter, (ii) the names of the arbitrators appointed by the disputants, (iii) the umpire appointed by him, and (iv) the agreement of those concerned, to abide by the decision of the majority. The award in the case of pecuniary damages, should not exceed six months' pay and allowances, and to be signed by the presiding officer. The commanding officer may not set aside a permissible award because he dissents from it.

The officer, who is named as arbitrator under the arbitration clause, should satisfy himself that the parties concerned have both agreed that the matter should be dealt with by him as arbitrator. The arbitrator should next ensure that both parties are clear as to exactly what is to be referred for arbitration. Before taking up the reference for final decision, the arbitrator should issue notices to both parties, giving a date for them either to submit their cases in writing or to appear before him. The parties should be given an opportunity to appear and produce documents and call witnesses, if they so desire. The arbitrator may refuse to admit irrelevant evidence but should be careful to admit all evidence material to the question which the parties may choose to put before him, as refusal might be fatal to the award. The award should set out the point or points referred and the arbitrator's decision. The arbitrator must be fair to both sides. He is not, however, bound by the rules of evidence under the BSA. [RA para 527 and 528].

Courts of Inquest

Section 194 of the BNSS, makes the local civil authorities responsible for holding an inquest in cases of unnatural deaths, i.e. deaths due to suicide, violence, accident or under suspicious circumstances. Written information regarding cases of such deaths of persons subject to the Army Act or of those not subject to the Army Act which occur within the unit lines is to be conveyed by commanding officer immediately, by hand, to the local civil police officer. If the civil police authorities do not intend sending the dead body for a post-mortem examination and decide not to hold an inquest, the concerned military authorities must obtain a declaration in writing.

Where the civil authorities are not easily accessible as for instance in operational areas and it is not practicable for them to hold an inquest before the dead body may become putrefied, a general approval for conducting Military Courts of Inquest may be obtained in advance from the State Governments concerned.

Where the sanction in writing has been obtained from the civil authorities to carry out the inquest under the aegis of the military authorities, a military court of inquest with comprehensive terms of reference should be held. The court of inquest should include medical officer as a member of the court, with comprehensive terms of reference. The court after having given permission to dispose of the dead body should further investigate the circumstances of occurrence of death, attributability and related matters by following the procedure for a court of inquiry. In the subsequent proceedings the attendance of the medical member may not be insisted upon depending upon the circumstances of the case because of the nature of his employment.

The funeral or cremation in such cases should take place only after obtaining the concurrence of the presiding officer and the medical member of the court of inquest. Where a court of inquest has been held by civil authorities, a court of inquiry should be held to investigate the circumstances of death and ascertain the military aspect of attributability for the purpose of pension benefits. A military court of inquest follows the same procedure as a court of inquiry. The convening officer is to forward a copy of the court's proceedings (only up to the inquest stage) to the magistrate of the area concerned having authority to hold an inquest. [For further details, see RA para 529].

Board of Officers

A board of officers differs from a court of inquiry in that the object for which it is assembled must not involve any issue of discipline. Such a board may follow the rules of court of inquiry for convenience, but it is not bound by them.

All proceedings of courts of inquiry, committees and boards for which special forms are not provided are to be written on IAFD-931. [RA para 516].

CHAPTER 8

ARMED FORCES TRIBUNAL

The Supreme Court of India, in the case of *Lt Col P P Singh Bedi* (1982), pointed out a glaring deficiency in the Army Act, *viz* the absence of the remedy of appeal against the order of a court-martial. The court had also expressed the necessity for an independent appellate forum for the armed forces. In order to meet the aspirations of the armed forces personnel, the Parliament passed the Armed Forces Tribunal Act (AFT Act), 2007. The Armed Forces Tribunal and its benches constituted under the Act of 2007 provide a forum where applications related to service matters as well as appeals against the decisions of courts-martial can be taken up.

Composition

The principal bench of the Armed Forces Tribunal, at Delhi, is headed by the chairperson, and has judicial and administrative members. A bench of the tribunal consists of one judicial member and one administrative member. The chairperson, depending upon the nature of a dispute, may order for a bench with more than two members. However, every bench constituted in pursuance of this clause shall include at least one judicial member and one administrative member.

A total of 15 benches have been created across India. A table indicating the number of benches and the locations is as follows.

S No	Location	No. of Benches
1	Delhi (Principal Bench)	3
2	Chandigarh	3
3	Lucknow	3
4	Kolkata	1
5	Guwahati	1
6	Mumbai	1
7	Kochi	1
8	Chennai	1
9	Jaipur	1

If at any time the vice-chairperson of a bench is satisfied that circumstances exist which render it necessary to have a sitting of the said bench at any place falling within its territorial jurisdiction other than the place or places at which it ordinarily sits, he may, with the consent of the chairperson, direct that the additional bench shall hold its sittings at any such appropriate place.

Only a former judge of the Supreme Court or a former chief justice of a high court can be the Chairperson of the tribunal.

Qualifications for Administrative Member: The qualifications, eligibility, salary and other terms and conditions of the appointment of a candidate is now governed by the Tribunal Reforms Act, 2021 and Tribunal (Conditions of Service) Rules, 2021. As per Rule 14(3) of the Tribunal (Conditions of Service) Rules 2021, a person shall not be qualified for appointment as Administrative Member, unless he/she:

(i) Has held or has been holding the rank of Major General or total period of three years in the Army or equivalent rank in the Air Force; or

(ii) Has served for not less than one year as Judge Advocate General in the Army or the Navy or the Air Force, and is not below the rank of Major General, Commodore and Air Commodore respectively; or

(iii) Is a person of ability, integrity and standing having special knowledge of, and professional experience of not less than thirty years in, economics, business, commerce, law, finance, accountancy/ management, industry, public affairs, administration or in any other matter useful to the Armed Forces Tribunal.

As per Rules 10 and 11 of the Tribunal (Conditions of Service) Rules, 2O21, the salary of a Member of Armed Forces Tribunal is Rs 2,25,000 per month plus other allowances as admissible.

Procedure for Selection: The Search-cum-Selection-Committee constituted under the Tribunal Reforms Act, 2O21 for recommending names for appointment to the said posts shall scrutinize the applications with respect to suitability of application for the posts by giving due weightage to qualifications and experience of candidates and shortlist candidates for conducting personal interaction. The final selection will be done on the basis of overall evaluation of candidates done by the Committee based on the qualification, experience and personal interaction.

Selection for re-appointment: The Member of Armed Forces Tribunal shall be eligible for re-appointment in the same manner as that for the original appointment, preferably, along with all the persons shortlisted in response to the vacancy circular or otherwise under the Tribunal Reforms Act, 2021 While making its assessment for suitability to a post, the Committee shall give additional weightage to the persons seeking re-appointment for their experience in the Tribunal and while doing so, shall take into account, the performance of the person while working as a Member in the Tribunal.

Jurisdiction

The tribunal has original jurisdiction over the service matters and appellate jurisdiction against order, finding or sentence passed by a court-martial.[AFT Act ss. 14 and 15].

Original Jurisdiction: The Armed Forces Tribunal has original jurisdiction over service matters. The term 'service matters' is defined in section 3 (o) of the Act, and includes:

(a) Remuneration, allowances, pension and retirement benefits.

(b) Tenure, including commission, appointment, enrolment, probation, confirmation, seniority, training, promotion, reversion, premature retirement, superannuation, termination of service and penal deductions.

(c) Summary disposal and trials where the punishment of dismissal is awarded.

(d) Any other matter, whatsoever.

The tribunal does not have jurisdiction in matters relating to (i) order of dismissal invoking the doctrine of Presidential pleasure (ii) transfers and postings, (iii) leave; (iv) summary trials, except where the punishment is of dismissal; and (iv) summary court-martial, except where the punishment is of dismissal or imprisonment for more than three months.

Appellate Jurisdiction: Under its appellate jurisdiction, the tribunal may allow an appeal against conviction by a court-martial where (a) the finding of the court-martial is legally not sustainable due to any reason whatsoever; or (b) the finding involves a wrong decision on a question of law; or (c) there was a material irregularity in the trial resulting in miscarriage of justice. In other cases, the tribunal shall be empowered to dismiss the appeal where it considers that no miscarriage of justice is likely to be caused or has actually resulted to the applicant. While dismissing an appeal the tribunal shall give reasons in writing. It may allow an appeal against conviction and pass an appropriate order. [AFT Act s. 15].

Power of the Tribunal in Service Matters

The tribunal, while disposing an application relating to a service matter, may summon and enforce the attendance of any person, require the production of any document, and may receive evidence of affidavit. While adjudicating an application under AFT Act s. 14, it is empowered to issue commission for the examination of witnesses or documents, or may requisition any public record or document from any office. However, this power shall be subject to the provisions of ss. 123 and 124 of the Indian Evidence Act, 1872. The tribunal may (i) review its decisions; (ii) dismiss an application for default or decide it *ex parte*; and (iii) set aside any order of dismissal of any application for default or any order passed by it *ex parte*. It shall decide both questions of law and fact. In case the tribunal dismisses an application, it will record reasons in writing.

Power of the Tribunal in Appeal

The tribunal, while disposing an appeal against the decision of a court-martial under AFT Act s. 15, is deemed to be a criminal court. It is empowered to:

(a) Substitute for the findings of the court-martial, a finding of guilty for any other offence for which the offender could have been lawfully found guilty by the court-martial and pass a fresh sentence;

(b) If the sentence is found to be excessive, illegal or unjust, the tribunal may (i) remit the sentence, (ii) mitigate the punishment awarded, or (iii) commute such punishment to any lesser punishment mentioned in the Army Act;

(c) Enhance the sentence awarded by a court-martial;

(d) Release the appellant, if sentenced to imprisonment, on parole with or without conditions;

(e) Suspend a sentence of imprisonment; or

(f) Pass any other order as it may think appropriate. The tribunal also has the power to quash a conviction and order a re-trail by a court-martial.

The AFT Act does not provide any fixed time-frame for deciding an application or appeal. The tribunal is a court of record. It shall not be bound by the procedure laid down in the Code of Civil Procedure (CPC), but shall be guided by the principles of natural justice.

Transfer of Pending Cases

The Act also provides for the transfer of pending cases from various high courts. Every suit or other proceeding pending before any court including a high court before the date of establishment of the tribunal would stand transferred to the tribunal. The court or other authorities after such transfer are also required to forward the records of such suit, or proceeding to the tribunal. The tribunal, on receipt of such records, will proceed to deal with such suit or proceeding, in the same manner as in the case of an application made under AFT Act s. 14 (2), from the stage which was reached before such transfer or from any earlier stage or de novo as the tribunal may deem fit.

Power to Punish for Contempt

The tribunal has power to punish for its contempt. Any person who is guilty of contempt of the tribunal by using any insulting or threatening language, or by causing any interruption or disturbance in the proceedings of the tribunal shall, on conviction, be liable to suffer imprisonment for a term which may extend to three years. For the purposes of trying an offence under this section, the provisions of sections 14, 15, 17, 18 and 20 of the Contempt of Courts Act, 1971 (70 of 1971) shall mutatis mutandis apply.

Power to Grant Bail

The tribunal is empowered to grant bail to a military accused [AFT Act s. 15 (3)], but not to a convict. However, an accused shall not be released on bail if he has been charged with an offence punishable with death or imprisonment for life. The power of the tribunal in this regards is lower than that bestowed on the sessions court in India.

Filing of Application and Court Fee

A person aggrieved by an order pertaining to any service matter over which the tribunal has jurisdiction may make an application to the tribunal along with the prescribed fee and necessary documents. The Procedure for filing application to the Tribunal is contained in Rule 4 of the Armed Forces Tribunal (Procedure) Rules, 2008. The application is required to be presented in **Form I** by the applicant in person or by an agent or by a duly authorized legal practitioner to the Registrar or any other officer authorized in writing by the chairperson or vice-chairperson to receive the same or be sent by registered post or by courier with acknowledgment due addressed to the registrar of the bench concerned. [Appendix A to the Armed Forces Tribunal (Procedure) Rules. 2008].

An application is to be filed with the registrar of the bench within whose jurisdiction (i) the applicant is posted for the time being, or was last posted or attached; or (ii) where the cause of action, wholly or in part, has arisen. However, with the leave of the chairperson the application may be filed with the registrar of the principal bench and such application shall be heard and disposed of by the bench which has jurisdiction over the matter.

Every application shall be accompanied by a fee of Rs 250/- to be remitted either through a crossed demand draft on a nationalized bank in favour of the registrar of the concerned bench and payable at the main branch of that bank at the station where the seat of the said bench is situated, or remitted through a crossed Indian Postal Order. In cases where the tribunal permits a single application to be filed on behalf of more than one person, the fee payable shall be Rs 1000/-. Where the Tribunal is satisfied that that an applicant is unable to pay the prescribe fee on grounds of indigent, it may exempt such an applicant from the payment of application fee. See Rules 8 and 9 of the Armed Forces Tribunal (Procedure) Rules, 2008 for contents of application and the documents to be annexed to the application.

The tribunal shall not admit an application unless it is satisfied that the applicant has availed himself of the remedies available to him under the Army Act. In case an individual has made an application and no final order has been made by the Central Government or other authority or a period of six months has expired, his application will be admitted by the tribunal. [AFT Act ss. 21 and 22].

Appeal by Ex-servicemen and their Families

Retired service personnel including their dependents, heirs and successors are authorized to approach the tribunal in case of disputes in the service matters. A person who has ceased to be in service by reason of retirement, dismissal, discharge, cashiering, release, removal, resignation or termination of service may, file an application with the registrar of the bench within whose jurisdiction such person is ordinarily residing at the time of filing the application. [Rule 6, The Armed Forces Tribunal (Procedure) Rules, 2008].

Appeal to Supreme Court

An appeal shall lie to the Supreme Court, against the final decision or order of the tribunal. The appeal is to be preferred within a period of ninety days of the decision or order. However, there shall be no appeal against an interlocutory order of the tribunal.

An appeal to the Supreme Court shall lie with the leave of the tribunal, and such leave shall not be granted unless it is certified by the tribunal that a point of law of general public importance is involved in the decision, or it appears to the Supreme Court that the point is one which ought to be considered by that Court.

The Supreme Court in a recent case has held that there is no vested right of appeal against a final order or decision of the Tribunal to the Supreme Court other than those falling under Section 30(2) of the Act (i.e., against an order or decisions of the Tribunal to punish for contempt). A conjoint reading of Sections 30 and 31 of the Armed Forces Tribunal Act leads to conclusion that only mode to appeal against an order of the Tribunal is:

(i) by way of certificate obtained from the Tribunal that decided the matter that 'a point of law of general public importance is involved in the decision', or

(ii) by obtaining leave of the Supreme Court under Section 31 for filing an appeal that 'the point is one which ought to be considered by the Supreme Court'.

[*Union of India v. Brigadier P. S. Gill*, AIR 2012 SC 1280, decided on 23 March, 2012]

An application to the tribunal for leave to appeal to the Supreme Court is required to be made within a period of thirty days beginning with the date of the decision of the tribunal. An application to the Supreme Court for leave shall be made within a period of thirty days beginning with the date on which the application for leave is refused by the tribunal. An appeal shall also lie to the Supreme Court as of right from any order or decision of the tribunal in the exercise of its jurisdiction to punish for contempt.

Armed Forces Tribunal and Court Martial

The Principal Bench of the Armed Forces Tribunal, New Delhi, has set aside a 1987 court-martial. The Bench in its decision in *Major S. S. Chillar v. Union of India* [WP(C)No. 2649 of 1989, TA No. 246 of 2009] of April 1, 2010 has made following concluding observations:

> Before parting with the case, we would like to observe that in conduct of Court Martial proceedings some elementary mistakes are commit-

ted. Neither the Judge Advocate, who advises the Court Martial proceedings, has, at any time, experience of conducting sessions trial, as a result of which he could not properly advise the Court Martial authorities nor the prosecutors are properly trained to conduct such criminal trials. As per AA s. 152, Court Martial shall be deemed to be a judicial proceeding within the meaning of ss. 193 and 228 of the Indian Penal Code and the Court Martial shall be deemed to be court within the meaning of ss. 345 and 346 of the Code of Criminal Procedure. For such matters, a properly trained prosecutor is required. This is highlighted in this case that such elementary mistakes were committed in conduct of the criminal prosecution. Therefore, the authorities should appoint proper prosecutors for conducting such criminal cases in Court Martial proceedings, likewise, a trained Presiding Officer, who knows how to conduct the criminal trial or a Judge Advocate who had an experience of conducting the criminal trials.

We have seen number of Court Martial cases, which have come before this Tribunal and we find that most of the elementary mistakes were committed in conduct of the criminal trials under Court Martial proceedings. Now a proper appeal lies against the Court Martial proceedings before this Tribunal, the Tribunal has to examine all the procedure as well as substance of the criminal trial like in Court of Appeal, including appreciation of the evidence, and our experience is that the trials in the Court Martial proceedings relating to civil offence[s] like murder or other penal code offences or offences under the other acts are not properly conducted like a regular criminal trial. The result is that they will turn into acquittal. Therefore, now in changed situation, when the Court Martial proceedings are amenable to regular appeal under the Act, the authorities have to undertake the overall review of conducting Court Martial trials pertaining to offences under penal code or other civil offences by a competent prosecutor, who has experience of trial as well as the Presiding Officer should also be a trained person, who has seen the trials conducted by Sessions Court, so that they can appreciate the difference between the two and regulate the Court Martial proceedings as if they are conducting a criminal trial before sessions. Such Presiding Officers should be sent for training in a criminal court, where trials are conducted, likewise, the Prosecutors and the Judge Advocate. Therefore, the matter requires a serious consideration of overhauling of the procedure.

Another important feature, which we would like to highlight that before presenting the matter for Court Martial; three tier proceedings are taken, first, a preliminary enquiry, then, at the charge stage, and, thirdly summary of evidence, ultimately the matter goes to Court Martial. Therefore, this is a four tier exercise, which is also cumbersome, time consuming and totally unwarranted. Once the investigation is done, then, the case should be immediately taken before the Court and Court find prima facie charges, then, either Court may send it to session court for trial or if authorities want to try by Court Martial, then, it can apply before the Court. The preliminary enquiry at three stages, i.e. Court of Inquiry, framing of charge and summary of evidence is a useless exercise and it creates more confusion and lot of time consuming also. Therefore, this exercise should be shorten[ed] like a criminal trial, so that the proceedings of [the] Court Martial can be expedited.

Rules

The following Rules have been made under Section 41 of the Armed Forces Tribunal Act, 2007:-

1. The Armed Forces Tribunal (Procedure) Rules, 2008.
2. The Armed Force Tribunal (Procedure for Investigation of Misbehaviour or Incapacity of Chairperson and other Members) Rules, 2008.
3. The Armed Forces Tribunal (Procedure for Appointment of Vice-Chairperson and other Members) Rules, 2008.
4. The Armed Forces Tribunal (Financial and Administrative Powers) Rules, 2008.
5. The Armed Forces Tribunal (Practice) Rules, 2009
6. The Armed Forces Tribunal (Salaries, Allowances and Conditions of service of Chairman and Members) Rules 2009.
7. Armed Forces Tribunal Procedure (Amendment) Rules 2011

CHAPTER 9

CIVIL OFFENCES

Introduction

The term civil offence for the purposes of the Army Act means an offence which is triable by a criminal court. A court martial can try all civil offences committed by a military person, subject to certain limitations. Courts martial are prohibited from trying cases of murder or culpable homicide of a person not subject to military, naval or air force law or cases of rape in relation to such a person, unless the offence is committed on active service or at a specified frontier post or at any place outside India. [AA s. 3 (ii), 69 and 70].

The Bharatiya Nyaya Sanhita (BNS) consisting of 358 sections is an updated version of the Indian Penal Code, 1860. Key changes in the BNS include:

- In BNS 20 new crimes such as organised crime, terrorism, and murder or grievous hurt by a group on certain grounds have been added. Sentences have been increased for 33 crimes. Fine amount has been increased and mandatory minimum punishment increased for 83 crimes.
- For the first time, "Community Service" has been introduced as one of the punishments in BNS s. 4.[i] It has been specifically

i The Indian Penal Code, 1860 has prescribed five types of punishments: (1) Death; (2) Imprisonment for life; (3) Imprisonment—rigorous and straightforward; (4) Forfeiture of property; and (5) Fine. However, the BNS has introduced a significant change, adding a sixth form of punishment—community service--under s. 4(f). Community service as a punishment has been widely adopted in Western legal systems and has been successfully integrated into their sentencing frameworks. These systems have demonstrated that community service can be an effective alternative to incarceration, especially for non-violent offenders. However, the law enforcement agencies and administrative bodies in India, lack clear guidelines on monitoring and enforcing community service sentences. This ambiguity extends to identifying responsible parties for overseeing and ensuring compliance with court-mandated community service.

provided for six petty offences: non-appearance in response to a proclamation, attempt to commit suicide to compel or restraint exercise of lawful power of public servant, petty theft on return of theft money, misconduct in public by a drunken person, and defamation, etc. It introduces the reformative approach in the punishment scheme which is aimed towards achieving *nyaya* in the society.

- Multiple considerations have been introduced through several sections for first-time offenders in the BNS. They are to be given relaxed punishment (one-fourth and one-half of the stipulated punishment) in plea bargaining; and first-time under-trial offender is given statutory bail after completion of one-third period of the maximum punishment prescribed.
- Multiple considerations have been introduced through several sections for first-time offenders in the BNS. They are to be given relaxed punishment (one-fourth and one-half of stipulated punishment) in plea bargaining; and first-time under-trial offender is given statutory bail after completion of one-third period of the maximum punishment prescribed.
- The IPC criminalised acts such as rape, voyeurism, stalking and insulting the modesty of a woman. The BNS retains these provisions. It increases the threshold for the victim to be classified as a major, in the case of gangrape, from 16 to 18 years of age. It also criminalises sexual intercourse with a woman by deceitful means or making false promises.
- Sedition: The BNS removes the offence of sedition. It instead penalises the following: (i) exciting or attempting to excite secession, armed rebellion, or subversive activities, (ii) encouraging feelings of separatist activities, or (iii) endangering the sovereignty or unity and integrity of India. These offences may involve exchange of words or signs, electronic communication, or use of financial means.
- Organised crime: Organised crime includes offences such as kidnapping, extortion, contract killing, land grabbing, financial scams, and cybercrime carried out on behalf of a crime syndicate. Attempting or committing organised crime will be punishable

with: (i) death or life imprisonment and a fine of Rs 10 lakh, if it results in death of a person, or (ii) imprisonment between five years and life, and a fine of at least five lakh rupees.

- Mob lynching: The BNS adds murder or grievous hurt by five or more people on specified grounds, as an offence. These grounds include race, caste, sex, language, or personal belief. The punishment for such murder is a minimum of seven years imprisonment to life imprisonment or death.
- Terrorism: The BNS defines terrorism as an act that intends to: (i) threaten the unity, integrity, and security of the country, (ii) intimidate the general public, or (iii) disturb public order. Punishment for attempting or committing terrorism includes: (i) death or life imprisonment and fine, if it results in death of a person, or (ii) imprisonment between five years and life, and fine.
- The BNS has made sexual offences "gender neutral" for the victim and the perpetrator. Both boys and girls could get procured for sexual exploitation. The word 'minor girl' in IPC sec 366A has been replaced with the word 'child' in BNS sec 96 to cover both male and female children below the age of 18 years and the offence of procurement has been made punishable.
- Rulings of the Supreme Court: The BNS conforms to some decisions of the Supreme Court. These include omitting adultery as an offence and adding life imprisonment as one of the penalties (in addition to the death penalty) for murder or attempt to murder by a life convict.

The Bhartiya Nyaya Sanhita, 2023 (Act No. 45 of 2023)[ii]

Application

Every person shall be liable to punishment under the Bhartiya Nyaya Sanhita (BNS), 2023 for every act or omission of which he shall be guilty within India. Any person liable and to be tried for an offence committed beyond India according to the provisions of this Sanhita for any act committed beyond India in the same manner as if such act had been committed within India. The provisions of this Sanhita shall also apply to any offence committed by: (a) any citizen of India in any place beyond

ii The Act No. 45, received the assent of the President on the 25th December, 2023.

India; (b) any person on any ship or aircraft registered in India wherever it may be; (c) any person in any place beyond India committing offence targeting a computer resource located in India. For instance, A, who is a citizen of India, commits a murder in any place beyond India. He can be tried and convicted of murder in any place in India in which he may be found. The provisions of the BNS shall not affect the provisions of any other Act for punishing mutiny and desertion of officers, soldiers, sailors or airmen in the service of the Government of India.

Common Intention

Whenever a criminal act is done by several persons, in furtherance of the common intention of all, each of such person is liable for that act in the same manner as if it was done by him alone. Where parties go with a common purpose to execute a common object, each and every one becomes responsible for the acts of each and every other in execution and furtherance of their common purpose. Since their purpose is common so must be their responsibility. All would be guilty of the principle offence. It is a well-recognized principle of criminal law that the courts cannot distinguish between co-conspirator, nor can they inquire, even if it was possible, as to the part taken by each in the crime. [Sec 3(5), BNS.].

Punishments

The punishments to which offenders are liable under the provisions of the Sanhita are (a) Death; (b) Imprisonment for life; (c) Imprisonment, which may be (i) Rigorous, that is, with hard labour; or (ii) Simple; (d) Forfeiture of property; (e) Fine; and (f) Community Service[iii] [Sec 4, BNS]. In calculating fractions of terms of punishment, imprisonment for life shall be reckoned as equivalent to imprisonment for twenty years unless otherwise provided [Sec 6, BNS].

In every case in which an offender is punishable with imprisonment which may be of either description, it shall be competent to the Court which sentences such offender to direct in the sentence that such imprisonment

iii The BNS adds community service as a punishment. It extends this punishment to offences such as: (i) theft of property worth less than Rs. 5,000, (ii) attempt to commit suicide with the intent to restrain a public servant, and (iii) appearing in a public place intoxicated and causing annoyance. The BNS does not define what community service will entail and how it will be administered.

shall be wholly rigorous, or that such imprisonment shall be wholly simple, or that any part of such imprisonment shall be rigorous and the rest simple [Sec 7, BNS]. Where no sum is expressed to which a fine may extend, the amount of fine to which the offender is liable is unlimited, but shall not be excessive [Sec 8(1), BNS]. Whenever any person is convicted of an offence for which under this Sanhita the Court has power to sentence him to rigorous imprisonment, the Court may, by its sentence, order that the offender shall be kept in solitary confinement for any portion or portions of the imprisonment to which he is sentenced, not exceeding three months in the whole, according to the following scale: (a) a time not exceeding one month if the term of imprisonment shall not exceed six months; (b) a time not exceeding two months if the term of imprisonment shall exceed six months and shall not exceed one year; (c) a time not exceeding three months if the term of imprisonment shall exceed one year [Sec 11, BNS].

General Exception

Chapter III of the BNS lists certain acts [Sections 14 to 44] which are not considered offence. This chapter has been framed in order to avoid the necessity of repeating in every penal clause a number of limitations. When a person is accused of any offence, the burden of proving the existence of circumstances bringing it within any of the provisions of general exception in the BNS is upon him. The court shall presume the absence of such circumstances.

For example: A, a soldier, fires on a mob by the order of his superior officer, in conformity with the commands of his superior. A has committed no offence, as his act would be covered under Sec 14 of BNS. But for an illegal superior order, e.g., to kill an innocent by-stander, or to torture an individual in custody, or fire on a group of people who have assembled for lawful purpose, the superior order affords no protection to a subordinate. Under the Army Act Sec. 41, only lawful commands are to be obeyed. Obedience to an illegal order can only be used in mitigation of punishment but cannot be used as a complete defence.

General exceptions under the BNS are:

Sec 14. Act done by a person bound, or by mistake of fact believing himself bound, by law

Sec 15. Act of Judge when acting judicially

Sec 16. Act done pursuant to judgment or order of Court

Sec 17. Act done by a person justified/ mistake of fact believing himself justified, by law

Sec 18. Accident in doing a lawful act

Sec 19. Act likely to cause harm, but done without criminal intent, and to prevent other harm

Sec 20. Act of a child under seven years of age

Sec 21. Act of a child above seven and under twelve years of age of immature understanding

Sec 22. Act of a person of unsound mind

Sec 23. Act of a person incapable of judgment by reason of intoxication caused against his will

Sec 24. Offence requiring a particular intent or knowledge committed by one who is intoxicated

Sec 25. Act not intended to be likely to cause death or grievous hurt, done by consent

Sec 26. Act not intended to cause death, done by consent in good faith for person's benefit

Sec 27. Act done in good faith for benefit of child/ person of unsound mind

Sec 28. Consent known to be given under fear or misconception

Sec 29. Exclusion of acts which are offences independently of harm caused

Sec 30. Act done in good faith for benefit of a person without consent

Sec 31. Communication made in good faith

Sec 32. Act to which a person is compelled by threats

Sec 33. Act causing slight harm

Sec 34. Things done in private defence

Sec 35. Right of private defence of body and of property

Sec 36. Right of private defence against act of a person of unsound mind, etc

Sec 37. Acts against which there is no right of private defence

Sec 38. When right of private defence of body extends to causing death

Sec 39. When such right extends to causing any harm other than death

Sec 40. Commencement and continuance of right of private defence of body

Sec 41. When right of private defence of property extends to causing death

Sec 42. When such right extends to causing any harm other than death

Sec 43. Commencement and continuance of right of private defence of property

Sec 44. Right of private defence against deadly assault / risk of harm to innocent person

Cognizable and Non-cognizable Offences

Placement and the punishment provided for an offence by the BNS indicates the legislative perceptions about its nature and seriousness. Serious offences are classified as cognizable and non-bailable by the BNSS. Classification of offences as cognizable [See BNSS Sec. 2(1)(g)], means that the police can initiate investigation into the offence on its own and arrest the accused without a warrant. In the case of a non- cognizable offence, the victim is required to obtain an order from the magistrate for even an investigation to begin. The procedure requires the complainant to be present in the court on all the days of the hearing for the trial to continue. If such an offence is also declared as bailable, the accused is entitled to be released on bail as a matter of right. The non- cognizable and/or bailable offences require the victim to have more perseverance, better resources and greater determination to prosecute. [Please see the First Schedule of the BNSS].

Concurrent jurisdiction

When a criminal court and a court-martial have each jurisdiction to try an offence, it is said that they have 'concurrent jurisdiction' in respect of that offence. Adjustment of jurisdiction as contained in AA ss. 125 and

126, gives the military authorities the right of deciding by which court the alleged offender is to be tried, subject to the reservation that when a criminal court considers that proceedings ought to be instituted before itself, it may require prescribed military authority to deliver the offender. In case of any dispute as to the trial of military offender matter may be referred to the Central Government for final decision. Please see the Criminal Courts and Court-Martial (Adjustment of Jurisdiction) Rules, 1978, in Chapter 10 as well as at RA para 418.

Serious Civil Offences Triable by Court-martial

The term civil offence has been defined in the Army Act (AA) Sec 3(ii) as an offence which is traible by a criminal court. Though courts-martial convened under the AA have jurisdiction to try all civil offences when committed by persons subject to the Act; s. 70 of the Act *inter alia* stipulates that a court-martial shall not try the offences of murder, rape or culpable homicide not amounting to murder, unless such offence is committed: (a) against a person subject to either military, naval or air force law, or (b) while on active service; or (c) at any place outside India; or (d) at a frontier post specified by the Central Government.

Terrorism

The BNS adds terrorism as an offence. Section 113 of the BNS defines 'Terrorist Act' as follows:

(1) Whoever does any act with the intent to threaten or likely to threaten the unity, integrity, sovereignty, security, or economic security of India or with the intent to strike terror or likely to strike terror in the people or any section of the people in India or in any foreign country:

(a) By using bombs, dynamite or other explosive substance or inflammable substance or firearms or other lethal weapons or poisonous or noxious gases or other chemicals or by any other substance (whether biological, radioactive, nuclear or otherwise) of a hazardous nature or by any other means of whatever nature to cause or likely to cause: (i) death or injury to any person; or (ii) loss or damage or destruction of property; or (iii) disruption of any supplies or services essential to the life of the community in India or in any foreign country; or (iv) damage to, the monetary stability of India by way of production or smuggling or circulation of counterfeit Indian paper currency, coin or of any other material; or (v) damage or destruction of any property in India or in a foreign country used or intended to be used for the defence of India or in connection with any other purposes of the Government of India, any State Government or any of their agencies; or

(b) Overawes by means of criminal force or the show of criminal force or attempts to do so or causes death of any public functionary or attempts to cause death of any public functionary; or

(c) Detains, kidnaps or abducts any person and threatening to kill or injure such person or does any other act in order to compel the Government of India, any State Government or the Government of a foreign country or an international or inter-governmental organisation or any other person to do or abstain from doing any act, commit a terrorist act. For the purpose of this sub-section, (a) "public functionary" means the constitutional authorities or any other functionary notified in the Official Gazette by the Central Government as public functionary; and (b) "counterfeit Indian currency" means the counterfeit currency as may be declared after examination by an authorised or notified forensic authority that such currency imitates or compromises with the key security features of Indian currency.

(2) Whoever commits a terrorist act shall (a) if such offence has resulted in the death of any person, be punished with death or imprisonment for life, and shall also be liable to fine; (b) in any other case, be punished with imprisonment for a term which shall not be less than five years but which may extend to imprisonment for life, and shall also be liable to fine.

(3) Whoever conspires or attempts to commit, or advocates, abets, advises or incites, directly or knowingly facilitates the commission of a terrorist act or any act preparatory to the commission of a terrorist act, shall be punished with imprisonment for a term which shall not be less than five years but which may extend to imprisonment for life, and shall also be liable to fine.

(4) Whoever organises or causes to be organised any camp or camps for imparting training in terrorist act, or recruits or causes to be recruited any person or persons for commission of a terrorist act, shall be punished with

imprisonment for a term which shall not be less than five years but which may extend to imprisonment for life, and shall also be liable to fine.

(5) Any person who is a member of an organisation which is involved in terrorist act, shall be punished with imprisonment for a term which may extend to imprisonment for life, and shall also be liable to fine.

(6) Whoever voluntarily harbours or conceals, or attempts to harbour or conceal any person knowing that such person has committed a terrorist act shall be punished with imprisonment for a term which shall not be less than three years but which may extend to imprisonment for life, and shall also be liable to fine. However, this sub-section shall not apply to any case in which the harbour or concealment is by the spouse of the offender.

(7) Whoever knowingly possesses any property derived or obtained from commission of any terrorist act or acquired through the commission of any terrorist act shall be punished with imprisonment for a term which may extend to imprisonment for life, and shall also be liable to fine.

It shall be the decision of a police officer not below the rank of Superintendent of Police whether to register the case under this section or under the Unlawful Activities (Prevention)Act, 1967.

PRAHAAR

India has been at the forefront of the ongoing fight against terrorism for several decades now. While the nature of threats continues to change and present new challenges, India has remained consistently opposed to terrorism in all its forms and manifestations. India has always stood by the victims of terrorism and has been steadfast in its belief that there can be no justification whatsoever, for violence in the world. It is this principled approach which informs the Indian policy of 'zero tolerance' against terrorism.

Disrupting/Intercepting terrorist efforts to access and use CBRNED (Chemical, Biological, Radiological, Nuclear, Explosive, Digital) material remains a challenge for Counter Terrorism (CT) agencies. The threat of state and non-state actors misusing drones and robotics for lethal purposes remains another area of concern, even as criminal hackers and nation states continue to target India through cyber-attacks.

Special laws are in place to tackle terrorism related crimes. The Unlawful Activities (Prevention) Act, 1967 is the principal legal regime to deal with terrorism in India, supplemented by the Bharatiya Nyaya Sanhita, 2023, Bharatiya Nagarik Suraksha Sanhita, 2023, Bharatiya Sakshya Adhiniyam, 2023 and various other Acts like the Explosives Substance Act, 1908, Arms Act 1959 and Prevention of Money Laundering Act, 2002.

The counter-terrorism strategy of India, 'PRAHAAR', is predicated on the following:

- **P**revention of terror attacks to protect Indian citizens and interests;
- **R**esponses, which are swift and proportionate to the threat posed;
- **A**ggregating internal capacities for achieving synergy in a whole-of-government approach;
- **H**uman rights and 'Rule of Law' based processes for mitigation of threats;
- **A**ttenuating the conditions enabling terrorism, including radicalization;
- **A**ligning and shaping the international efforts to counter terrorism;
- **R**ecovery and resilience through a whole-of-society approach.

India remains committed to international cooperation and collaboration. To build consensus on the understanding of terrorism and the rights of victims of terrorism, India continues to work for a comprehensive framework on international terrorism while pursuing its counter-terrorism policy and strategy PRAHAAR, which aims to criminalize all terrorist acts and deny access to funds, weapons and safe havens to the terrorists, their financiers and supporters.

The Right of Private Defence

The right of private defence is a very valuable right recognized in all democratic and civilized societies. It says that every person has a right to defend himself and his property against any threat, danger or violence. The law does not expect a person to behave like a coward when confronted with dangerous situations. Law requires people to rise to the occasion in such situations. It is perfectly justifiable to use force, if it is needed, to protect oneself from an unlawful attack. However, the kind and amount of force is minutely regulated by law.

Sections 34 to 44 of the BNS state the law relating to the right of private defence of person and property. BNS s. 34 provides "Nothing is an offence, which is done in the exercise of the right of private defence." The right of private defence is of two types: (i) right of private defence of body—his own body, and the body of any other person, and (ii) right of private defence of property—of himself or of any other person. The offences against which the right of private defence can be exercised have been listed [Sec 35, BNS]. The right of self-defence is not absolute but is clearly qualified by Sec 37, which says that the right in no case extends to the inflicting of more harm than it is necessary for the purpose of defence. In a free fight, no right of private defence is available to either party and each individual is responsible for his own acts. While it is true that law does not expect from the person, whose life is placed in danger, to weigh, with nice precision, the extent and the degrees of the force which he employs in his defence. It also does not countenance that the person claiming such a right should resort to force which is out of all proportion to the injuries received or threatened and far in excess of the requirement of the case. The onus of proving the right ofprivate defence is on the accused. There is no right of private defence (i) against the acts of a public servant or their subordinates; and (ii) where there is sufficient time for recourse to public authorities; and the quantum of harm that may not be in excess of harm that may be necessary for the purpose of defence. Sec 38, BNS justifies the killing of an assailant in the following cases: (a) In case of apprehension of death as consequence of assault. (b) In case of apprehension of grievous hurt as consequence of assault. (c) Assault with the intention of committing rape. (d) Assault with the intention of gratifying unnatural lust. (e) Assault with the intention of kidnapping or abducting. (f) Assault with the intention of wrongfully confining a person.

In case the offence is not of any of the category stated in Sec 38, the right of private defence of the body extend to the voluntary causing to the assailant of any harm other than death [Sec 39, BNS]. The right of private defence of the body commences as soon as a reasonable apprehension of danger to the body arises from an attempt or threat to commit the offence though the offence may not have been committed; and it continues as long as such apprehension of danger to the body continues. The apprehension of danger must be reasonable, not fanciful [Sec 40 BNS]. Section 41 justifies homicide in case of robbery, house breaking by night, arson and the theft, mischief or house trespass which cause apprehension or grievous harm. If a person does not have possession over the property, he cannot claim any right of private defence regarding such property. If the offence is not of any categories mentioned in Sec 41, the right extends to the voluntary causing to the wrongdoer of any harm other than death [Sec 42, BNS]. The Right of private defence of property commences when a reasonable apprehension of danger to the property commences [Sec 43, BNS]. Injury to innocent persons in the exercise of the right of defence is excusable under Sec 44, BNS.

Abetment

Sections 45 to 57, deal with the offence of abetment under the Chapter IV of the BNS. A person may make himself responsible for the crime of another by instigating, conspiring with, or aiding the actual criminal. Abetment is constituted by (i) instigating a person to commit an offence; or (ii) engaging in a conspiracy to commit it; or (iii) intentionally aiding a person to commit it. It is not necessary that the person abetted should be capable of committing an offence or he should have the same guilty intention as that of the abettor. Under Sec 48, a person who abets an offence beyond India, to be committed in India, would be guilty of abetting the offence in India. For example: A, in country X, instigates B to commit a murder in India, A is guilty of abetting murder. The abetment of an offence being an offence, the abetment of such an abetment is also an offence. The abetment of an offence is punishable under IPC ss. 49 to 57 of the BNS and under the Army Act Sec(s) 66 to 68.

Offences against the State

Chapter VII of the BNS (sections 147 to 158) contains offence against the State which could be grouped into five categories:

- Waging, or attempting or conspirating to wage, or collecting men and ammunition to wage war against the Government of India (Sec 147-150).
- Assaulting President, or Governor of a State with intent to compel or restrain the exercise of lawful power (Sec 151).

- Act endangering sovereignty, unity and integrity of Inda (new provision, Sec 152).
- Waging war against a power at peace with the Government of India or committing depredation on the territories of such power (Sec 153 to 155).
- Permitting or aiding or negligently suffering the escape of, or rescuing or harbouring a State prisoner (Sec 156-158).

Attempt to commit offence

A person who attempts to commit an offence or to cause such an offence to be committed, and in such attempt does any act towards the commission of theoffence, is criminally responsible even though the attempt is unsuccessful [Sec 62, BNS].

A mere intention to commit an offence unaccompanied by acts will not amount to an actual 'attempt', nor will acts themselves if they are merely preparatory to the commission of the offence. For instance, if A, intending to murder B by poison, purchases poison and mixes it with food which remains in A's keeping, the mere mixing with food is not an attempt to murder by poison. Some act must be done which is more than an intention or preparation, and which is a real step towards the commission of the offence; thus, if A had placed the food on B's table, or delivered it to B's servants to place it on B's table, he would be guilty of an attempt to murder. It is no defence to a charge of attempting to commit a crime that it was legally or physically impossible for the offender to have committed the full offence. For example, with the intention of stealing B's wallet, A puts his hand in the B's pocket but finds the pocket empty. A will still be guilty of an attempt to commit theft.

Offences against Public Tranquillity: Unlawful Assembly

An unlawful assembly, as defined in Sec 189(1), is an assembly of five or more persons, if their common objective is: (a) To overawe by criminal force the Central or State Government, or the legislature, or any public servant exercising power lawfully; or (b) To resist the execution of law; or (c) To commit mischief or criminal trespass; or (d) To obtain possession of any property or to enforce any right by using criminal force; or (e) By using criminal force, compelling any person to do what he is not legally bound to do or omit what he is legally entitled to do. The assembly must consist of five or more persons having one of the five specified objects as their common object. An assembly which is lawful in its inception may become unlawful by the subsequent act of its members. The object of sec 189(1) is that the law discourages disorderly assembly of men to preserve the public peace. Sec 189(3) provides punishment for members of an unlawful assembly as it endangers public peace

Sec 190 states that if an offence is committed by any member of an unlawful assembly in prosecution of the common object of that assembly, or such as the members of that assembly knew to be likely to be committed in prosecution of that object, every person who, at the time of the committing of that offence, is a member of the same assembly, is guilty of that offence

Offences against Public Tranquillity: Riot

A riot is an unlawful assembly in which force or violence is used by the members of assembly in prosecution of the common object [Sec 191, BNS]. Punishment of imprisonment up to 2 years, or fine or both could be awarded for rioting, which is enhanced to five years or/and fine, in case the offence is committed using deadly weapons.

Culpable Homicide and Murder

Homicide is the killing of a human being by a human being. It could be either lawful or unlawful. Section 100 of BNS provides: "Whoever causes the death of a human being by doing an act with the intention of causing death, or with the intention of causing such bodily injury as is likely to cause death, or with the knowledge that he is likely by such act to cause death, commits the offence of culpable homicide".

For example, A knows X to be behind a bush. B does not know it. A, with the intention of causing X's death, induces B to fire at the bush. B fires and kills X. In this case, B may not be guilty of any offence, but A has committed the offence of culpable homicide. Sec 100, provides three Explanations, as follows:

1. A person who causes bodily injury to another who is labouring under a disorder, disease or bodily infirmity, and thereby accelerates the death of that other, shall be deemed to have caused his death.

2. Where death is caused by bodily injury, the person who causes such bodily injury shall be deemed to have caused the death, although by resorting to proper remedies and skilful treatment the death might have been prevented.

3. The causing of the death of a child in the mother's womb is not homicide. But it may amount to culpable homicide to cause the death of a living child, if any part of that child has been brought forth, though the child may not have breathed or been completely born.

According to sec 101, the culpable homicide is a murder:

(a) If the act by which the death is caused is done with the intention of causing death; or

(b) If the act by which the death is caused is done with the intention of causing such bodily injury as the offender knows to be likely to cause the death of the person to whom the harm is caused; or

(c) If the act by which the death is caused is done with the intention of causing bodily injury to any person and the bodily injury intended to be inflicted is sufficient in the ordinary course of nature to cause death; or

(d) If the person committing the act by which the death is caused, knows that it is so imminently dangerous that it must in all probability would cause death

The culpable homicide which would otherwise be murder is reduced to "culpable homicide not amounting to murder" in certain circumstances which are specified in the exceptions to Sec 101 of the BNS:

1. Grave and sudden provocation.
2. Right of private defence of person or property exceeded.
3. Powers of public servant acting for the advancement of public justice.
4. If committed without provocation in a sudden fight
5. Consent by the person killed

Sec 103 provides punishment for murder and states: (1) Whoever commits murder shall be punished with death or imprisonment for life, and shall also be liable to fine. (2) When a group of five or more persons acting in concert commits murder on the ground of race, caste or community, sex, place of birth, language, personal belief or any other similar ground each member of such group shall be punished with death or with imprisonment for life, and shall also be liable to fine. Section 104 states that whoever, being under sentence of imprisonment for life, commits murder, shall be punished with death or with imprisonment for life, which shall mean the remainder of that person's natural life. The punishment for culpable homicide not amounting to murder/ abetment/ attempt to murder are covered under section 105 to 109 of the BNS.

Criminal Force and assault Against Women

Sections 74 to 79 of the BNS deal with the offences against women. These are as follows:

- Assaults or use of criminal force to a woman with intention to outrage her modesty [Sec 74, BNS].
- Sexual harassment by any of the following acts: (*i*) physical contact and advances involving unwelcome and explicit sexual overtures; or (ii) demand or request for sexual favours; or (*iii*) showing pornography against the will of a woman; or (*iv*) making sexually coloured remarks [Sec 75].
- Assault or use of criminal force to any woman with the intention of disrobing her [Sec 76, BNS].

Voyeurism: Sec 77 of the BNS deals with the offence of voyeurism. whoever watches, or captures the image of a woman engaging in a private act in circumstances where she would usually have the expectation of not being observed either by the perpetrator or by any other person at the behest of the perpetrator or disseminates such image shall be punished on first conviction with imprisonment of minimum one year, which may extend to three years, and fine. Punishment on a second or subsequent conviction shall be imprisonment for a minimum period of three years, which may extend to seven years, and fine.

For the purpose of Sec 77, "private act" includes an act of watching carried out in a place which, in the circumstances, would reasonably be expected to provide privacy and where the victim's genitals, posterior or breasts are exposed or covered only in underwear; or the victim is using a lavatory; or the victim is doing a sexual act that is not of a kind ordinarily done in public. Further, where the victim consents to the capture of the images or any act, but not to their dissemination to third persons and where such image or act is disseminated, such dissemination shall be considered an offence under this section.

Stalking: Section 78 of the BNS provides that any man who (i) follows a woman and contacts, or attempts to contact such woman to foster personal interaction repeatedly despite a clear indication of disinterest by such woman; or (ii) monitors the use by a woman of the internet, e-mail or any other form of electronic communication, commits the offence of stalking. However, such conduct shall not amount to stalking if the man who pursued it proves that: (i) it was pursued for the purpose of preventing or detecting crime and the man accused of stalking had been entrusted with the responsibility of prevention and detection of crime by the State; or (ii) it was pursued under any law or to comply with any condition or requirement imposed by any person under any law; or (iii) in the particular circumstances such conduct was reasonable and justified. A man accused of a crime of stalking shall be punished on first conviction with imprisonment of either description for a term which may extend to three years, and shall also be liable to fine; and be punished on a second or subsequent conviction, with imprisonment of either description for a term which may extend to five years, and shall also be liable to fine.

Words, Gesture or act intended to insult modesty of a women: Whoever, intending to insult the modesty of any woman, utters any words, makes any sound or gesture, or exhibits any object in any form, intending that such word or sound shall be heard, or that such gesture or object shall be seen, by such woman, or intrudes upon the privacy of such woman, shall be punished with simple imprisonment for a term which may extend to three years, and also with fine [Sec 79, BNS].

Offences relating to Marriage

Dowry Death: In the 1980s, the incidences of 'dowry deaths' were steadily rising in India. A dowry death is the murder of a young woman; committed by the in-laws, when she was unable to fulfill their coercive demands for money, articles or property, categorized as dowry. Organizations across the country pressurized and urged the government to provide legislative protection to women against domestic violence and dowry. The objective was to allow the state to intervene rapidly and prevent the murders of young girls who were unable to meet the dowry demands of their in-laws. As a result of the intense campaigning and lobbying, sec. 304B dealing with dowry death was inserted under IPC in 1986.

Section 80 of BNS embodies a legal fiction whereby the husband or the concerned relative is deemed to have caused the dowry death in a case where the conditions prescribed in the section are present and then the onus shifts on the husband, or as the case may be, on the relative concerned to rebut the presumption enshrined in the section by cogent evidence to show that he has not caused such dowry death. Punishment for dowry death, under Section 80 of the BNS, is imprisonment for not less than seven years, which may extend to imprisonment for life. Besides, Sec 117 of the BSA provides for presumption as to abetment of suicide by a married woman if the conditions specified in that section are satisfied.

Hurt and Grievous Hurt

The BNS sec 114 states: "Whoever causes bodily pain, disease, or infirmity to any person is said to cause "hurt". Whoever does any act of causing hurt to any person, or with the knowledge that he is likely thereby to cause hurt to any person, and does thereby cause hurt to any person, is said "voluntarily to cause hurt" and punished with imprisonment of either description up to one year, or with fine which may extend to Rs 10,000, or with both. Punishment for causing grievous hurt on 'provocation' is governed by Sec 122(1) of the BNS.

The term "Grievous hurt" is hurt of more serious kind as specified in 116 of the BNS. The following kinds of hurt are designated as "grievous hurt": (a) Emasculation. (b) Permanent privation of the sight of either eye. (c) Permanent privation of the hearing of either year. (d) Privation of any member or joint. (e) Permanent disfiguration of the head or face. (f) Fracture or dislocation of a bone or tooth; and (g) Any hurt which endangers life or causes the individual to suffer in pain or unable to follow his pursuit for 12 days. Voluntarily to cause hurt or grievous hurt to anyone is an offence (Sections 117 and 118, BNS) which varies in its gravity according to the instrument used, the provocation given, the status of the person hurt, and the object of the offender.

Section 117(3) states: Whoever commits an offence under Sec 117(1) and in the course of such commission causes any hurt to a person which causes that person to be in permanent disability or in persistent vegetative state, shall be punished with rigorous imprisonment for a term which shall not be less than ten years but which may extend to imprisonment for life, which shall mean imprisonment for the remainder of that person's natural life. Section 117(4) further provides that when a group of five or more persons acting in concert, causes grievous hurt to a person on the ground of his race, caste or community, sex, place of birth, language, personal belief or any other similar ground, each member of such group shall be guilty of the offence of causing grievous hurt, and shall be punished with imprisonment of either description for a term which may extend to seven years, and shall also be liable to fine.

Criminal Force and Assault

Section 128 of BNS defines the term force. A person is said to use force to another if he causes motion, change of motion, or cessation of motion to that other, or if he causes to any substance such motion, or change of motion, or cessation of motion as brings that substance into contact with any part of that other's body, or with anything which that other is wearing or carrying, or with anything so situated that such contact affects that other's sense of feeling. It is necessary that the person causing the motion, or change of motion, or cessation of motion, causes that motion, change of motion, or cessation of motion in one of the following three ways: (a) by his own bodily power;(b) by disposing any substance in such a manner that the motion or change or cessation of motion takes place without any further act on his part, or on the part of any other person; or (c) by inducing any animal to move, to change its motion, or to cease to move. Under Sec 129, the 'force' becomes criminal when it is (i) used without consent and in order to the committing of an offence, or (ii) intentionally used to cause injury, fear or annoyance to another to whom force is used. For example, A intentionally pulls up a woman's veil. Here A intentionally uses force to her, and if he does so without her consent intending or knowing it to be likely that he may thereby injure, frighten or annoy her, he has used criminal force to her.

An assault (Sec 130, BNS), is less than the use of criminal force, the force being cut short before the blow actually falls. An assault requires making of any gesture or preparation by a person in presence of another, and intentionally causing that person present to apprehend that the person making it is about to use criminal force to him. An assault is included in every use of criminal force. Section 131 provides punishment for assault or use of criminal force. Under section 74, whoever assaults or uses criminal force to any women, intending to outrage her modesty can be punished with imprisonment up to two years, or fine or with both. Under the Army Act, offences of assault and the use of criminal force have been dealt in ss. 40 (a) and 47.

Offences Against Women and Child

Rape: The term "rape" has been defined under Sec 63 of the BNS. A man is said to commit "rape" if he:

(a) Penetrates his penis, to any extent, into the vagina, mouth, urethra or anus of a woman or makes her to do so with him or any other person; or

(b) Inserts, to any extent, any object or a part of the body, not being the penis, into the vagina, the urethra or anus of a woman or makes her to do so with him or any other person; or

(c) Manipulates any part of the body of a woman so as to cause penetration into the vagina, urethra, anus or any part of body of such woman or makes her to do so with him or any other person; or

(d) Applies his mouth to the vagina, anus, urethra of a woman or makes her to do so with him or any other person,

under the circumstances falling under any of the following seven descriptions:

(i) Against her will;

(ii) Without her consent;

(iii) With her consent, when her consent has been obtained by putting her or any person in whom she is interested, in fear of death or of hurt;

(iv) With her consent, when the man knows that he is not her husband and that her consent is given because she believes that he is another man to whom she is or believes herself to be lawfully married;

(v) With her consent when, at the time of giving such consent, by reason of unsoundness of mind or intoxication or the administration by him personally or through another of any stupefying or unwholesome substance, she is unable to understand the nature and consequences of that to which she gives consent;

(vi) With or without her consent, when she is under 18 years of age;

(vii) When she is unable to communicate consent.

BNS Sec 63 also explains the terms, "vagina" and "consent." The term "vagina" also includes labia majora; and "consent" means an unequivocal voluntary agreement when the woman by words, gestures or any form of communication, communicates willingness to participate in the specific sexual act. However, a woman who does not physically resist to the act of penetration shall not by the reason only of that fact, be regarded as consenting to the sexual activity. There are two exceptions to the offence of "rape". Medical procedure or intervention shall not constitute rape; and sexual intercourse or sexual acts by a man with his own wife, the wife not being under 18 years of age, is not rape.

Punishment for rape: The punishment for rape is minimum 10 years of rigorous imprisonment which may extend to imprisonment for life, and fine. In special circumstances, rape by (i) a police officer, committed within the limits of the police station, or in the premises of any police station; or on a woman in such police officer's custody; (ii) a public servant on a woman in such public servant's custody; or (iii) a member of the armed forces deployed in an area; (iv) a management staff of a jail, institution or remand home; (v) a hospital management staff; etc, shall be punished with rigorous imprisonment for a term which shall not be less than ten years, but which may extend to imprisonment for life, which shall mean imprisonment for the remainder of that person's natural life, and fine [Sec 64, BNS].

Under certain cases, the punishment for rape is enhanced. Sec 65 of the BNS states that whoever, commits rape on a woman under 16 years of age shall be punished with rigorous imprisonment for a term which shall not be less than 20 years, but which may extend to imprisonment for life, which shall mean imprisonment for the remainder of that person's natural life, and fine. Such fine shall be just and reasonable to meet the medical expenses and rehabilitation of the victim. Further, punishment for rape on a woman under 12 years of age shall be punished with rigorous imprisonment for a term of not be less than twenty years, but which may extend to imprisonment for life, which shall mean imprisonment for the remainder of that person's natural life, and with fine or with death. Such fine shall be just and reasonable to meet the medical expenses and rehabilitation of the victim. Fine imposed under this section shall be paid to the victim [Sec 65, BNS].

The BNS section 67 states that whoever has sexual intercourse with his own wife, who is living separately, whether under a decree of separation or otherwise, without her consent, shall be punished with imprisonment for not less than two years but which may extend to seven years, and also fine.

Gang Rape: In case of gang rape, *w*here a woman is raped by one or more persons constituting a group, each of those persons shall be deemed to have committed the offence of rape and shall be punished with rigorous imprisonment for a term which shall not be less than 20 years, but which may extend to imprisonment for life which shall mean imprisonment for the remainder of that person's natural life, and with fine. Such a fine shall be just and reasonable to meet the medical expenses and rehabilitation of the victim and shall be paid to the Victim. Where a woman under 18 years of age is raped by one or more persons constituting a group each of those persons shall be deemed to have committed the offence of rape and shall be punished with imprisonment for life, and with fine, or with death. Such fine shall be just and reasonable to meet the medical expenses and rehabilitation of the victim and shall be paid to the victim [Sec 70, BNS].

Repeat Offence of Rape: Whoever has been previously convicted of an offence punishable under section 64 or section 65 or section 66 or section 70 and is subsequently convicted of an offence punishable under any of the said sections shall be punished with imprisonment for life which shall mean imprisonment for the remainder of that person's natural life, or with death [Sec 71, BNS].

The Sexual Harassment of Women at Workplace (Prevention, Prohibition and Redressal) Act, 2013

The Constitution of India guarantees all its citizens equality of status and opportunity. Sexual harassment is considered as a violation of the fundamental rights of a woman to equality under Articles 14 and 15 of the Constitution of India and right to life and to live with dignity under Article 21 of the Constitution. The Sexual Harassment of Women at Workplace (Prevention, Prohibition and Redressal) Act 2013 was enacted in order to provide a safe and secure working environment to women at workplace. With the enactment of the Act, India is now a part of the group of countries to have prohibited sexual harassment at workplace through national legislation. The Act is unique in its broad coverage which includes all working women from organized and unorganized sectors alike, as also public and private sectors, regardless of hierarchy.

Under the Act of 2013, 'sexual harassment' includes any one or more of the following unwelcome acts or behaviour (whether directly or by implication), such as (i) physical contact and advances; (ii) a demand or request for sexual favours; (iii) making sexually coloured remarks; (iv) showing pornography; or (v) any other unwelcome physical, verbal or non-verbal conduct of a sexual nature. Section 3 of the Act dictates that no woman shall be subjected to sexual harassment at any workplace. The following circumstances, among other circumstances, if it occurs or is present in relation to or connected with any act or behaviour of sexual harassment may amount to sexual harassment: (i) implied or explicit promise of preferential treatment in her employment; (ii) implied or explicit threat of detrimental treatment in her employment; (iii) implied or explicit threat about her present or future employment status; (iv) interference with her work or creating an intimidating or offensive or hostile work environment for her; or (v) humiliating treatment likely to affect her health or safety.

The Protection of Children from Sexual Offences Act, 2012

To deal with child sexual abuse cases, the Government has brought in a special law, namely, The Protection of Children from Sexual Offences

(POCSO) Act, 2012. The Act has come into force with effect from 14 November 2012. The POCSO Act is a comprehensive law to provide for the protection of children from the offences of sexual assault, sexual harassment and pornography, while safeguarding the interests of the child at every stage of the judicial process by incorporating child-friendly mechanisms for reporting, recording of evidence, investigation and speedy trial of offences.

The POCSO Act defines a child as any person below 18 years of age, and regards the best interests and well-being of the child as being of paramount importance at every stage, to ensure the healthy physical, emotional, intellectual and social development of the child. It defines different forms of sexual abuse, including penetrative and non-penetrative assault, as well as sexual harassment and pornography, and deems a sexual assault to be "aggravated" under certain circumstances, such as when the abused child is mentally ill or when the abuse is committed by a person in a position of trust or authority vis-a-vis the child, like police officer, members of the armed forces or security forces, teacher, or doctor. People involved in child trafficking for sexual purposes are also punishable under the provisions relating to abetment in the Act. The Act prescribes stringent punishment graded as per the gravity of the offence, with a maximum term of rigorous imprisonment for life, and fine.

Some of the important definitions and provisions of the POCSO Act are as follows.

Penetrative sexual assault and punishment

A person is said to commit "penetrative sexual assault" if: (a) He penetrates his penis, to any extent, into the vagina, mouth, urethra or anus of a child or makes the child to do so with him or any other person; or (b) He inserts, to any extent, any object or a part of the body, not being the penis, into the vagina, the urethra or anus of the child or makes the child to do so with him or any other person; or (c) He manipulates any part of the body of the child so as to cause penetration into the vagina, urethra, anus or any part of body of the child or makes the child to do so with him or any other person; or (d) He applies his mouth to the penis, vagina, anus, urethra of the child or makes the child to do so to such person or any other person. Whoever commits penetrative sexual assault shall be punished with imprisonment for minimum 7 years which may extend to imprisonment for life, and shall also be liable to fine.

[Section 3 and 4 of the POCSO Act]

Aggravated penetrative sexual assault and punishment

(a) Whoever, being a police officer, commits penetrative sexual assault on a child (i) Within the limits of the police station or premises at which he is appointed; or (ii) In the premises of any station house, whether or not situated in the police station, to which he is appointed; or In the course of his duties or otherwise; or Where he is known as, or identified as, a police officer; or

(b) Whoever being a member of the armed forces or security forces commits penetrative sexual assault on a child (i) Within the limits of the area to which the person is deployed; or (ii) In any areas under the command of the forces or armed forces; or (iii) In the course of his duties or otherwise; or (iv) Where the said person is known or identified as a member of the security or armed forces; or

(c) Whoever being a public servant commits penetrative sexual assault on a child; or

(d) Whoever being on the management or on the staff of a jail, remand home, protection home, observation home, or other place of custody or care and protection established by or under any law for the time being in force, commits penetrative sexual assault on a child, being inmate of such jail, remand home, protection home, observation home, or other place of custody or care and protection; or

(e) Whoever being on the management or staff of a hospital, whether Government or private, commits penetrative sexual assault on a child in that hospital; or

(f) Whoever being on the management or staff of an educational institution or religious institution, commits penetrative sexual assault on a child in that institution; or

(g) Whoever commits gang penetrative sexual assault on a child. [Explanation: When a child is subjected to sexual assault by one or more persons of a group in furtherance of their common intention, each of such persons shall be deemed to have committed gang penetrative sexual assault within the meaning of this clause and each of such person shall be liable for that act in the same manner as if it were done by him alone]; or

(h) Whoever commits penetrative sexual assault on a child using deadly weapons, fire, heated substance or corrosive substance; or

(i) Whoever commits penetrative sexual assault causing grievous hurt or causing bodily harm and injury or injury to the sexual organs of the child; or

(j) Whoever commits penetrative sexual assault on a child, which (i) Physically incapacitates the child or causes the child to become mentally ill as defined under the Mental Health Act, 1987 or causes impairment of any kind so as to render the child unable to perform regular tasks, temporarily or permanently; or (ii) In the case of female child, makes the child pregnant as a consequence of sexual assault; (iii) Inflicts the child with Human Immunodeficiency Virus or any other life-threatening disease or infection which may either temporarily or permanently impair the child by rendering him physically incapacitated, or mentally ill to perform regular tasks; or

(k) (k) Whoever, taking advantage of a child's mental or physical disability, commits penetrative sexual assault on the child; or

(l) Whoever commits penetrative sexual assault on the child more than once or repeatedly; or

(m) Whoever commits penetrative sexual assault on a child below 12 years; or

(n) Whoever being a relative of the child through blood or adoption or marriage or guardianship or in foster care or having a domestic relationship with a parent of the child or who is living in the same or shared household with the child, commits penetrative sexual assault on such child; or

(o) Whoever being, in the ownership, or management, or staff, of any institution providing services to the child, commits penetrative sexual assault on the child; or

(p) Whoever being in a position of trust or authority of a child commits penetrative sexual assault on the child in an institution or home of the child or anywhere else; or

(q) Whoever commits penetrative sexual assault on a child knowing the child is pregnant; or

(r) Whoever commits penetrative sexual assault on a child and attempts to murder the child; or

(s) Whoever commits penetrative sexual assault on a child in the course of communal or sectarian violence; or

(t) Whoever commits penetrative sexual assault on a child and who has been previously convicted of having committed any offence under this Act or any sexual offence punishable under any other law for the time being in force; or

(u) Whoever commits penetrative sexual assault on a child and makes the child to strip or parade naked in public, is said to commit aggravated penetrative sexual assault.

Whoever commits aggravated penetrative sexual assault, shall be punished with rigorous imprisonment for a minimum period of 10 years which may extend to imprisonment for life and shall also be liable to fine [Section 5 and 6 of the POCSO Act]

Sexual assault and punishment

Whoever, with sexual intent touches the vagina, penis, anus or breast of the child or makes the child touch the vagina, penis, anus or breast of such person or any other person, or does any other act with sexual intent which involves physical contact without penetration is said to commit sexual assault. Whoever, commits sexual assault, shall be punished with imprisonment of minimum three years which may extend to five years and fine [Section 7 and 8 of the POCSO Act]

Aggravated sexual assault

(a) Whoever, being a police officer, commits sexual assault on a child (i) Within the limits of the police station or premises where he is appointed; or (ii) In the premises of any station house whether or not situated in the police station to which he is appointed; or (iii) In the course of his duties or otherwise; or (iv) Where he is known as, or identified as a police officer; or

(b) Whoever, being a member of the armed forces or security forces, commits sexual assault on a child (i) Within the limits of the area to which the person is deployed; or (ii) In any areas under the command of the security or armed forces; or (iii) In the course of his duties or otherwise; or (iv) Where he is known or identified as a member of the security or armed forces; or

(c) Whoever being a public servant commits sexual assault on a child; or

(d) Whoever being on the management or on the staff of a jail, or remand home or protection home or observation home, or other place of custody or care and protection established by or under any law for the time being in force commits sexual assault on a child being inmate of such jail or remand home or protection home or observation home or other place of custody or care and protection; or

(e) Whoever being on the management or staff of a hospital, whether Government or private, commits sexual assault on a child in that hospital; or

(f) Whoever being on the management or staff of an educational institution or religious institution, commits sexual assault on a child in that institution; or

(g) Whoever commits gang sexual assault on a child. [Explanation: when a child is subjected to sexual assault by one or more persons of a group in furtherance of their common intention, each of such persons shall be deemed to have committed gang sexual assault within the meaning of this clause and each of such person shall be liable for that act in the same manner as if it were done by him alone]; or

(h) Whoever commits sexual assault on a child using deadly weapons, fire, heated substance or corrosive substance; or

(i) Whoever commits sexual assault causing grievous hurt or causing bodily harm and injury or injury to the sexual organs of the child; or

(j) Whoever commits sexual assault on a child, which (i) Physically incapacitates the child or causes the child to become mentally ill as defined under section 2 (1) of the Mental Health Act, 1987 or causes impairment of any kind so as to render the child unable to perform regular tasks, temporarily or permanently; or (ii) Inflicts the child with Human Immunodeficiency Virus or any other life threatening disease or infection which may either temporarily or permanently impair the child by rendering him physically incapacitated, or mentally ill to perform regular tasks; or

(k) Whoever, taking advantage of a Childs mental or physical disability, commits sexual assault on the child; or

(l) Whoever commits sexual assault on the child more than once or repeatedly; or

(m) Whoever commits sexual assault on a child below twelve years; or

(n) Whoever, being a relative of the child through blood or adoption or marriage or guardianship or in foster care, or having domestic relationship with a parent of the child, or who is living in the same or shared household with the child, commits sexual assault on such child; or

(o) Whoever, being in the ownership or management or staff, of any institution providing services to the child, commits sexual assault on the child in such institution; or

(p) Whoever, being in a position of trust or authority of a child, commits sexual assault on the child in an institution or home of the child or anywhere else; or

(q) Whoever commits sexual assault on a child knowing the child is pregnant; or

(r) Whoever commits sexual assault on a child and attempts to murder the child; or

(s) Whoever commits sexual assault on a child in the course of communal or sectarian violence; or

(t) Whoever commits sexual assault on a child and who has been previously convicted of having committed any offence under this Act or any sexual offence punishable under any other law for the time being in force; or

(u) Whoever commits sexual assault on a child and makes the child to strip or parade naked in public, is said to commit aggravated sexual assault.

Whoever, commits aggravated sexual assault shall be punished with imprisonment of either description for a term which shall not be less than five years but which may extend to seven years, and shall also be liable to fine [Section 9 and 10 of the POCSO Act].

Sexual harassment and punishment

A person is said to commit sexual harassment upon a child when such person with sexual intent,

(i) Utters any word or makes any sound, or makes any gesture or exhibits any object or part of body with the intention that such word or sound shall be heard, or such gesture or object or part of body shall be seen by the child; or (ii) Makes a child exhibit his body or any part of his body so as it is seen by such person or any other person; or (iii) Shows any object to a child in any form or media for pornographic purposes; or (iv) Repeatedly or constantly follows or watches or contacts a child either directly or through electronic, digital or any other means; or (v) Threatens to use, in any form of media, a real or fabricated depiction through electronic, film or digital or any other mode, of any part of the body of the child or the involvement of the child in a sexual act; or (vi) Entices a child for pornographic purposes or gives gratification

therefor.

Whoever, commits sexual harassment upon a child shall be punished with imprisonment up to 3 years and fine [Section 11 and 12 of the POCSO Act].

Use of child for pornographic purposes

Whoever, uses a child in any form of media (including programme or advertisement telecast by television channels or internet or any other electronic form or printed form, whether or not such programme or advertisement is intended for personal use or for distribution), for the purposes of sexual gratification, which includes: (a) Representation of the sexual organs of a child; (b) Usage of a child engaged in real or simulated sexual acts (with or without penetration); (c) The indecent or obscene representation of a child; shall be guilty of the offence of using a child for pornographic purposes.

Explanation: For the purposes of this section, the expression "use a child" shall include involving a child through any medium like print, electronic, computer or any other technology for preparation, production, offering, transmitting, publishing, facilitation and distribution of the pornographic material.

Punishment for using child for pornographic purposes

(1) Whoever uses a child or children for pornographic purposes shall be punished with imprisonment up to five years and fine. In the event of second or subsequent conviction with imprisonment may extend to seven years and fine.

(2) If the person using the child for pornographic purposes commits an offence of penetrative sexual assault (section 3), by directly participating in pornographic acts, he shall be punished with imprisonment of minimum 10 years, which may extend to imprisonment for life and fine.

(3) If the person using the child for pornographic purposes commits an offence of aggravated penetrative sexual assault (section 5), by directly

participating in pornographic acts, he shall be punished with rigorous imprisonment for life and fine.

(4) If the person using the child for pornographic purposes commits an offence of sexual assault (section 7), by directly participating in pornographic acts, he shall be punished with imprisonment of minimum six years, which may extend to eight years, and fine.

(5) If the person using the child for pornographic purposes commits an offence of aggravated sexual assault (section 9), by directly participating in pornographic acts, he shall be punished with imprisonment of minimum eight years, which may extend to ten years, and fine [Section 13 and 14, POCSO Act].

Punishment for storage of pornographic material involving child

Any person, who stores, for commercial purposes any pornographic material in any form involving a child shall be punished with imprisonment of either description which may extend to three years or with fine or with both [Section 15, POCSO Act].

Indian Armed Forces and Security Forces

The term "armed forces or security forces" in the POCSO Act means armed forces of the Union or security forces or police forces, constituted under (a) The Air Force Act, 1950, (b) The Army Act, 1950, (c) The Assam Rifles Act, 2006, (d) The Bombay Home Guard Act, 1947, (e) The Border Security Force Act, 1968, (f) The Central Industrial Security Force Act, 1968, (g) The Central Reserve Police Force Act, 1949, (h) The Coast Guard Act, 1978, (i) The Delhi Special Police Establishment Act, 1946, (j) The Indo-Tibetan Border Police Force Act, 1992, (k) The Navy Act, 1957, (l) The National Investigation Agency Act, 2008, (m) The National Security

Guard Act, 1986, (n) The Railway Protection Force Act, 1957, (o) The Sashastra Seema Bal Act, 2007, (p) The Special Protection Group Act, 1988, (q) The Territorial Army Act, 1948, and (r) The State police forces (including armed constabulary) constituted under the State laws to aid the civil powers of the State and empowered to employ force during internal disturbances or otherwise.

In keeping with the best international child protection standards, the POCSO Act also provides for mandatory reporting of sexual offences. This casts a legal duty upon a person who has knowledge that a child has been sexually abused to report the offence; if he fails to do so, he may be punished with six months' imprisonment and/ or a fine. Thus, a teacher who is aware

that one of her students has been sexually abused by a colleague is legally obliged to bring the matter to the attention of the authorities. The Act, on the other hand, also prescribes punishment for a person, if he provides false information with the intention to defame any person, including the child.

The POCSO Act also casts the police in the role of child protectors during the investigative process. Thus, the police personnel receiving a report of sexual abuse of a child are given the responsibility of making urgent arrangements for the care and protection of the child, such as obtaining emergency medical treatment for the child and placing the child in a shelter home, should the need arise. The Act also makes provisions for the medical examination of the child designed to cause as little distress as possible. The examination is to be carried out in the presence of the parent or other person whom the child trusts, and in the case of a female child, by a female doctor. The POCSO Act further makes provisions for avoiding the re-victimisation

of the child at the hands of the judicial system. It provides for special courts that conduct the trial in-camera and without revealing the identity of the child, in a manner that is as child-friendly as possible. Hence, the child may have a parent or other trusted person present at the time of testifying and can call for assistance from an interpreter, special educator, or other professional while giving evidence; further, the child is not to be called repeatedly to testify in court and may testify through video-link rather than in the intimidating environs of a courtroom. The Act stipulates that a case of child sexual abuse must be disposed of within one year from the date the offence is reported. The Act also provides for the Special Court to determine the amount of compensation to be paid to a child who has been sexually abused, so that this money can then be used for the child's medical treatment and rehabilitation.

Adultery Law and the Armed Forces

On 27 September 2018, a five-judge Bench of the Supreme Court in the case of *Joseph Shine v. Union of India*, unanimously struck down Section 497 of the Indian Penal Code (IPC), thereby decriminalizing adultery. It struck down section 497 on the grounds that it violates Articles 14, 15 and 21 of the Constitution. The Bench held that the section is an archaic and paternalistic law, which infringes upon a woman's autonomy and dignity. The Court however, observed that while adultery could be a civil wrong, it cannot be a criminal offence.

In January 2021, the Supreme Court has admitted an application from the Central Government to decide if the members of the armed forces may be exempted from the ruling of the court in the case of *Joseph Shine v. Union of India* which decriminalized adultery. In its application, the government has referred to article 33 of the Indian Constitution, which authorizes the Parliament to restrict or abrogate (by law) any of the fundamental rights in terms of their applications to the members of the armed forces so to ensure proper discharge of their duties and to maintain discipline amongst them.

The two questions that the government has asked the court to clarify are the following: (i) Whether persons subject to the Army Act can still be subject to section 497 of the Indian Penal Code? (ii) Whether adulterous or promiscuous acts by a person subject to Army, Navy and Air Force Act can be punished under the provisions of these statutes dealing with unbecoming conduct and maintenance of good order and discipline? Even if the court rules in favour of the government, it will not create criminal liability for anybody who is not a member of the armed forces as the application focuses solely on members of the armed forces.

Simply because something is not a crime does not mean that it cannot be prohibited within the context of different professional settings. It is not a crime for two consenting adults to engage in a sexual relationship. When a person engages in such prohibited conduct, he would be guilty of a wrong only in the context of their employment and not as per the general law of the land. Action may not be taken for the adulterous act per se, but can certainly be taken for engaging in an act which is against the good order and military discipline or amounts to an unbecoming conduct. To qualify as act against good order and military discipline, such an act or an omission does not have to be a crime under the general law of the land.

The criteria of good order and military discipline have to be ascertained from the perspective of the custom, internal code and ethics of the armed forces.

Further Development: The Supreme Court of India has stated that the armed forces can take action against officers for adultery. Observing that military discipline will be affected if there is an army with "completely loose morals", the Supreme Court on 31 January 2023 ruled that the armed forces can take action against their officers for adulterous acts and decriminalisation of adultery would not stand in the way of initiating disciplinary proceedings. Clarifying its 2018 judgment which had struck down Section 497 of the IPC that criminalised adultery, a five-judge Constitution bench headed by Justice K M Joseph said the verdict was not concerned with the provisions of the armed forces acts. The order by the bench, also comprising justices Ajay Rastogi, Aniruddha Bose, Hrishikesh Roy, and C T Ravikumar, said it is not as if this court approved of adultery. Further, the bench said, "This court was neither called upon nor has pronounced on Sections 45 and 63 of the Army Act and corresponding provisions of the other Acts. We only make this position clear and dispose of the application (filed by the Central Government). The Supreme Court had earlier said that armed forces must have some kind of mechanism for disciplinary proceedings against their officers for adultery as "this is a conduct that can shake up the life of officers." It had said adultery creates "pain" in a family and it should not be treated in a lighter manner.

CHAPTER 10

THE BHARATIYA NAGARIK SURAKSHA SANHITA

The Bharatiya Nagarik Suraksha Sanhita (BNSS), 2023 has replaced the Code of Criminal Procedure (CrPC), 1973. The new law has been designed to ensure faster justice and address modern forms of crime. Total sections have been increased from 484 to 531. The BNSS is mainly an adjective law of procedure. Its object is to provide the machinery for the punishment of offenders against the substantive criminal law, i.e., the Bhartiya Nyaya Sanhita (BNS), 2023. In fact, the two codes are read together. Some terms are specially defined in the BNSS, but in the absence of such definition, the definitions set out in the BNS are to be adopted. The BNSS also provides the machinery for the punishment of offences under other Acts. It is, however, not a pure adjective law; there are certain provisions of the code which partake of the nature of substantive law, e.g., maintenance proceedings (Chapter X) and prevention of offences (Chapter XII).

The BNSS provides for the use of technology and forensic sciences in the investigation of crime and furnishing and lodging of information, service of summons, etc., through electronic communication. Specific time-lines have been prescribed for time-bound investigation, trial and pronouncement of judgments. Citizen centric approach has been adopted for supply of copy of FIR to the victim and to inform them about the progress of investigation, including by digital means. In cases where the punishment is seven years or more, the victim shall be given an opportunity of being heard before withdrawal of the case by the Government. Summary trial has been made mandatory for petty and less serious cases. The accused persons may be examined through electronic means, like video conferencing. The magisterial system has also been streamlined.[i]

i The Statement of Objects and Reasons, The Bharatiya Nagarik Suraksha Sanhita (BNSS), 2023 (46 of 2023). Received the ascent of the President on 25-12-2023 and published in the Gazette of India on 25-12-2023.

Some of the highlights of the BNSS are as follows:

- New definitions for key terms like 'audio-visual electronic means' and 'electronic communication' have been introduced.
- Judgments are now required within 45 days of the trial's completion, and charges must be framed within 60 days of the first hearing.
- Timelines for the completion of trials and the pronouncement of judgments by courts has been provided.
- Trials can proceed in the absence of an accused declared a proclaimed offender, and judgments can be pronounced against such accused.
- Any person can now file a Zero First Information Report (FIR) at any police station, regardless of jurisdiction.
- Complainant can visit any police station to report a crime; the case must be transferred to the police station with jurisdiction in 5 days. FIR can be registered even if a complaint is submitted on WhatsApp or e-mail; however, the complainant will have to visit the police station within 72 hours afterwards.
- For certain offences against women, a women police officer is to lodge FIR.
- Section 530 envisages that all trials, inquiries and proceedings under the BNSS may be made compatible with technology and held in electronic mode by use of electronic communication or through the use of us audio-video electric means.

Applicability

The provisions of Bharatiya Nagarik Suraksha Sanhita, 2023, other than those relating to Chapters IX, XI and XII, shall not apply (a) to the State of Nagaland; and (b) to the tribal areas. However, the concerned State Government may, by notification, apply such provisions or any of them to the whole or part of the State of Nagaland or such tribal areas, as the case may be, with such supplemental, incidental or consequential modifications, as may be specified in the notification.

Definitions

- "Audio-video electronic means" shall include use of any communication device for the purposes of video conferencing, recording of processes of identification, search and seizure or evidence, transmission of electronic communication and for such other purposes and by such other means as the State Government may, by rules provide [Sec 2(1)(a), BNSS].
- "Bail" means release of a person accused of or suspected of commission of an offence from the custody of law upon certain conditions imposed by an officer or Court on execution by such person of a bond or a bail bond [Sec 2(1)(b), BNSS].
- "Bailable offence" means an offence which is shown as bailable in the First Schedule, or which is made bailable by any other law for the time being in force; and "non-bailable offence" means any other offence [Sec 2(1)(c), BNSS].
- "Bail bond" means an undertaking for release with surety [Sec 2(1)(d), BNSS].
- "Bond" means a personal bond or an undertaking for release without surety [Sec 2(1)(e), BNSS].
- "Cognizable offence" means an offence for which, and "cognizable case" means a case in which, a police officer may, in accordance with the First Schedule or under any other law for the time being in force, arrest without warrant [Sec 2(1)(g), BNSS].
- "Complaint" means any allegation made orally or in writing to a Magistrate, with a view to his taking action under this Sanhita, that some person, whether known or unknown, has committed an offence, but does not include a police report [Sec 2(1)(h), BNSS]. For instance, a report made by a police officer in a case which discloses, after investigation, the commission of a non-cognizable offence shall be deemed to be a complaint; and the police officer by whom such report is made shall be deemed to be the complainant.
- "Electronic communication" means the communication of any written, verbal, pictorial information or video content transmitted or transferred (whether from one person to another or from one device to another or from a person to a device or from a device to

a person) by means of an electronic device including a telephone, mobile phone, or other wireless telecommunication device, or a computer, or audio-video player or camera or any other electronic device or electronic form as may be specified by notification, by the Central Government; [Sec 2(1)(i), BNSS].

- "Investigation" includes all the proceedings under the BNSS for the collection of evidence conducted by a police officer or by any person (other than a Magistrate) who is authorised by a Magistrate in this behalf. Where any of the provisions of a special Act are inconsistent with the provisions of the BNSS, the provisions of the special Act shall prevail [Sec 2(1)(l), BNSS].
- "Non-cognizable offence" means an offence for which, and "non-cognizable case" means a case in which, a police officer has no authority to arrest without warrant; [Sec 2(1)(o), BNSS].
- "Officer in charge of a police station" includes, when the officer in charge of the police station is absent from the station-house or unable from illness or other cause to perform his duties, the police officer present at the station-house who is next in rank to such officer and is above the rank of constable or, when the State Government so directs, any other police officer so present [Sec 2(1)(r), BNSS].
- "Victim" means a person who has suffered any loss or injury caused by reason of the act or omission of the accused person and includes the guardian or legal heir of such victim; [Sec 2(1)(y), BNSS].
- Words and expressions used in BNSS and not defined but defined in the Information Technology Act, 2000 and the Bharatiya Nyaya Sanhita, 2023 shall have the meanings respectively assigned to them in that Act and Sanhita. [Sec 2(2), BNSS].

Classes of Criminal Courts

There are six different classes of criminal courts in a State:

(a) High Court

(b) Courts of Session

(c) Judicial Magistrate of the first class

(d) Judicial Magistrate of the second class

(e) Executive Magistrate

Besides these, courts may also be constituted under any other law [Sec 6, BNSS].

Directorate of Prosecution

The State Government may establish a Directorate of Prosecution in the State consisting of a Director of Prosecution and as many Deputy Directors of Prosecution as it thinks fit; and a District Directorate of Prosecution in every district consisting of as many Deputy Directors and Assistant Directors of Prosecution, as it thinks fit. A person shall be eligible to be appointed as a Director of Prosecution or a Deputy Director of Prosecution, if he has been in practice as an advocate for not less than 15 years or is or has been a Sessions Judge. The powers and functions of the Director of Prosecution shall be to monitor cases in which offences are punishable for ten years or more, or with life imprisonment, or with death; to expedite the proceedings and to give opinion on filing of appeals. The other powers and functions of the Director of Prosecution, Deputy Directors of Prosecution and Assistant Directors of Prosecution and the areas for which each of the Deputy Directors of Prosecution or Assistant Directors of Prosecution have been appointed shall be such as the State Government may, by notification, specify [Sec 20, BNSS].

Aid to Magistrates and the Police

A three-fold duty has been imposed on members of public to assist a magistrate or police officer: (i) in the taking or preventing the escape of an offender, (ii) in the prevention or suppression of a breach of the peace; and (iii) in the prevention of any injury attempted to be committed to any public property [Sec 31, BNSS].

Public to give information of certain offences

Under Sec 33 of the BNSS, every person, aware of the commission of, or of the intention of any other person to commit, any offence punishable under any of the following sections of the Bharatiya Nyaya Sanhita, 2023, shall be required to give information to the nearest Magistrate or police officer of such commission or intention:

- Sections 103 to 105;
- Sections 111 to 113;
- Sections 140 to 144;
- Sections 147 to 154 and section 158;
- Sections 178 to 182;
- Sections 189 and 191;
- Sections 274 to 280;
- Section 307;
- Sections 309 to 312;
- Section 316 (5);
- Sections 326 to 328; and
- Sections 331 and 332,

Arrest of Persons

When Police may Arrest Without Warrant

Section 35(1) of the BNSS enumerates 10 categories of cases in which a police officer may arrest a person without an order from a Magistrate without a warrant. The police officer may arrest a person:

- Who commits a cognizable offence in the presence of a police officer;
- Against whom a reasonable complaint has been made, or credible information has been received, or a reasonable suspicion exists that he has committed a cognizable offence punishable with imprisonment for a term which may be less than seven years;
- Against whom credible information has been received that he has committed a cognizable offence punishable with imprisonment for a term which may extend to more than seven years;
- Who has been proclaimed as an offender under BNSS or by order of the State Government;
- In whose possession anything is found which may reasonably be suspected to be stolen property and who may reasonably be

suspected of having committed an offence with reference to such thing;

- Who obstructs a police officer while in the execution of his duty, or who has escaped, or attempts to escape, from lawful custody; or
- Who is reasonably suspected of being a deserter from any of the Armed Forces of the Union;
- Who has been concerned in any act committed out of India which, if committed in India, would have been punishable as an offence, and for which he is, under any law relating to extradition, liable to be apprehended or detained in custody in India; or
- Who, being a released convict, commits a breach of any rule made under sec 394(5) of BNSS;
- For whose arrest any requisition has been received from another police officer specifying that the person to be arrested.

Sec 25(2) specifies that no arrest shall be made without prior permission of an officer not below the rank of Deputy Superintendent of Police in case of an offence which is punishable for imprisonment of less than three years and such person is infirm or is above 60 years of age.

Procedure for Arrest

Every police officer while making an arrest shall bear an accurate, visible and clear identification of his name which will facilitate easy identification. He shall prepare a memorandum of arrest which shall be (i) attested by at least one witness, who is a member of the family of the person arrested or a respectable member of the locality where the arrest is made; and (ii) countersigned by the person arrested. He shall also inform the person arrested, unless the memorandum is attested by a member of his family, that he has a right to have a relative or a friend or any other person named by him to be informed of his arrest [Sec 36, BNSS].

Designated Police Officer to maintain/ display information about Arrested Person

Sec 37 of the BNSS states that the State Government shall establish a police control room in every district and at State level and designate a police officer in every district and in every police station, not below the rank of Assistant Sub-Inspector who shall be responsible for maintaining the information about the names and addresses of the persons arrested, nature of the offence with which charged, which shall be prominently displayed in any manner including in digital mode in every police station and at the district headquarters.

Right of Arrested Person

When any person is arrested and interrogated by the police, he shall be entitled to meet an advocate of his choice during interrogation, though not throughout interrogation [Sec 38, BNSS].

Arrest on refusal to give name and residence

When any person who, in the presence of a police officer, has committed or has been accused of committing a non-cognizable offence refuses, on demand of such officer, to give his name and residence or gives a name or residence which such officer has reason to believe to be false, he may be arrested by such officer in order that his name or residence may be ascertained. When the true name and residence of such person have been ascertained, he shall be released on his executing a bond, with or without sureties, to appear before a Magistrate if so required. However, if such person is not resident in India, the bond shall be secured by a surety resident in India. Should the true name and residence of such person not be ascertained within twenty-four hours from the time of arrest or should he fail to execute the bond, or sufficient sureties, he shall be sent to the nearest Magistrate having jurisdiction. [Sec 39, BNSS].

Arrest by private person

Any private person is authorized to arrest or cause to be arrested any person (i) who in his presence commits a nonbailable and cognizable offence, or (ii) who is a proclaimed offender. He must without unnecessary delay, make over such person to a police officer, or, in the absence of a police officer, or either take him or cause him to be taken to the nearest police station. If such person is liable to arrested under Sec 35(1) of BNSS, he shall be re-arrested by the police officer. If there is reason to believe that he has committed a non-cognizable offence, his name and residence are to be ascertained. However, if there is no sufficient reason to believe that he has committed any offence, he is to be released at once. [Sec 40, BNSS].

Protection of members of the Armed Forces from arrest

Sec 42(1) of the BNSS protects members of the armed forces from arrest where they do or purport to do something in the discharge of their official duty. They can be proceeded against only after obtaining consent of the Central Government. The State Government is similarly empowered under Sec 42(2) to extend the protection to specified class of members of the force maintaining public order.

Arrest how made

The word arrest when used in its ordinary sense means to apprehension or restraint or deprivation of one's personal liberty to go where he pleases. In legal sense, arrest means taking into custody of another person under authority empowered by law.

Under Sec 43 of the BNSS, in making an arrest the police officer or other person making the same is to actually touch or confine the body of the person to be arrested, unless there is a submission to the custody by word or action. If such person forcibly resists the endeavour to arrest him, or attempts to evade the arrest, the police officer or other person may use all means necessary to affect the arrest.

The police officer may, keeping in view the nature and gravity of the offence, use handcuff while making the arrest of a person or while producing such person before the court who is a habitual or repeat offender, or who escaped from custody, or who has committed offence of organised crime, terrorist act, drug related crime, or illegal possession of arms and ammunition, murder, rape, acid attack, counterfeiting of coins and currency-notes, human trafficking, sexual offence against children, or offence against the State. The procedure to arrest does not give a right to cause the death of a person who is not accused of an offence punishable with death or with imprisonment for life.

In cases where a woman is to be arrested, unless the circumstances indicate to the contrary, her submission to custody on an oral intimation of arrest shall be presumed and, unless the circumstances otherwise require or unless the police officer is a female, the police officer shall not touch the person of the woman for making her arrest. Except in exceptional circumstances, no woman shall be arrested after sunset and before sunrise, and where such exceptional circumstances exist, the woman police officer shall, by making a written report, obtain the prior permission of the Magistrate of the first class within whose local jurisdiction the offence is committed or the arrest is to be made.

Search of place entered by person sought to be arrested

If a person, acting under a warrant of arrest, or any police officer having authority to arrest, has reason to believe that the person to be arrested has entered into or is within any place; any person residing in, or being in charge of such place shall allow him free ingress and afford all reasonable facilities for a search.

If ingress to such place cannot be obtained, it shall be lawful for a person acting under a warrant, or for a police officer to enter such place and search. In order to enter into such place and make arrest, the police officer can break open any outer or inner door or window of any house or place. In case, such place is an apartment in the occupancy of a female (not being the person to be arrested) who, according to custom, does not appear in public, such person or police officer, before entering such apartment, is to give notice to such female that she is at liberty to withdraw and afford her reasonable facility for withdrawing, and may then break open the apartment and enter.

Any police officer or other person authorized to make an arrest may break open any outer or inner door or window of any house or place in order to liberate himself or any other person who, having lawfully entered for the purpose of making an arrest, is detained therein [Sec 44, BNSS].

Pursuit of Offender into other Jurisdiction

A police officer may, for the purpose of arresting without warrant any person whom he is authorised to arrest, pursue such person into any place in India [Sec 45, BNSS].

No unnecessary restraint

The person arrested shall not be subjected to more restraint than is necessary to prevent his escape [Sec 46, BNSS].

Person arrested to be informed of grounds of arrest and of right to bail

Every police officer or other person arresting any person without warrant shall inform the arrested person full particulars of the offence and other grounds for which he is arrested. Where a police officer arrests without warrant any person other than a person accused of a non-bailable offence, he shall inform the person arrested that he is entitled to be released on bail and that he may arrange for sureties on his behalf [Sec 47, BNSS].

Search of arrested persons

Whenever (*i*) a person is arrested by a police officer under a warrant which does not provide for the taking of bail, or under a warrant which provides for the taking of bail but the person arrested cannot furnish bail; and (ii) a person is arrested without warrant, or by a private person under a warrant, and cannot legally be admitted to bail, or is unable to furnish bail: the officer making the arrest or, when the arrest is made by a private person, the police officer to whom he makes over the person arrested, may search such person, and place in safe custody all articles, other than necessary wearing-apparel, found upon him. Where any article is seized from the arrested person, a receipt showing the articles taken in possession by the police officer shall be given to such person [Sec 49(1), BNSS]. Whenever it is necessary to search a female, the search shall be made by another female with strict regard to decency [Sec 49(2), BNSS].

Power to Seize Offensive Weapons

The police officer or other person making any arrest under the BNSS may, immediately after the arrest is made, take from the person arrested any offensive weapons which he has about his person, and shall deliver all weapons so taken to the Court or officer before which or whom the officer or person making the arrest is required by this Sanhita to produce the person arrested [Sec 50, BNSS].

Medical examination of accused by Medical Practitioner at request of police officer

When a person is arrested on a charge of committing an offence of such a nature that there are reasonable grounds for believing that an examination of his person will afford evidence as to the commission of an offence, the police officer can request a registered medical practitioner for medical examination. Whenever a female is being examined, the examination shall be conducted by or under the supervision of a female registered medical practitioner. The registered medical practitioner shall, without any delay, forward the examination report to the investigating officer [Sec 51 (1), (2) and (3), BNSS].

The medical examination shall include the examination of blood, blood stains, semen, swabs in case of sexual offences, sputum and sweat, hair samples and finger nail clippings by the use of modern and scientific techniques including DNA profiling and such other tests which the registered medical practitioner thinks necessary in a particular case. The term "registered medical practitioner" means a medical practitioner who possesses any medical qualification recognised under the National Medical Commission Act, 2019 and whose name has been entered in the National Medical Register or a State Medical Register under that Act [Sec 51, explanation, BNSS].

Examination of Person Accused of Rape by Medical Practitioner

According to Sec 52, BNSS, when a person is arrested on a charge of committing an offence of rape or attempt to rape and there are reasonable grounds for believing that an examination of his person will afford evidence as to the commission of such offence, he shall be examined by a registered medical practitioner of the Government or by any other registered medical (the radius of 16 km from the place where the offence has been committed), and to use such force as is reasonably necessary for that purpose. The registered medical practitioner conducting medical examination shall examine such person and prepare an examination report giving the following particulars: (i) the name and address of the accused and of the person by whom he was brought; (ii) the age of the accused; (iii) marks of injury, if any, on the person of the accused; (iv) the description of material taken from the accused for DNA profiling; and (v) other material particulars in reasonable detail. The report shall state precisely the reasons for each conclusion arrived at. The exact time of commencement and completion of the examination shall also be noted in the report. The registered medical practitioner shall forward the report to the investigating officer, who shall forward it to the Magistrate as required under Sec 193(6)(a), BNSS.

Examination of Arrested Person by Medical Officer

When any person is arrested, he shall be examined by a medical officer in the service of the Central/ State Government, or by a registered medical practitioner soon after the arrest is made. In case, the medical officer or the registered medical practitioner is of the opinion that one more examination of such person is necessary, he may do so. Where the arrested person is a female, her medical examination shall be done only by or under the supervision of a female medical officer, or by a female registered medical practitioner. The medical officer or a registered medical practitioner so examining the arrested person shall prepare the record of such examination, mentioning therein any injuries or marks of violence upon the person arrested, and the approximate time when such injuries or marks may have been inflicted. A copy of the medical examination report shall be furnished by the medical officer or registered medical practitioner to the arrested person or the person nominated by such arrested person [Sec 53, BNSS].

Health and Safety of Arrested Person

It shall be the duty of the person having the custody of an accused to take reasonable care of the health and safety of the accused [Sec 56, BNSS].

Person arrested not to be detained more than twenty-four hours

When a person has been arrested without warrant, a police officer shall not detain him in custody for a longer period than under all the circumstances of the case is reasonable, and such period shall not, in the absence of a special order of a Magistrate under section 187, exceed 24 hours exclusive of the time necessary for the journey from the place of arrest to the Magistrate's Court, whether having jurisdiction or not. [Sec 58, BNSS].

Police to report apprehensions

Officers in charge of police stations must report to the District Magistrate, or, the Sub-divisional Magistrate, the cases of all persons arrested without warrant, within the limits of their respective stations, whether such persons have been admitted to bail or otherwise [Sec 59, BNSS].

Summons

Every summons issued by a Court under the BNSS must be in writing, in duplicate, signed by the presiding officer of such Court or by such other officer as directed by the High Court, and must bear the seal of the Court. In case summon is in encrypted or any other form of electronic communication, it shall bear the image of the seal of the Court or digital signature [Sec 63, BNSS].

Summon how Served

Every summons shall be served by a police officer or subject to such rules as the State Government may make in this behalf, by an officer of the Court issuing it or other public servant. The summons shall, if practicable, be served personally on the person summoned, by delivering one of the duplicates of the summons to him. Summons bearing the image of Court's seal may also be served by electronic communication in such form and in such manner, as decided by the State Government. Every person on whom a summons is so served personally shall, if so, required by the serving officer, sign a receipt therefor on the back of the other duplicate [Sec 64, BNSS].

Summon, when person summoned cannot be found

Where the person summoned cannot be found, the summons may be served by leaving one of the duplicates for him with some adult member of his family residing with him, and the person with whom the summons is so left shall sign a receipt therefor on the back of the other duplicate. However, a servant is not a member of the family within the meaning of this section [Sec 66, BNSS].

Summon, Service on Government Servant

Where the person summoned is in the active service of the Government, the Court issuing the summons shall send it in duplicate to the head of the office in which such person is employed. The head of the officer shall thereupon cause the summons to be served in the manner provided by section 64, and shall return it to the Court under his signature with the endorsement required by that section. Such signature shall be evidence of due service [Sec 68, BNSS].

Dispersal of assembly by use of civil force

BNSS Section 148 deals with the dispersal of an unlawful assembly or which is likely to cause a breach the peace. An assembly of such kind may be commanded to disperse by an Executive Magistrate or officer in charge of a police station, not below the rank of a sub-inspector. In case assembly shows no disposition to disperse quietly, force may be employed to disperse. The said Executive Magistrate or police officer may require the assistance of any person, (not being an officer or member of the armed forces) for the purpose of dispersing such assembly, and, if necessary, arresting and confining the persons who form part of it so that they may be punished according to law.

Use of armed forces to disperse assembly

If an unlawful assembly cannot be otherwise dispersed (as stated in Sec 148), and if it is necessary for the public security that it should be dispersed, the District Magistrate or any other Executive Magistrate authorised by him, who is present, may cause it to be dispersed by the armed forces.

Such Magistrate may require any 'officer' in command of any group of persons belonging to the armed forces to disperse the assembly with the help of the armed forces under his command, and to arrest and confine such persons forming part of it as the Executive Magistrate may direct, or as it may be necessary to arrest and confine in order to disperse the assembly or to have them punished according to law

Every such officer of the armed forces shall obey such requisition and shall use as little force, and do as little injury to person and property, as may be consistent with dispersing the assembly and arresting and detaining such persons [Sec 149, BNSS].

The term "officer", in this section means a person commissioned, gazetted or in pay as an officer of the armed forces and includes a junior commissioned officer, a warrant officer, a petty officer, a non-commissioned officer and a non-gazetted officer [Sec 151(3)(b), BNSS].

Power of Armed Forces Officers to Disperse Assembly

When the public security is manifestly endangered by any such assembly and no Executive Magistrate can be communicated with, any commissioned or gazetted officer of the armed forces may disperse such assembly with the help of the armed forces under his command. Such officer in order to disperse such assembly, may arrest and confine any persons forming part of it so that they may be punished according to law. While he is acting under this section, it becomes practicable for him to communicate with an Executive Magistrate, he shall do so, and shall thereafter obey the instructions of the Magistrate, as to whether he should continue such action [Sec 150, BNSS].

Protection against prosecution for acts done under preceding sections 148-150

Sanction of the Central Government is necessary for prosecution against a military officer, who has acted in good faith under Sec 150. Any act done in good faith and any act done by an inferior officer or soldier in obedience to any order is not an offence. Further, no action can be taken against the member of the armed forces who has acted in obedience to any order which he was bound to obey. The expression "armed forces" means the military, naval and air forces, operating as land forces and includes any other Armed Forces of the Union so operating [Sec 151, BNSS].

Information in Cognizable cases [First Information Report]

The information about a cognizable offence given to a police officer and reduced to writing as required by BNSS sec 173 is known as first information. The term 'First Information Report' (FIR) is not mentioned in the BNSS, but these words are understood to mean information received under Sec 173.

Every information relating to the commission of a cognizable offence, irrespective of the area where the offence is committed [concept of Zero FIR], may be given orally or by electronic communication to an officer in charge of a police station. If given orally, it shall be reduced to writing by him or under his direction, and be read over to the informant; and every such information, whether given in writing or reduced to writing as aforesaid, shall be signed by the person giving it. If information is given by electronic communication, it shall be taken on record by him on being signed within three days by the person giving it, and the substance thereof shall be entered in a book to be kept by such officer in such form as the State Government may by rules prescribe in this behalf [concept of e-FIR].

However, if the information is given by the woman against whom an offence under sections 64 to 71, sections 74 to 79, or section 124 of the BNSS is alleged to have been committed or attempted, then such information shall be recorded, by a woman police officer or any woman officer. Further, in the event that the person against whom an offence under sections as stated above is alleged to have been committed or attempted, is temporarily or permanently mentally or physically disabled, then such information shall be recorded by a police officer, at the residence of the person seeking to report such offence or at a convenient place of such person's choice, in the presence of an interpreter or a special educator. Recording of such information shall be video-graphed and the police officer shall get the statement of the person recorded by a Magistrate under sec 183(6)(a) as soon as possible.

A copy of the information as recorded above shall be given forthwith, free of cost, to the informant or the victim [Sec 173 (1) and (2), BNSS].

The officer in charge of a police station may also on receipt of information relating to the commission of any cognizable offence, which is made punishable for three years or more but less than seven years, with the prior permission from an officer not below the rank of Deputy Superintendent of Police, considering the nature and gravity of the offence (i) proceed to conduct preliminary enquiry to ascertain whether there exists a prima facie case for proceeding in the matter within a period of 14 days; or (ii) proceed with investigation when there exists a prima facie case [Sec 173(3), BNSS].

Any person aggrieved by a refusal on the part of an officer in charge of a police station to record the information referred in Sec 173 (1) may send the substance of such information, in writing and by post, to the Superintendent of Police concerned who, if satisfied that such information discloses the commission of a cognizable offence, shall either investigate the case himself or direct an investigation to be made by any police officer subordinate to him as provided by BNSS, and such officer shall have all the powers of an officer in charge of the police station in relation to that offence failing which such aggrieved person may make an application to the Magistrate [Sec 173 (4), BNSS].

Plea Bargaining

To reduce delay in disposing of criminal cases the Law Commission of India recommended introduction of "plea-bargaining" as an alternative method to deal with huge arrears of criminal cases. Chapter XXIII of the BNSS, Sections 289-300 deal with plea-bargaining.

A plea-bargaining may be made by an accused above the age of 18 years, when the challan has been presented by the police in the court alleging that an offence, punishable with seven years or less imprisonment, appears to have been committed by an accused or on a private complaint the accused has been summoned by the court for an offence punishable with 7 years or less imprisonment. A person accused of an offence may file an application for plea bargaining within a period of thirty days from the date of framing of charge in the Court in which such offence is pending for trial. The accused's application for plea-bargaining shall contain brief description of the case including the offence to which the case relates and shall be accompanied by an affidavit sworn by the accused stating that he knows the extent of punishment of the offence or offences he is indicted for and that he is willing to plead guilty to the charge of the particular offence or offences and that he has not been previously convicted of the same offence.

The court will then issue notice to the public prosecutor concerned, investigating officer of the case, the victim of the case and the accused for the date fixed for the purpose. When the parties appear, the court shall examine the accused in camera where the other parties in the case shall not be present, to satisfy itself that the accused has filed the application voluntarily. If satisfied, the court shall then give time to the above parties to sit together and workout mutually, a satisfactory disposition of the case. The court will ensure that the process is completed voluntarily and the accused can also seek the help of an advocate in the process. When the parties work out the disposition, a report shall be prepared which shall be signed by all the parties. This shall be followed by judgment imposing lighter sentence on the accused and providing compensation to the victims. The Court shall deliver its judgment in terms of Sec 293 in the open Court and the same shall be signed by the presiding officer of the Court.

The provisions also mandate the court to give accused the benefit of Probation of Offenders Act, if permissible. If the court finds that the benefit of probation is not available to the accused, then the court may sentence the accused to half of such minimum punishment, and where the accused is a first-time offender and has not been convicted of any offence in the past, it may sentence the accused to one-fourth of such minimum punishment provided for such an offence. The period of sentence already undergone by the accused during investigation and trial of the case shall be set off against the sentence imposed by the court. The judgment of the court will be final and no appeal shall lie against such judgment. This provision enables early release of under trial prisoners, who are the real victims of our delayed judicial process.

Trial in Absentia

The BNSS has introduced new provisions for conducting trial in absentia of certain kinds of accused. It refers to conducting a criminal trial without the presence of the accused person in court. Under Section 355 of the BNSS, the Judge or Magistrate may conduct a trial of an accused in his absence if it is deemed that the personal attendance of the accused is not necessary in the interests of justice, or if the accused persistently disturbs the proceedings in court.

The BNSS allows in-absentia trial of proclaimed offenders under specific conditions. Section 356 of the BNSS mandates the court to proceed with the trial in absentia when a person declared as a proclaimed offender has absconded to evade trial, and there is no immediate prospect of arresting him. It also specifies a mandatory waiting period of 90 days from the date of framing of the charge before commencing the trial. The BNSS states that the voluntary absence of the accused after the trial has commenced shall not prevent the continuation of the trial, including the pronouncement of the judgment, even if the accused is arrested or appears at the conclusion of the trial.

Trial of Persons Subject to Mil Law

Section 521 of the BNSS governs the delivery of persons, who are subject to military law, to their respective commanding officers for trial by court-martial. It ensures that personnel liable under military law are tried by specialized military tribunals rather than by civilian courts. The Central Government is empowered to make rules consistent with the BNSS and the military law (the Army Act, 1950, the Navy Act, 1957, and the Air Force Act, 1950), as to when persons subject to such military law will be tried by a criminal court or by a court-martial. When an accused, subject to the military is brought before the Magistrate, the Magistrate shall have regard to such rules (a mandatory provision), and is to handover the accused to his commanding officer or to the nearest military station, with a statement of offence for trial by a court-martial. [Sec 521(1), BNSS].

Every Magistrate shall, on receiving a written application for that purpose by the commanding officer of any unit shall use his utmost endeavours to apprehend and secure any person accused of such offence [Sec 521(2), BNSS]. A High Court may direct that a prisoner detained in any jail situated within the State be brought before a court-martial for trial or to be examined touching any matter pending before the court-martial [Sec 521(3), BNSS].

The Criminal Courts and Court-Martial (Adjustment of Jurisdiction) Rules, 1978

In exercise of the powers conferred by Cr PC s. 475 (1), and in supersession of the Criminal Courts and Court-Martial (Adjustment of Jurisdiction) Rules 1952, the Central Government has made the following rules for the trial of the persons subject to military, naval, air force or coast guard law, or any other law relating to the Armed Forces of the Union by a Court to which the said Code applies, or by a Court-Martial or Coast Guard court, as the case may be, namely:

1. These rules may be called the Criminal Courts and Court-Martial (Adjustment of Jurisdiction) Rules, 1978.

2. In these rules, unless the context otherwise requires

(a) "Commanding Officer" (i) in relation to a person subject to military law, means the Officer Commanding the unit to which such person belongs or is attached; (ii) in relation to a person subject to naval law, means the Commanding Officer of the ship or naval establishment or unit to which such person belongs or is attached. (iii) in relation to a person subject to air force law, means the officer for the time being in command of the unit to which such person belongs or is attached. (iv) in relation to a person subject to the Coast guard law, means the Commanding Officer of the Coast guard ship or establishment or unit to which such person belongs or is attached.

(b) "Competent Air Force Authority" means the Chief of the Air Staff, the air or other officer commanding any Command, Group, Wing or Station in which the accused person is serving,

or where such person is serving in field area, the Officer Commanding the forces or the air forces in the field;

(c) "Competent Military Authority" means the Chief of Army Staff or Officer Commanding the army, army corps, division, area, sub-area or independent brigade in which the accused person is serving, and except in cases falling under section 69 of the Army Act, 1950 in which death has resulted, the officer commanding the brigade or sub-area or station in which the accused person is serving.

(d) "Competent Naval Authority" means the Chief of the Naval Staff or the Flag Officer, Commanding-in-Chief, Western Naval Command, Bombay or the Flag Officer Commanding-in-chief, Eastern Naval Command Vishakhapatnam or the Flag Officer Commanding, Southern Naval Area, Cochin or the Flag Officer Commanding, Western Fleet or the Flag Officer Commanding, Eastern Fleet or Senior Naval Officer where the accused person is serving.

(e) "Competent Coast Guard Authority" means the Director General or Inspector General or Deputy Inspector General within whose command the accused person is serving.

3. Where a person subject to military, naval, air force or coast guard law, or any other law relating to the Armed Forces of the Union for the time being in force is brought before a Magistrate and charged with an offence for which he is also liable to be tried by a Court Martial or Coast guard Court, as the case may be such Magistrate shall not proceed to try such person or to commit the case to the Court of Session, unless: (a) he is moved thereto by a competent military, naval, air force or Coast guard authority; or (b) he is of opinion, for reasons to be recorded, that he should so proceed or to commit without being moved thereto by such authority.

4. Before proceeding under clause (b) of rule 3, the Magistrate shall give a written notice to the Commanding Officer or the competent military, naval, air force or coast guard authority, as the case may be, of the accused and until the expiry of a period of 15 days from the date of service of the notice he shall not: (a) Convict or acquit the accused under BNSS ss. 275,

s. 278 (1) and (2), 279 (1), or s. 280, or hear him in his defence under s. 277; or (b) frame in writing a charge against the accused under ss. 263 or s. 269 (1); or (c) make an order committing the accused for trial to the Court of Session under BNSS s. 232, or (d) make over the case for inquiry or trial under NBSS s. 212.

5. Where a Magistrate has been moved by the competent military, naval, air force or Coast guard authority, as the case may be, under clause (a) of rule 3, and such authority, as the case may be, subsequently gives notice to such Magistrate that, in opinion of such authority, the accused should be tried by a Court Martial or Coast Guard court as the case may be such Magistrate if he has not taken any action or made any order under rule 4, before receiving the notice shall stay the proceedings and if the accused is in his power or under his control, shall deliver him together with the statement referred to in BNSS s. 521 (1) to the officer specified in the said sub section.

6. Where within the period of fifteen days mentioned in rule 4, or at any time thereafter but before the Magistrate takes any action or makes any order referred to in that rule, the commanding officer of the accused or the competent military, naval, air force or Coast guard authority, as the case may be, gives notice to the Magistrate that in the opinion of such officer or authority, the accused should be tried by a Court Martial or Coast guard court as the case may be the Magistrate shall stay the proceedings, and if the accused is in his power or under his control, shall deliver him together with the statement referred to in BNSS s. 521 (1) to the officer specified in the said sub-section.

7. (1) When an accused has been delivered by the Magistrate under rule 5 or 6, the commanding officer of the accused or the competent military, naval, air force or Coast guard authority, as the case may be, shall as soon as may be, inform the Magistrate whether the accused has been tried by a Court Martial or Coast guard court as the case may be or other effectual proceedings have been taken or ordered to be taken against him.

(2) When the Magistrate has been informed under sub-rule (1) that the accused has not been tried or other effectual proceedings have not been taken or ordered to be taken against him, the Magistrate shall report the circumstances to the State Government which may, in consultation with

the Central Government, take appropriate steps to ensure that the accused person is dealt with in accordance with law.

8. Notwithstanding anything in the foregoing rules, where it comes to the notice of a Magistrate that a person subject to military, naval, air force or coast guard law, or any other law relating to the Armed Forces of the Union for the time being in force has committed an offence, proceedings in respect of which ought to be instituted before him and that the presence of such person cannot be procured except through military, naval, air force or coast guard authorities, the Magistrate may by a written notice require the commanding officer of such person either to deliver such person to a Magistrate to be named in the said notice for being proceeded against according to law, or to stay the proceedings against such person before the Court Martial or coast guard court, as the case may be if since instituted, and to make a reference to the Central Government for determination as to the court before which proceedings should be instituted.

9. Where a person subject to military, naval, air force or coast guard law, or any other law relating to the Armed Forces of the Union for the time being in force has committed an offence which in the opinion of competent military, naval, air force or coast guard authority, as the case may be, ought to be tried by a Magistrate in accordance with the civil law in force or where the Central Government has, on a reference mentioned in Rule 8, decided that proceedings against such person should be instituted before a Magistrate, the commanding officer of such person shall after giving a written notice to the Magistrate concerned, deliver such person under proper escort to that Magistrate. [Amended by SO 4010 dated 24 November 86. See RA para 418].

CHAPTER 11

BHARATIYA SAKSHYA ADHINIYAM

The Bharatiya Sakshya Adhiniyam, 2023 has replaced the Indian Evidence Act (IEA), 1872 in that total provisions have been increased from 167 to 170. Technological advancements have been integrated into the new law, incorporating several modern aids, including forensic, for police investigations, court trials, and closing loopholes that previously delayed justice. Technology integration includes forensic investigations for offences punishable by seven years or more, with forensic experts required to visit crime scenes and record processes. All proceedings, including trials and inquiries, are to be conducted electronically. All electronic communications, including social media and Voice over Internet Protocol (VoIP), are now admissible in evidence.

The BSA classifies electronic records as primary evidence, enabling investigators to use information stored in electronic devices during trials. Additional facts, to which Court shall take judicial notice are: Laws having extraterritorial operation; International treaty, agreement or convention with country or countries by India, or decisions made by India at international associations or other bodies; and the seals of Courts of Admiralty and Maritime Jurisdiction, etc. The details of certain aspects of BSA Act, 2023,[i] are as follows:

Application of the Act

The Bhartiya Sakshya Adhiniyam (BSA) applies to all judicial proceedings in or before any Court, including courts-martial, but not to affidavits presented to any Court or officer, nor to proceedings before an arbitrator.

Definitions

Section 2 of the BSA defines certain terms as follows.

---

i The Bhartiya Sakshya Adhiniyam, 2023 (No 47 of 2023), An Act to consolidate and to provide for general rules and principles of evidence for fair trial.

- "Court" includes all Judges and Magistrates, and all persons, except arbitrators, legally authorised to take evidence [Sec 2(1)(a), BSA].
- "Conclusive proof" means when one fact is declared by this Adhiniyam to be conclusive proof of another, the Court shall, on proof of the one fact, regard the other as proved, and shall not allow evidence to be given for the purpose of disproving it [Sec 2(1)(b), BSA].
- "disproved" in relation to a fact, means when, after considering the matters before it, the Court either believes that it does not exist, or considers its non-existence so probable that a prudent man ought, under the circumstances of the particular case, to act upon the supposition that it does not exist [Sec 2(1)(c), BSA].
- "Document" means any matter expressed or described or otherwise recorded upon any substance by means of letters, figures or marks or any other means or by more than one of those means, intended to be used, or which may be used, for the purpose of recording that matter and includes electronic and digital records [Sec 2(1)(d), BSA]. For example:
    * A writing is a document.
    * Words printed, lithographed or photographed are documents.
    * A map or plan is a document.
    * An inscription on a metal plate or stone is a document.
    * A caricature is a document.
    * An electronic record on emails, server logs, documents on computers, laptop or smartphone, messages, websites, locational evidence and voice mail messages stored on digital devices are documents.
- The term "evidence" means and includes (i) Oral Evidence: all statements including statements given electronically which the Court permits or requires to be made before it by witnesses in relation to matters of fact under inquiry; (ii) Documentary Evidence: all documents including electronic or digital records produced for the inspection of the Court [Sec 2(1)(e), BSA].

Oral Evidence: All facts, except the contents of documents may be proved by oral evidence. Oral evidence shall, in all cases whatever, be direct; if it refers to (i) a fact which could be seen, it must be the evidence of a witness who says he saw it; (ii) a fact which could be heard, it must be the evidence of a witness who says he heard it; (iii) a fact which could be perceived by any other sense or in any other manner, it must be the evidence of a witness who says he perceived it by that sense or in that manner; or (iv) an opinion or to the grounds on which that opinion is held, it must be the evidence of the person who holds that opinion on those grounds [Sec 54 and 55, BSA].

Documentary Evidence: The contents of documents may be proved either by primary or by secondary evidence. Primary evidence means the document itself produced for the inspection of the Court. In cases where there is documentary evidence, oral evidence does not have any value. The original document is the best evidence. Where a document is executed in several parts, each part is primary evidence of the document. Where a number of documents are all made by one uniform process, as in the case of printing, lithography or photography, each is primary evidence of the contents of the rest; but, where they are all copies of a common original, they are not primary evidence of the contents of the original. Where an electronic or digital record is created or stored, and such storage occurs simultaneously or sequentially in multiple files, each such file is primary evidence. Under Sec. 57, the ambit of Primary Evidence has been expanded to include the following: (i) Digital electronic record created or stored simultaneously or sequentially in multiple files, each file is primary evidence. (ii) Electronic record produced from proper custody if not disputed. (iii) Video recording simultaneously stored, broadcasted and transmitted to another device. Each of its stored recordings is primary evidence. (iv) Electronic record automatically stored in a multiple storage space in a computer resource. Each automated storage is primary evidence [Sec 56, 57, BSA and Explanations 4 to 7 of the Sec 57, BSA]

Secondary Evidence: Secondary evidence includes: (i) certified copies; (ii) copies made from the original by mechanical processes which in themselves ensure the accuracy of the copy, and copies compared with such copies; (iii) copies made from or compared with the original; (iv) counterparts of documents as against the parties who did not execute them; (v) oral accounts of the contents of a document given by some person who has himself seen it; (vi) oral or written admissions; (viii) evidence of a person who has examined a document, the original of which consists of numerous accounts or other documents which cannot conveniently be examined in Court, and who is skilled in the examination of such documents. For example: A copy compared with a copy of a letter made by a copying machine is secondary evidence of the contents of the letter, if it is shown that the copy made by the copying machine was made from the original [Sec 58, BSA].

Secondary Evidence in Certain Cases. Secondary evidence may be given in the following cases: (a) when the original is shown or appears to be in the possession or power of the person against whom the document is sought to be proved; (b) when the existence, condition or contents of the original have been proved to be admitted in writing by the person against whom it is proved or by his representative in interest; (c) when the original has been destroyed or lost; (d) when the original is of such a nature as not to be easily movable; (e) when the original is a public document within the meaning of section 74; (f) when the original is a document of which a certified copy is permitted under the BSA, or by any other law in force in India to be given in evidence; (g) when the originals consist of numerous accounts or other documents which cannot conveniently be examined in Court, and the fact to be proved is the general result of the whole collection [Sec 60, BSA].

Electronic or Digital Records: Admissibility of an electronic or digital record in evidence cannot be denied in the evidence on the ground that it is an electronic or digital record and such record shall have the same legal effect, validity and enforceability as other document [Sec 61, BSA]. The contents of electronic records may be proved in accordance with the section 63; which includes any information contained in an electronic record which is printed on paper, stored, recorded or copied in optical or magnetic media or semiconductor memory which is produced by a computer or any communication device or otherwise stored, recorded or copied in any electronic form (computer output) shall be deemed to be also a document [Sec 62 and 63, BSA].

Circumstantial Evidence: It has become a proverb that 'facts cannot lie,' whilst witnesses may. Direct evidence can prove the commission of an offence by a particular suspect. However, there are times when direct evidence is not available to prove as to who committed the crime. In such cases, circumstantial evidence hints at or directly associated with the facts in issue leading to a satisfactory conclusion towards the commission of the offence, which lead to inference of guilt. Circumstantial evidence is in no way inferior to direct evidence and in some respect superior to it. Since the circumstantial evidence make a chain, it is important that the chain is so conclusive and sufficient that it only shows the guilt of the accused, and there is no scope for doubt or any other conclusion.

Just like the Indian Evidence Act, the circumstantial evidence in BSA has not been expressly defined. Sec 2(k) of BSA defines what is 'relevant' in evidence. In case of circumstantial evidence, relevancy of circumstances is all that matters while linking the chain to prove the guilt. When a case rests on circumstantial evidence, such evidence must satisfy the following tests:

- Circumstances from which an inference of guilt is sought to be drawn must be firmly established.
- Those circumstances should be pointing towards the guilt of the accused.
- Circumstances taken cumulatively should form a chain so complete that there is no escape from the conclusion that the crime was committed by the accused and none else.

"Fact" means and includes: (a) anything, state of things, or relation of things, capable of being perceived by the senses; (b*i*) any mental condition of which any person is conscious. For example, (i) There are certain objects arranged in a certain order in a certain place, is a fact. (*ii*) That a person heard or saw something, is a fact. (*iii*) That a person said certain words, is a fact. (iv) That a person holds a certain opinion, has a certain intention, acts in good faith, or fraudulently, or uses a particular word in a particular sense, or is or was at a specified time conscious of a particular sensation, is a fact [Sec 2(f) BSA].

Proved, Disproved and Not Proved: A fact is said to be 'proved', when after considering the matters before it, the court either believes it to exist or considers its existence so probable that a prudent man ought, under the circumstances of the particular case, to act upon the supposition that it exists. Whereas a fact is said to be 'disproved' when, after considering the matters before it, the court either believes that it does not exist, or considers its non-existence so probable that a prudent man ought, under the circumstances of the particular case, to act upon the supposition that it does not exist. A fact is said 'not proved' when it is neither proved nor disproved. [Sec 2(1)(j), (c) and (i), BSA].

May Presume, Shall Presume and Conclusive Proof: Whenever it is provided by the BSA that the Court may presume a fact, it may either regard such fact as proved, unless and until it is disproved, or may call for proof of it. Whenever it is directed by the BSA that the Court shall presume a fact, it shall regard such fact as proved, unless and until it is disproved. Where one fact is declared by the BSA to be conclusive proof of another, the Court shall, on proof of the one fact, regard the other as proved, and shall not allow evidence to be given for the purpose of disproving it. [Sec 2(1)(h), (l) and (b), BSA].

When Facts not otherwise relevant become relevant: Facts not otherwise relevant are relevant (i) if they are inconsistent with any fact in issue or relevant fact; (ii) if by themselves or in connection with other facts they make the existence or non-existence of any fact in issue or relevant fact highly probable or improbable. [Sec 9, BSA]. Any fact which either disproves or tends to prove or disprove any claim or charge in a case is made relevant. For example; the question is, whether A committed a crime at Mumbai on a certain day. The fact that, on that day, A was at Kolkata is relevant.

Plea of Alibi

Alibi is a Latin term meaning elsewhere. The plea of alibi is important defence strategy. It essentially asserts that the accused was elsewhere at the time of the alleged crime, thus making his involvement impossible. For example, if A has been accused of committing a crime at Delhi on a particular date and time, and he can show that he was at Leh at or about the same time, his innocence is clear. The concept of Alibi is not defined under the law, but it is impliedly enshrined under Sec 9 of the BSA. While the plea of alibi places the primary burden of proof on the accused, information that supports or disproves that claim is admissible under Sec 9.

Admissions

An admission is a statement, oral or documentary or contained in electronic form, which suggests any inference as to any fact in issue or relevant fact, and which is made by any of the persons, and under certain circumstances [Sec 15, BSA]. Admissions are very weak kind of evidence and the Court may reject them if it is satisfied from other circumstances that they are untrue. Section 16 lays down five classes of persons who can make admission: (i) Party to the proceeding; (ii) Agent authorized by such party; (iii) Party suing or sued in a representative character making admissions holding such character; (iv) Person who has any proprietary or pecuniary interest in the subject matter of the proceeding; and (v) Person from whom the parties to the suit have derived their interest in the subject matter of the suit. Other provisions relating to admission are contained in Sec 17-21 of BSA.

Confession

The substantive law of confession is contained in Sections 22 to 24 of BSA. The word 'confession' has not been defined in the BSA. A confession is an admission of guilt. It is made at any time by a person charged with a crime stating or suggesting the inference that he committed the crime. A confession must either admit in terms the offence, or substantiate all the facts which constitute the offence. In order to decide whether a statement is confessional or not, it must be read as a whole.

A confession made by an accused is irrelevant if it is caused by (i) inducement; (ii) threat, coercion; or (iii) promise. The inducement, threat or promise should have (i) reference to the charge against the accused; (ii) proceeded from a person in authority; and (iii) assured the accused that by making confession he would gain any advantage in the proceedings against him [Sec 22, BSA]. However, a confession is relevant if it is made after the impression caused by any such inducement, threat or promise has been fully removed [Proviso to Sec 22, BSA].

A confession is inadmissible in evidence if made to a police officer or a Provost Marshal. A confession is relevant if it is made in the immediate presence of a Magistrate when the accused is in the custody of police officer [Sec 23, BSA].

When more persons than one are being tried jointly for the same offence, and a confession made by one of such persons affecting himself and some other of such persons is proved, the Court may take into consideration such confession as against such other person as well as against the person who makes such confession. For example, A and B are jointly tried for the murder of C. It is proved that A said, "B and I murdered C". The court may consider the effect of this confession as against B [Sec 24, BSA].

Precautions in Recording Confession

Before recording a confession, the military officer must ensure that the accused is removed from the police custody. He must explain to the accused the legal implications of making a confessional statement. He should also inform that the accused that he is not in any police custody. He should not record any statement unless, upon questioning the accused, he has reasons to believe that it is being made voluntarily. After giving sufficient time to consider his decision to make confessional statement, if an accused still wants to make the confession, the officer must administer him the following caution in accordance with Army Rule 23 (3), in the presence of an independent officer (not a military police officer): "I understand you wish to make a statement. You are not obliged to do so but if you do so, it will be taken down in writing and may be used as evidence." Thereafter, he should record the statement verbatim. He should read it over to the accused and obtain his signature. He should also endorse the caution administered to the accused at the end of and sign on the said certificate, along with the signature of the independent officer who witnessed the accused making the statement.

Difference between Admission and Confession

- Statement is a genus, admission is the species and confession is the sub-species. A confession therefore, is a statement made by the accused person admitting his guilt.
- A confession is a statement made by an accused person which is sought to be proved against him in criminal proceedings to establish the commission of an offence by him.
- A confession if deliberately and voluntarily made may be accepted as conclusive in itself of the matter confessed. An admission is not

a conclusive proof of the matters admitted, but may operate as estoppel.

- A confession always goes against the person making it. An admission may be used on behalf of the person making it under the exception provided in Sec 18 BSA.
- The confession of one or more accused jointly tried for the same offence can be taken into consideration against the co-accused. But an admission by one or of the several defendants in a suit is no evidence against another defendant.
- Hearsay Evidence

Hearsay evidence is a fundamental concept in the law of evidence, and it plays a crucial role in determining the admissibility of statements made outside the courtroom. In simpler terms, it involves the use of statements made by someone who is not testifying in court to prove the facts stated in those statements. Generally, such evidence is excluded from court proceedings because it lacks the reliability and trustworthiness that come from direct testimony and cross-examination of witnesses. The general rule under the BSA is that any evidence that is hearsay is not admissible. The reason behind this rule is to ensure that evidence presented in court is reliable, trustworthy, and subject to cross-examination.[ii]

Exception to hearsay evidence: Sec 26 and 27, BSA are exception to the general rule that hearsay evidence is not admissible. These exceptions (dying declaration, persons who are dead, or statements made in ordinary course of business, etc), are based on the principle that hearsay evidence may be considered reliable in certain circumstances. Section 27 of the BSA provides that that evidence given by witness in a judicial proceeding, or before any person authorized by law to take it, is relevant in a subsequent judicial proceeding when: (i) the witness is dead, (ii) he cannot be found, (iii) is incapable of giving evidence, (iv) he is kept out of the way by the adverse party, or (v) his presence cannot be obtained without unreasonable delay or expense.

---

ii See generally Sec 60, BSA. Though the term 'hearsay' has not been used in the IEA, hearsay evidence is excluded on the ground that it is always desirable in the interest of justice to get the person, whose statement is relied upon during his examination, and its accuracy can be tested by cross-examination.

Opinions of Expert

Section 39 of the BSA relates to opinions of experts. It provides, "When the Court has to form an opinion upon a point of foreign law or of science or art, or any other field, or as to identity of handwriting or finger impressions, the opinions of experts may be taken. An expert witness is one who has devoted time and study to a special branch of learning and thus, is especially skilled on those points on which he is asked to state his opinion. His evidence on such point is admissible to enable the court to come to satisfactory conclusion. Sec 39(2) of the BSA states that when in a proceeding, the court has to form an opinion on any matter relating to any information transmitted or stored in any computer resource or any other electronic or digital form, the opinion of the Examiner of Electronic Evidence referred to in section 79A of the Information Technology Act, 2000, may be taken.

How to Prove handwriting: In case of opinion of experts as to handwriting of any person, it can be proved by the following ways: (a) By the evidence of writer himself; (b) By the evidence of a person who has seen the person, whose handwriting is in question, write; (c) By evidence of person who is acquainted with such handwriting; (d) By the evidence of an expert in comparing handwriting (e) By the court comparing the documents in question; the court may direct a person present in court to write any word or figures and compare with the document in question. (f) In the case of digital signature of any person, the opinion of certifying authority which has issued digital signature certificate [Sec 41, BSA].

Judicial Notice

Judicial notice means the judge's belief in the existences of a fact for which no evidence is required. Judicial notice is based upon reasons of the wisdom of dispensing with proof of matters within the common knowledge of everyone. Sec 51 of the BSA states, "No fact of which the Court will take judicial notice need be proved." The BSA requires courts to take judicial notice of certain matters by general knowledge. Thus, the court may take judicial notice of the following: (a) All laws in force in the territory of India including laws having extra-territorial operation; (b) international treaty, agreement or convention with country or countries by India, or decisions made by India at international associations or other bodies; (c) the course of proceeding of the Constituent Assembly of India, of Parliament of India and of the State Legislatures; (d) the seals of all Courts and Tribunals; etc. [Sec 51 and 52, BSA]. AA s. 134 similarly provides that a court-martial may take judicial notice of any matter within the general knowledge of the members.

Public and Private Documents

Documents are of two kinds public and private. The BSA Sec. 74 gives a list of documents which are regarded as public documents. For example, documents forming the acts, or records of the acts: (i) of the sovereign authority; (ii) of official bodies and tribunals; and (iii) of public officers, legislative, judicial and executive of India or of a foreign country. Public documents also include public records kept in any State or Union territory of private documents, for example contracts, leases, mortgage-deeds, etc. All other documents except the documents referred above are private [Sec 74, BSA].

Certified Copies of Public Document: Every public officer having the custody of a public document, which any person has a right to inspect, shall give that person on demand a copy of it on payment of the legal fees therefor, together with a certificate written at the foot of such copy that it is a true copy of such document. Such a certificate shall be dated and subscribed by such officer with his name and his official title, and shall be sealed, whenever such officer is authorised by law to make use of a seal; and such copies so certified shall be called certified copies. Such certified copies may be produced in proof of the contents of the public documents or parts of the public documents of which they purport to be copies [Sec 75 and 76, BSA].

Primary and Secondary Evidence

The contents of documents must be proved either by primary or by secondary evidence [Sec 56, BSA]. Sec 57 of the BSA states, "Primary evidence means the document itself produced for the inspection of the Court." It further provides following explanations: (1) Where a document is executed in several parts, each part is primary evidence of the document. (2) Where a document is executed in counterpart, each counterpart being executed by one or some of the parties only, each counterpart is primary evidence as against the parties executing it. (3) Where a number of documents are all made by one uniform process, as in the case of printing, lithography or photography, each is primary evidence of the contents of the rest; but, where they are all copies of a common original, they are not primary evidence of the contents of the original. (4) Where an electronic or digital record is created or stored, and such storage occurs simultaneously or sequentially in multiple files, each such file is primary evidence. (5) Where an electronic or digital record is produced from proper custody, such electronic and digital record is primary evidence unless it is disputed. (6) Where a video recording is simultaneously stored in electronic form and transmitted or broadcast or transferred to another, each of the stored recordings is primary evidence. (7) Where an electronic or digital record is stored in multiple storage spaces in a computer resource, each such automated storage, including temporary files, is primary evidence.

Secondary Evidence. Secondary evidence includes: (1) Certified copies given under the provisions of BSA. (2) Copies made from the original by mechanical processes which in themselves ensure the accuracy of the copy, and copies compared with such copies. (3) Copies made from or compared with the original. (4) Counterparts of documents as against the parties who did not execute them. (5) Oral accounts of the contents of a document given by some person who has himself seen it. (6) Oral admissions. (7) Written admissions. (8) Evidence of a person who has examined a document, the original of which consists of numerous accounts or other documents which cannot conveniently be examined in Court, and who is skilled in the examination of such documents [Sec 58, BSA]. For example, A copy compared with a copy of a letter made by a copying machine is secondary evidence of the contents of the letter, if it is shown that the copy made by the copying machine was made from the original.

Section 59 of the BAS states that Documents shall be proved by primary evidence except in the cases mentioned under Sec 60 of the Act, where secondary evidence may be given of the existence, condition, or contents of a document. Thus, secondary evidence may be given in the following cases

- When the original is in the possession or power of the person against whom the document is sought to be proved, or person is out of reach of, or not subject to the process of the Court.
- When the existence, condition or contents of the original have been admitted in writing by the person against whom it is proved;

- When the original has been destroyed or lost;
- When the original is of such a nature as not to be easily movable;
- When the original is a public document;
- When the original is a document of which a certified copy is permitted by the BSA or by any other law in force in India to be given in evidence;
- When the originals consist of numerous accounts or other documents which cannot conveniently be examined in court.

Sec 61and 62 of the BSA make special provisions as to evidence relating to electronic records. Section 61, makes the provision for the admissibility of an electronic or digital record in the evidence on the ground that it is an electronic or digital record and such record shall, subject to section 63, have the same legal effect, validity and enforceability as other document. Sec 62 states that the contents of electronic records may be proved in accordance with the provisions of sec 63 of the BSA.

Privileged Communication

Privileged communications are of two kinds, namely those which are privileged from disclosure and those which are prohibited from being disclosed. Sec 128-134 of the BSA deals with privileged communication. A person is not permitted to give any evidence derived from unpublished records relating to any affairs of State, except with the permission of the head of the department, who may withhold such permission as he thinks fit. A public officer cannot be compelled to disclose communication made to him in confidence when he considers that the public interests would suffer by this disclosure. [Sec 129 and 130 BSA]. Sec 131 states that no magistrate or police officer shall be compelled to disclose the source of information regarding the commission of an offence if the disclosure would cause harm to the informant or other persons. This section aims to protect informants and encourage the reporting of crimes without fear of retribution. Also see RA para 319 and 320 for official documents and their production in a court.

A few exceptions to the privilege contained under Sec 132 are: (1) Communications made in furtherance of an illegal purpose are not protected. (2) If an advocate finds in the course of his employment that any crime/fraud has been committed since the employment began, he can disclose such information.

Presumption as to Abetment of suicide by Married Women and Dowry Death

The legislative intent for sections 117 and 118 was to curb the menace of dowry deaths. When the question is whether the commission of suicide by a woman had been abetted by her husband or any relative of her husband and it is shown that she had committed suicide within a period of seven years from the date of her marriage and that her husband or such relative of her husband had subjected her to cruelty, the Court may presume, having regard to all the other circumstances of the case, that such suicide had been abetted by her husband or by such relative of her husband [Sec 117, BSA]. When the question is whether a person has committed the dowry death of a woman and it is shown that soon before her death, such woman had been subjected by such person to cruelty or harassment for, or in connection with, any demand for dowry, the Court shall presume that such person had caused the dowry death [Sec 118, BSA]. For the purposes of Sec 117 and 118, the terms "cruelty" and "dowry death" shall have the same meaning as in sec 86 and 80 respectively.

Dumb witnesses

Sec 125 of the BSA deals with witnesses who are unable to communicate verbally. It provides that a witness who is unable to speak may give his evidence in any other manner in which he can make it intelligible, as by writing or by signs; but such writing must be written and the signs made in open Court and evidence so given shall be deemed to be oral evidence. Further, if the witness is unable to communicate verbally, the Court shall take the assistance of an interpreter or a special educator in recording the statement, and such statement shall be video-graphed.

Examination of Witnesses

The order in which witnesses are produced and examined is regulated by the law and practice relating to civil and criminal procedure respectively, and in the absence of any such law, by the discretion of the Court. [Sec 140, BSA]. The examination of a witness, by the party who calls him, is called his examination-in-chief. The examination of a witness by the adverse party is called his cross-examination. The examination of a witness, subsequent to the cross-examination by the party who called him, is called his re-examination [Sec 142, BSA].

Order of Examination: Witnesses are to be first examined-in-chief then (if the adverse party so desires) cross-examined, then (if the party calling him so desires) re-examined. The examination and cross-examination must relate to relevant facts but the cross-examination need not to be confined to the facts which the witness testified on his examination-in-chief. The re-examination shall be directed to the explanation of matters referred to in cross-examination, and if new matter by permission of the Court, introduced in re-examination, the adverse party may further cross-examine upon that matter. [Sec. 143, BSA]. A person summoned to produce a document does not become a witness by the mere fact that he produces it, and cannot be cross-examination, unless and until he is called as a witness. [Sec. 144, BSA]

Witnesses to character may be cross-examined and re-examined [Sec. 145, BSA].

Any questions suggesting the answer which the person putting it wishes or expects to receive is called a leading question. Leading questions must not, if objected to by the adverse party, be asked in an examination-in-chief, or in re-examination, except with the permission of the Court. The Court shall permit leading questions as to matters which are introductory or undisputed or which have, in its opinion, been already sufficiently proved. Leading questions may be asked in cross-examination [Sec. 146, BSA]

Hostile Witness

The term "hostile witness" does not appear in the BSA. The term is a judicial creation originating from English law. Under Sec 157/158 of the BSA, a witness is considered hostile when he shows a "hostile mind" or exhibits that he has no desire to tell the truth to the party that called them. A witness who is unfavourable to a party is not necessarily hostile. In other words, a witness who is gained over by the opponent and is unwilling to tell the truth is a hostile witness. In such a case, the court may permit the person who calls a witness, to put any question to him, which may be put in cross-examination by the adverse party under Sec 157/158 of the BSA.

CHAPTER 12

The Inter-Services Organization (Command, Control and Discipline) Act, 2023

The Armed Forces in India are governed by the three distinct Service Acts like the Army Act, 1950, the Air Force Act, 1950 and the Navy Act of 1957. However, the diverse nature of these acts has sometimes posed challenges in maintaining uniform discipline, coordination, and expeditious proceedings across the inter-service formations established by the Government. In 2023, the Government notified the Inter-Services Organization (Command, Control and Discipline) Act (or ISO Act), empowering the Commander-in-Chief or Officer-in-Command of Inter-services Organisations (ISO) to exercise effective disciplinary or administrative power over the personnel from all branches of the military, streamlining operations and fostering collaboration.

Few highlights of the ISO Act are as follows:

- The Act grants Commanders-in-Chief and Officers-in-Command of ISOs the authority to exercise disciplinary and administrative control over service personnel under their command, regardless of their specific branch (Army, Navy, Air Force). This allows a simplified command structure and ensures efficient decision-making within ISOs.
- The ISO Act establishes the position of a CO, responsible for a specific unit, ship, or establishment within an ISO.
- The existing ISOs like the Andaman and Nicobar Command or NDA will be will be formally recognised under the Act.
- The Government may constitute an ISO which has personnel belonging to at least two of the three services: the army, the

navy, and the air force. ISO will be placed under the command of an Officer-in-Command.

- A Joint Services Command (tri-service) can also be formed, which will be placed under the command of a Commander-in-Chief.
- The Central Government may notify any force raised and maintained in India to which the ISO Act will apply. This would be in addition to army, navy, and air force personnel.
- The Rules formulated under the Inter-Services Organisations (Command, Control and Discipline) Act 2023 have been notified through a Gazette Notification and came into effect from May 27, 2025.

This significant step aims to bolster effective command, control, and efficient functioning of Inter-Services Organisations (ISOs), thereby strengthening jointness among the Armed Forces. The details of ISO Act 2023 and ISO Rules 2025 are as follows.

The Inter-services Organisations (Command, Control and Discipline) Act, 2023

The provisions of ISO Act apply to all persons who are subject to the Air Force Act, 1950, the Army Act, 1950 and the Navy Act, 1957, and to persons of such other forces as the Central Government may specify, by notification, under section 4, who are serving in or attached to an Inter-services Organisation [Section 2, ISO Act].

Definitions: Section 3 of the ISO Act defines certain terms as follows:

- "Air Officer" means any officer of the Air Force above the rank of group Captain [section 3(a)].
- "Chief of Defence Staff" means an officer of the regular Army, or the Indian Navy, or the Air Force, as the case may be, appointed as such by the Central Government [section 3(b)].
- "Commander-in-Chief" means a General Officer of the regular Army, or a Flag Officer of the Indian Navy, or an Air Officer of the Air Force, appointed as Commander-in-Chief of a Joint Services Command, and in his absence, the officer on whom the command devolves [section 3(c)].

- "Commanding Officer" means the officer in actual command of the unit, ship or establishment and includes an officer appointed as such by the Commander-in-Chief or the Officer-in-Command, as the case may be, of an Inter-services Organisation [section 3(d)].
- "Flag Officer" means an officer of the rank of Admiral of the Fleet, Admiral, Vice-Admiral or Rear-Admiral [section 3(e)].
- "General Officer" means an officer of the regular Army above the rank of Brigadier [section 3(f)].
- "Inter-services Organisation" means a body of troops including a Joint Services Command consisting of persons, subject to the Air Force Act, 1950, the Army Act, 1950 and the Navy Act, 1957 or any two of the said Acts [section 3(g)].
- "Officer" in relation to an Inter-services Organisation, means an officer as defined in section 4(xxiii) of the Air Force Act, 1950, or section 3 (xviii) of the Army Act, 1950, or section 3(16) of the Navy Act, 1957 [section 3(i)].
- "Officer-in-Command" of an Inter-services Organisation means either a General Officer of the regular Army, or a Flag Officer of the Indian Navy, or an Air Officer of the Air Force, appointed as the Officer-in-Command of an Inter-services Organisation, other than Joint Services Command, and in his absence, the officer on whom the command devolves [section 3(j)].
- "Regulations" means the regulations made under the Air Force Act, 1950, the Army Act, 1950, or the Navy Act, 1957 [section 3(k)].
- "Rules" means the rules made under the ISO Act 1923; and under the Air Force Act, 1950, the Army Act, 1950, or the Navy Act, 1957 [section 3(l)].
- "Service Acts" means the Air Force Act, 1950, or the Army Act, 1950, or the Navy Act, 1957 or any two of the said Acts or all the said Acts [section 3(m)].
- "Service personnel" means persons who are subject to any of the Service Acts: the Air Force Act, 1950, or the Army Act, 1950, or the Navy Act, 1957 [section 3(n)].

The words and expressions used in the ISO Act 2023 and not defined but defined in the Air Force Act, 1950, or the Army Act, 1950, or the Navy Act, 1957 shall have the meanings, respectively, assigned to them under the said Acts.

Special provision for Certain Forces under Central Government

Section 4 of the Act states that the Central Government may, by notification, specify any force or any part thereof, raised and maintained in India under the authority of the said Government, to which all or any of the provisions of this Act shall apply and accordingly all the officers referred to in section 3(1)(i) of the Act, shall be deemed to be officers within the meaning of the respective Acts relating to the said forces. Once a notification has been issued, the authority to exercise all the disciplinary and administrative powers under the respective Acts governing such force or any part thereof including the powers conferred by warrants or commissions issued under such Acts governing that force or any part thereof, shall vest in the Commander-in-Chief or the Officer-in-Command of the Inter-services Organisation. Further, where any of the provisions of the ISO Act applies to a force or any part thereof as referred above, the Central Government may direct that by what authority or which officer, the jurisdiction, powers or duties incidental to the operation of the provisions of this Act shall be exercised or performed in respect of that force.

Constitution of Inter-services Organisation or Joint Services Command

The Central Government, under section 5 of the Act may issue a notification to constitute an Inter-services Organisation, which may include a Joint Services Command, comprising of units or service personnel who are subject to any of the Service Acts, as may be placed under the command of the Commander-in-Chief, or the Officer-in-Command. The Central Government may, by an order published in the Official Gazette, direct that any power exercisable by the Commander-in-Chief or the Officer-in-Command may also be exercisable by any other officer specially empowered in this behalf by the Government.

Existing Inter-services Organisations and Commander-in-Chief or Officer-in-Command to Continue

The ISO Act, section 6 clarifies that (a) the Inter-services Organisations constituted by the Central Government and functioning as such immediately before the date of commencement of this Act, shall be deemed to have been constituted under the provisions of this Act; and (b) the Commander-in-Chief or the Officer-in-Command of an Inter-services Organisation, who has been appointed and functioning as such immediately before the date of commencement of this Act, shall be deemed to have been appointed under the provisions of this Act. Further, nothing contained in this Act shall render invalid any action taken or acts performed, immediately before the commencement of this Act, by the Inter-services Organisation, or by the Commander-in-Chief or by the Officer-in-Command of an Inter-services Organisation, while functioning as such under any law applicable at that time.

Powers of Commander-in-Chief or Officer-in-Command

The Commander-in-Chief or Officer-in-Command of an Inter-services Organisation, shall be the head of such Inter-services Organisation and shall exercise command and control over the personnel serving in or attached to that Inter-services Organisation, for the purpose of maintenance of discipline and proper discharge of their duties [Section 7(1), ISO Act]. For this purpose, the Commander-in-Chief or the Officer-in-Command of an Inter-services Organisation shall be competent to exercise all the disciplinary and administrative powers vested in and exercised by (*a*) the General Officer Commanding the Army; (*b*) the Flag Officer Commanding-in-Chief of a Naval Command; (*c*) the Air Officer Commanding-in-Chief of an Air Command; (*d*) any other officer or authority specified in the Service Acts or in the rules and regulations made thereunder, including the powers conferred by warrants or commissions issued under the provisions of such Service Acts; and (*e*) any other officer or authority as may be specified in the notification issued under section 4 of the ISO Act [Section 7, ISO Act].

Commanding Officer

The Commanding Officer of an Inter-services Organisation shall, in addition to having command over any unit, ship or establishment, also perform such duties as may be assigned to him in respect of such Inter-services Organisation by its Commander-in-Chief or the Officer-in-Command and shall be empowered to initiate all disciplinary or administrative actions over the personnel appointed, deputed, posted or attached to that Inter-services Organisation [Section 8, ISO Act].

Superintendence of Central Government

The superintendence of the Inter-services Organisation shall vest in the Central Government, which shall have the power to issue directions to each of such organisations, on any matters concerning national security or general administration, if it considers necessary and expedient so to do in the public interest [Section 9, ISO Act].

Power to declare persons to be on active service

Notwithstanding anything contained in the Service Acts, the Central Government may, by notification, declare that any service personnel or class of service personnel to whom the Service Acts apply shall, with reference to any Inter-services Organisation in which he or they may be serving in or attached to or with reference to any provision of this Act, be deemed to be on active service within the meaning of this Act and the Service Acts [Section 10, ISO Act].

Power to make rules

Section 11 of the Act provides that the Central Government may make rules for the purposes of carrying out the provisions of this Act.

Overriding effect of ISO Act

The provisions of the ISO Act shall have effect notwithstanding anything inconsistent therewith contained in any other law for the time being in force or in any instrument having effect by virtue of any law other than this Act [Section 12, ISO Act].

Protection of action taken in good faith

No suit, prosecution or any other legal proceeding shall lie against any person for anything which is in good faith done or intended to be done under this Act [Section 13, ISO Act].

Power to remove difficulties

If any difficulty arises in giving effect to the provisions of this Act, the Central Government may, by order published in the Official Gazette, make such provisions not inconsistent with the provisions of this Act, as may appear to be necessary for removing the difficulty; provided that no such order shall be made under this section after the expiry of a period of three years from the commencement of this Act. Further, every order made under this section shall be laid, as soon as may be after it is made, before each House of Parliament [Section 14, ISO Act].

Laying of Rules before Parliament.

Section 15 of the Act states that every rule made by the Central Government under the ISO Act shall be laid, as soon as may be after it is made, before each House of Parliament, while it is in session, for a total period of 30 days which may be comprised in one session or in two or more successive sessions, and if, before the expiry of the session immediately following the session or the successive sessions aforesaid, both Houses agree in making any modification in such rule or both Houses agree that the rule should not be made, the rule shall thereafter have effect only in such modified form or be of no effect, as the case may be; so, however, that any such modification or annulment shall be without prejudice to the validity of anything previously done under that rule.

The Inter-Services Organisations (Command, Control and Discipline) Rules, 2025

In exercise of the powers conferred by section 11 of the Inter-services Organisations (Command, Control and Discipline) Act, 2023, the Central Government has made the Inter-services Organisations (Command, Control and Discipline) Rules, 2025. These Rules have come into effect from 27 May 2025, the date of their publication in the Official Gazette. The term "Act" referred in these Rules means the Inter-services Organisations (Command, Control and Discipline) Act, 2023 [Rule 2(a)]. The term "Inter-services establishment" means an establishment consisting of persons, subject to the Army Act, 1950, the Air Force Act, 1950 and the Navy Act, 1957, or any two of the said Acts, and commanded by an Officer-in-Command, of the rank of Major General or Air Vice Marshal or Rear Admiral or above [Rule 2(b)].

According to ISO Rules, 2025, the term "Inter-services Organisation" shall have the meaning as defined under section 3(1)(g) of the Inter-services Organisations (Command, Control and Discipline) Act, 2023. The term "Inter-services unit" means a unit or ship or establishment, consisting of persons, subject to the Army Act, 1950, the Air Force Act, 1950 and the Navy Act, 1957, or any two of the said Acts, and commanded by an Officer subject to any of the said Acts, empowered in terms of section 8 of the Inter-services Organisations (Command, Control and Discipline) Act, 2023.

The term "Joint Services Command" means a Command consisting of persons, subject to the Army Act, 1950, the Air Force Act, 1950 and the Navy Act, 1957 or any two of the said Acts, and commanded by a Commander-in-Chief, of the rank of Lieutenant General or Air Marshal or Vice Admiral. Further, the words and expressions used in these Rules and not defined in the ISO Act or in these rules, but defined either in the Army Act, 1950, the Air Force Act, 1950 and the Navy Act, 1957, or in the rules or regulations made thereunder, shall have the meaning respectively assigned to them under the said Acts, rules or statutory regulations.

According to **Rule 3(1)**, when the Commander-in-Chief, the Officer-in-Command or the Commanding Officer is absent, on leave or otherwise, the officer to officiate as the Commander-in-Chief, Officer-in-Command or the Commanding Officer shall be notified in the Inter-services Organisation, Establishment or Unit Orders, as the case may be and in case of emergency where such Orders have not been notified, by such officer as deputed to officiate by the next higher formation, until the appointment is notified. Further, under Rule 3(2), the officer officiating as the Commander-in-Chief, the Officer-in-Command or the Commanding Officer, shall, subject to such restrictions as contained in the respective Service Acts, rules or regulations, exercise any power conferred on the Commander-in-Chief, the Officer-in-Command or the Commanding Officer, as the case may be.

Rule 4 relates to disciplinary and administrative power and states that the Commander-in-Chief of a Joint Services Command, Officer-in-Command of Inter-services establishment and Commanding Officer of Inter-services unit shall exercise all disciplinary and administrative power over a person subject to any of the Service Acts, posted or attached to that Inter-services Organisation, in accordance with the Service Acts, rules or regulations applicable to such person.

Rule 5 deals with residuary provision. It states that matter relating to command, control and disciplinary and administrative powers of the Commander-in-Chief or, as the case may be, Officer-in-Command of the Inter-services Organisation or the Commanding Officer of an Inter-services unit with respect to which no express provision has been made in these rules or in the Service Acts or in the rules or regulations made thereunder, shall be referred to the Central Government for its decision.

Advantages:

The enactment of the ISO Act and ISO Rules will serve to enhance India's military command structure. Under the provisions of the Act, Commanders-in-Chief and Officers-in-Command of ISOs are vested with statutory authority to exercise command, control, and administrative oversight regarding discipline over personnel from different branches of the Armed Forces serving within their formations. Importantly, this command is exercised without infringing upon the individual service conditions unique to the Indian Army, Indian Navy, and Indian Air Force. It will significantly improve coordination, decision-making, and operational joint operability among tri-service organization. The ISO Act and Rules will have the following advantages:

(a) Enhanced Operational Effectiveness by way of joint planning, training, and better coordination between services, crucial for modern warfare;

(b) Faster Decision-Making, streamlined command structures within integrated units allow for quicker decision-making on the battlefield; and

(c) Optimum Resource Utilisation as integration will reduce duplication of efforts and optimises resource allocation across all services.

CHAPTER 13

AID TO CIVIL POWER

Besides carrying out its primary task of defending the country against external aggression, the armed forces may be asked to assist the civil government for various internal duties, both in peace and in war. The types of aid so sought by the government could be for (i) maintenance of law and order; (ii) maintenance of essential services; (iii) assistance during natural and other calamities; and (iv) any other type of assistance, including assistance in development projects. The term 'duties in aid of the civil power' in its wider sense could cover all the above types of assistance, however, in the restricted sense, it means the aid given by the Army for the maintenance of law and order. This chapter covers the issue of aid rendered by the Army to the civil administration in the maintenance of law and order, martial law, the Armed Forces (Special Powers) Act and the role of the National Human Rights Commission.

Maintenance of Law and Order

The State Governments are primarily responsible for maintaining law and order. They have adequate machinery at their disposal for the dispersal of unlawful assemblies, suppression of disturbances and riots and the power to arrest and prosecute the offenders. The civil authorities are first required to utilize the police forces at their disposal for restoring law and order, and seek the aid of the Army only when the police forces are inadequate to deal with the situation.

The terms 'unlawful assembly' and 'riot' have been defined in BNS ss. 189 and 191. Please refer Chapter 9 of the book.

Dispersal of unlawful assemblies

Chapter XI of the BNSS deals with the dispersal of unlawful assemblies. Section 148 provides that any executive magistrate or officer in charge of a police station or, in the absence of such officer in charge, any police officer, not below the rank of a sub-inspector may command any unlawful assembly or any assembly of five or more persons likely to cause a disturbance of the public peace, to disperse; and it becomes the duty of every member of such an assembly to disperse accordingly.

If, upon being so commanded, such assembly does not disperse, or if, without being so commanded, it conducts itself in such a manner as to show a determination not to disperse, any executive magistrate or officer in charge of police station, may proceed to disperse such assembly by force, and may require the assistance of any male civilian for the purpose of dispersing such assembly and, if necessary, for arresting and confining the persons, so that they may be punished according to law. When the civil authorities are incapable of dispersing such an unlawful assembly by the use of all the resources at their disposal, they can seek the aid of the armed forces for the dispersal of such assembly.

Dispersal of Unlawful Assembly with the help of the Armed Forces

BNSS s. 149 provides that the executive magistrate of the highest rank who is present may cause an unlawful assembly to be dispersed by the armed forces. The executive magistrate may require any officer in command of any group of persons belonging to the armed forces to disperse such assembly with the help of armed forces under his command and to arrest and confine such persons forming part of it, to have them punished according to law. Every officer of the armed forces is required to obey the requisition of the magistrate in such manner as he thinks fit but in doing so, he is to use as little force and do as little injury to person and property as may be consistent with dispersing the assembly and arresting and detaining such persons.

Every requisition made on an officer in command of troops, in writing or by telegram, by a civil authority for military aid for maintenance of law and order must be complied with immediately. The request by the magistrate should preferably be in writing, but if made verbally, the officer commanding troops should ask the magistrate to repeat the request in the presence of two military personnel. The strength and composition of the force, the amount of ammunition, arms and equipment to be taken and the manner of carrying out the operations are matters for the military authorities alone. [RA para 303 and 305].

Principles governing use of force

The use of force in dispersal of unlawful assembly is governed by the following principles [MML Vol. I, Ch. VII, para 8]:

(a) Necessity: The necessity is deemed to be established when the executive magistrate requisitions the aid. The troop commander must ensure that (i) each and every act is justified; (ii) action taken in one place does not effect another place; (iii) there are no reprisals; and (iv) action is preventive and not punitive.

(b) Minimum force: No more force is to be used than is necessary to achieve the immediate object. This refers to the actual amount of force used and not to the number of troops employed.

(c) Impartiality: Officers and other persons must be impartial in communal disturbances or labour strikes. They should not accept gifts or show favours.

(d) Good faith: Officers and other persons must act in good faith (BNS s. 2(II)), i.e., with due care and attention.

Liaison Officer

In order to ensure that the military authorities have the earliest possible opportunity of gauging the requirements of the situation, the military commander on receipt of a warning by the civil authorities that troops may be required in aid of the civil authorities is to detail a military liaison officer to get in touch with the civil authority in the affected area. The liaison officer is to furnish reports regarding the situation.

The liaison officer is to maintain close contact with the local civil and police authorities, and with the officer commanding the troops employed for dispersal of unlawful assembly. He will be under the orders of the commander of troops during the presence of the latter at the scene of action, if that officer is senior to him. Alternatively, should the liaison officer be the senior, he will automatically be in military command unless specially ordered to the contrary by the officer who detailed him. If possible, the liaison officer should be of such a rank that he will not have to take command of the troops.

Written Report

On the withdrawal of the troops the liaison officer is to submit a written report to the officer who detailed him. The report will comprise a brief narrative of events and a brief summary of his observations and his appreciation of the cause of the trouble. The liaison officer will remain in the disturbed area until ordered to rejoin his unit. The report will be forwarded to Army HQ through the authorized channels. [RA para 304 and 307].

Method of dispersal of unlawful assembly

Troops employed are not to use police methods or be armed with police weapons like lathies and truncheons. All orders to the troops are to be given by their commander. They will on no account fire except by his word of command. They are to use their own weapons and military tactics to deal with the situation. When fire is to be opened on a mob, the procedure [MML Vol. I, Ch. VII, para 9] should be as follows:

(a) Before firing: If possible the crowd should be warned that unless the unlawful assembly disperses, fire is to be opened and that it will be effective. If possible, the magistrate present should give this warning in vernacular. Attention of the crowd can be attracted by sounding a bugle or whistle. A warning notice in appropriate vernacular, where possible, should be carried and exposed to the mob at the required moment. The police force present at the spot does not come under the command of the officer commanding the body of troops. Troops should be kept out of sight of the mob, until they are to be actively used.

(b) During firing: Firing is to be strictly controlled. If officer commanding the body of troops considers that firing by a single or a few individuals is likely to prove sufficient, he is to issue orders to one person of a few specified individuals. If more fire is required, he will issue orders to specified section commanders. While giving fire orders, he will indicate definite targets and state the number of rounds to be fired. The most effective targets are usually the ring leaders. Troops should shoot for effect. They should normally direct their fire low in order to injure and incapacitate rather than to kill.

Firing with blank ammunition or over the heads of the crowd is strictly forbidden. Rapid fire should never be necessary except in self-defence. Pauses in firing will give the crowd an opportunity to disperse. Firing should be stopped immediately the crowd begins to disperse. It should be ensured that the mob does not get too close, to the troops, so as to hamper their tactical handling of weapons or to get involved into hand to hand fighting.

(c) After firing: Immediate steps should be taken to assist the injured by providing first-aid, medical attention, and evacuation to the hospital. All empty cases should be recovered and the number of rounds fired counted and recorded in a diary. Important witnesses to the incident should be detained with the help of the executive magistrate. All arrested rioters should be handed over to the civil authority for being dealt with in accordance with the law. It is absolutely essential that a minute to minute and item by item diary of events is maintained by the officer commanding the body of troops. In case of any future inquiry about the firing, the diary would be useful.

Power of Commissioned Officers to disperse Unlawful Assembly

It may happen that when troops are called out for dispersing unlawful assemblies, an executive magistrate may not be present on the spot to handle the situation. In such cases when public security is manifestly endangered by such assembly and when no executive magistrate can be communicated with, any commissioned or gazetted officer of the armed forces may disperse such assembly with the help of the troops under his command and may arrest and confine any person forming part of it, so that they may be punished according to law. While so acting, the officer or JCO must, when it is practicable for him to do so, communicate with an executive magistrate, and thereafter obey the instructions of such magistrate, as to whether or not he should continue the action. (BNSS s. 150). If the magistrate directs to cease action, it must be obeyed.

In the absence of a magistrate, only a commissioned officer is competent to take action for dispersal of an unlawful assembly when public security is manifestly endangered. A warrant officer, JCO or OR cannot do so on his own. However, a WO or OR can exercise the right of private defence of person or property, under the ordinary civil law to safeguard the lives of himself, the persons under his command and other persons and to protect any property against theft, robbery, mischief, or criminal trespass.

Protection of officers and men acting in aid to civil power

A commissioned officer acting in good faith, or an officer acting at the request of an executive magistrate, or a JCO, WO or OR acting in obedience to any order of his superior officer which he was bound to obey by law, is deemed to have committed any offence and no prosecution can be instituted in any civil (criminal) court against such person except with the sanction of the Central Government (BNSS s. 151).

Power of WO and OR to Arrest

A warrant officer or OR has no power to arrest on his own, any rioters or members of an unlawful assembly. However, under the powers conferred by BNSS s. 40, every citizen including a WO or OR can arrest any person, who, in his view, commits a non-bailable and cognizable offence and hand him over to the police authorities without unnecessary delay. A few example of non-bailalbe and cognizable offences are: murder, culpable homicide, attempt to murder, voluntarily causing grievous hurt by dangerous weapon, theft, robbery and docoity. While arresting, when such person forcibly resists the endeavour to arrest him or attempts to evade the arrest, a WO or OR can use force but no more force is to be used than is necessary. In using force, under these circumstances, he has no right to cause the death of such person unless he is accused of an offence punishable with death or imprisonment for life.

Maintenance of Essential service during Strikes and Emergency

Troops can lawfully be commanded to maintain essential services during strikes or in an emergency if it is likely to affect some military object or purpose. The Central Government can also issue a notification under the Armed Forces (Emergency Duties) Act, 1947, if the maintenance of a particular service is vital importance to the community, and call the military for its maintenance. The notification declaring a service as essential does not *ipso facto* imply that the State Government can requisition Army assistance without explicit sanction of the Central Government. (RA para 302).

Martial Law

Article 34 of the Constitution uses the term 'martial law' without defining it. The term 'martial law' could be used in international as well as domestic sense. Under the international law, it is used to express the powers exercisable by the general in command of army over the inhabitants of an enemy country during war. In domestic sense, it is used to denote the action of the military authorities, when in order to deal with a situation amounting to insurrection or war within the country.

Conditions of extreme disorder may sometimes arise when the civil authorities, even with the help of the armed forces, are unable to bring the situation under control. In such situation, with prior approval of the Central Government, martial law may be imposed in the disturbed area by a military commander. Martial law means the suppression of the civil authority, by military authority, whose sole object is to restore conditions, as expeditiously as possible, to enable the civil authority to resume charge. By imposing martial law a military commander assumes the appointment of Martial Law Administrator and takes control of the affected area. During the period of a major emergency, the military authorities may exercise abnormal powers outside the ordinary law. Such right is essential for the very survival of an ordinary government. Martial law is, therefore, the exercise of the right of private defence by repelling force by force. The military commander may, however, require the civil authorities to discharge their normal functions under such conditions as may be prescribed by him.

Being an extreme step, the decision to declare martial law has to be taken at the highest level possible. Before imposing martial law, as far as practicable, the military commander should obtain the approval of the Central Government. Where the situation is grave, and the circumstances are such that it is not possible to obtain the prior approval of the Central Government, the military commander may, on his own, assume supreme authority for the maintenance of law and order. He should, however, inform the Central Government as soon as possible after martial law is proclaimed. He should also issue proclamation for the information of the inhabitants that martial law has been declared.

Since the main object of imposition of martial law is to restore law and order and the functioning of essential services vital to the community, the military commander should issue Martial Law Regulations, specifying therein the martial law offences, punishments for such offences, and constitute military courts for the trial of offenders against martial law. The military courts consist of military officers and should include one civil member having judicial experience. These courts are to deal with all offences including breaches of Martial Law Regulations. As these courts are not courts in the eyes of law, no court can exercise any appellate jurisdiction over them, or issue any writ against them, or take cognizance of sentences passed by them.

The military, however, can use only so much force, and no more, as may be necessary to put down breaches of peace. In every case, action taken by the military is to be judged by the teat of necessity—whether it was necessary in order to perform its duty of repelling force and restoring order. If the force used is excessive and unnecessary, the military authorities can be held liable for it.

Act of Indemnity

When law and order has been restored, and civil authority resumes charge, civil courts may inquire into the legality of acts of military authorities while martial law was in force. For this reason it is necessary to protect persons from prosecution, those who have been administering martial law. This is done by an Act of Indemnity passed by the Parliament under Article 34 of the Constitution. Such an Act would make transactions legal which were illegal when they took place; free the individuals concerned from legal liability, and make the judgment of Military Courts valid. The protection is afforded under an Act of Indemnity only to those where acts were bonafide and performed in the honest belief that they were part of their duty. The power of Parliament under Article 34 is subject to two conditions: (i) the act to be indemnified must have been done in connection with the maintenance or restoration of order; or (ii) martial law must be in force in the area where the act was done.

In recent years, to fight insurgency and break-down of law and order, Parliament has had to enact special laws conferring broad powers on the military personnel but falling short of martial law. The Armed Forces (Special Powers) Act, authorizes the state as well as the Central Government to call the armed forces to their aid in case of disturbed or dangerous condition and the army officers are given extensive powers to maintain public order.

The Armed Forces (Special Powers) Act (AFSPA)

In India, under normal circumstances, law and order is a provincial (state) subject. However, when a state becomes helpless in dealing with the law and order situation and discharging its primary duty of affording protection to citizens, the Union (Central) Government may declare the whole state or a part of it a disturbed area under the special law and send armed forces in aid of civil powers. While working in aid to civil power, the armed forces get enhanced protection under the special law: The Armed Forces (Special Powers) Act, 1958; and The Armed Forces (Jammu and Kashmir) Special Powers Act, 1990. These Acts contain similar provisions and are hereinafter referred to as AFSPA.

The AFSPA is a small legislation with six sections. Section 1 contains the title of the Act and the territorial limits to which the provisions of the Act are applicable. Section 2 sets out the definition of terms like "armed forces". In the 1972 version of the AFSPA, the armed forces were defined as "the military and Air Force of the Union so operating". In the 1958 version of the Act, the definition was of the "military forces and the air forces operating as land forces". The term "disturbed area" has not been defined. It has been stated as "an area which is for the time being declared by notification under Section 3 to be a disturbed area". Section 2(c) states that all other words not defined in the AFSPA have the meanings assigned to them in the Army Act of 1950.

Section 3 of the Act states how an area can be declared disturbed. It grants the power to declare an area disturbed to the Central Government and the Governor of the state, but does not describe the circumstances under which the authority would be justified in making such a declaration. It only requires that such authority be "of the opinion that the whole or parts of the area are in a dangerous or disturbed condition such that the use of the Armed Forces in aid of civil powers is necessary." This definition was challenged in the case of *Indrajit Barua v. State of Assam* AIR 1983 Del 513. The Delhi High Court ruled that the lack of precision in the definition of a disturbed area was not an issue since the government and the people of India understand its meaning. The Court held that the term "disturbed area" defies any definition. It held, "A disturbed area has to be adjudged according to the location, situation and circumstances of a particular case". Section 3 of the AFSPA lays down that a notification in respect of disturbed area may be issued in regard to an area which "is in such a disturbed or dangerous condition that the use of armed forces in aid of civil power is necessary". The 1972 amendments to the AFSPA extended the power to declare an area disturbed to the Central Government. In the 1958 version of the AFSPA only the state governments had this power. The Central Government has the power to overrule the opinion of the Governor of a state and declare an area disturbed.

Power under Section 4 of AFSPA

Section 4 sets out the powers granted to the military stationed in a disturbed area. These powers are granted to commissioned officers, warrant officers, or non-commissioned officers (NCO). This section allows armed forces personnel to use force for a variety of reasons. The designated member of the armed forces can shoot to kill, for the commission or suspicion of the commission of the following offences: acting in contravention of any law or order for the time being in force in the disturbed area prohibiting the assembly of five or more persons, carrying weapons, or carrying anything which is capable of being used as a fire-arm or ammunition. To justify the invocation of this provision, the officer need to be "of the opinion that it is necessary to do so for the maintenance of public order" and give "such due warning as he may consider necessary".

The armed forces officer/warrant officer or NCO can destroy property, if it is an arms dump, a fortified position or shelter from where armed attacks are made or are suspected of being made, if the structure is used as a training camp, or as a hide-out by armed gangs or absconders. They can arrest anyone without a warrant who has committed, is suspected of having committed a cognisable offence and use any amount of force "necessary to effect the arrest". They can enter and search without a warrant to make an arrest or to recover any property, arms, ammunition or explosives, which are believed to be unlawfully kept on the premises. Section 4 of the AFSPA also allows the use of force necessary for the search.

There is a contention that drastic powers have been conferred on low-ranking officials like NCO. In the armed forces, an NCO holds a responsible position. When troops are deployed, the sections/patrols which go for search and patrolling operations are commanded by the NCO. In isolated places/ remote areas, while encountering insurgents, the NCO is expected to take a decision as regards the suitable use of force in the particular situation, for which he is trained. The Supreme Court in the case of *Naga People's Movement of Human Rights v. Union of India* AIR 1998 SC 431, held that the powers conferred under Sections 4 and 5 on the officers and NCOs are not arbitrary and unreasonable, and are not violative of the provisions of Article 14, 19 and 21 of the Constitution.

Section 5 states that after the military has arrested someone under the AFSPA, they must hand that person over to the nearest police station with the "least possible delay". There is no definition in the Act of what constitutes the least possible delay. This provision has been interpreted as depending on the specific circumstances of each case; there is no precise amount of time after which the section is violated. In *Bacha Bora v. State of Assam* (1991) 2 GLR, 119, the Divisional Bench of the Guwahati HC held that the words 'least possible delay' mean 'within the shortest possible time', though no arbitrary time limit can be set down as it may not be possible in many cases to precisely quantify the period of time in the terms of hours, dates or months.

Section 6 of the AFSPA stipulates that no legal proceeding can be brought against any member of the armed forces acting under the AFSPA without the permission of the Central Government. This does not amount to the granting of immunity to members of the armed forces. It only requires that permission be taken from the Central Government before prosecution. Section 6 gives the Central Government the discretion to grant or refuse sanction for instituting prosecution against any person in respect of anything done in the exercise of the powers conferred by the Act. This discretion cannot be termed arbitrary as any order of the Central Government refusing or granting sanction under Section 6, is subject to judicial review. Section 6 of the AFSPA was reviewed in the case of *Indrajit Barua v. Union of*

India AIR 1983 Del 513. The High Court justified this provision on the grounds that it prevents the filing of "frivolous claims".

The Supreme Court of India has recently held that military personnel cannot be prosecuted without prior sanction of the Central Government for an act committed during the course of duty in places where AFSPA was applicable. The case dealt with two instances of encounters in places where AFSPA was applicable. In the first case, five people were killed by the Army in a counterinsurgency operation in Assam in 1994, while in the second, another five were killed in J&K in March 2000. In both instances, the CBI was directed to investigate the matter, and alleged that Army officers had staged fake encounters. CBI claimed that the people who were killed were indeed victims of fake encounters and moved the court to initiate prosecution against the accused Army officers. It was claimed by the officers that they could only be prosecuted with the prior sanction of the Central Government.

The Supreme Court held that the AFSPA, or the Armed Forces (J&K) Special Powers Act, empowers the Central Government to ascertain if an action is 'reasonably connected with the discharge of official duty' and is not a misuse of authority. The officer only enjoys immunity from prosecution in cases when he has 'acted in exercise of powers conferred under the Act'. The courts have no jurisdiction in the matter. In making a decision, the Government must make an objective assessment of the exigencies leading to the officer's actions.

The Court ruled that under the AFSPA, or the Armed Forces (J&K) Special Powers Act, sanction is mandatory. But, the need to seek sanction would only arise at the time of cognizance of the offence. Cognizance is the stage when the prosecution begins. Sanction is, therefore, not required during investigation. The Court ruled that there is no requirement of sanction under the Army Act, 1950. Hence, if the Army chooses, it can prosecute the accused through court-martial instead of going through the criminal court.

[*General Officer Commanding v. Central Bureau of Investigation*, AIR 2012 SC 1890, decided 1 May 2012.]

Draconian Legislations?

A few human rights organizations have claimed that the AFSPA is one of the most draconian legislations that the Indian Parliament has passed. Even an NCO is granted the right to shoot to kill on the basis of the mere suspicion that it is necessary to do so in order to "maintain the public order". In reality, the imposition of the AFSPA and subsequent safeguards avoids any possibility of arbitrariness in the exercise of power under the Act. The provisions of the AFSPA can be applied in only the following special cases: (i) The Central Government is satisfied that the normal law and order situation has deteriorated up to the extent that it has created a disturbed or dangerous situation; (ii) the state police force is not in a position to stop infiltration or the activities of undesirable forces; (iii) the power conferred by the statute can be exercised only in the specified area and in no other state; (iv) even in a disturbed area, the law has to be followed, for example, an order under s. 163 BNNS must be in force before the powers under s. 4 of the Act can be exercised; (v) the powers can be exercised only in respect of those who are violating law and order; (vi) before exercising the power, a warning is required to be given to those who are violating the law in force; and (vii) The military person exercising the power is answerable to the organization for any breach in the policy directives (Do's and Don'ts) issued by the organization. The BNNS confers wide powers on an Executive Magistrate to deal with emergent situations. Under s. 163 BNNS the Magistrates have powers to impose restrictions on the personal liberties of individuals, in a specific locality or town, where the situation has the potential to cause unrest or danger to peace and tranquility.

Another condition is that in the event of deployment of armed forces, the said forces will operate in the state concerned in cooperation with the civil administration so that the situation that has necessitated the deployment of the armed forces is effectively dealt with and normalcy is restored. Thus, there are ample safeguards to prevent the wanton abuse of the power conferred by the AFSPA

The armed forces need special legal protection and powers in the areas where they operate. It is imperative to use special legislation "from the point of view of morale as well as operational efficiency to protect the rights of soldiers". The Supreme Court of India, in the case of *Naga*

People's Movement of Human Rights upheld the AFSPA. Upholding the instructions issued by the Central Government, a five-judge bench gave a list of do's and don'ts to be observed while acting under the AFSPA that provide effective checks against any misuse or abuse of the powers conferred. The Supreme Court opined that these instructions should be treated as binding by members of the armed forces while exercising their powers under the Act.

The ten commandments of human rights which could be followed in the Army are as follows: (i) Do not use excessive force, (ii) Avoid indiscriminate firing (iii) Do not ill-treat anyone, in particular women and children, (iv) Do not damage civilian property, (v) Do not torture anyone, (vi) No discrimination on any grounds while dealing with civilians, (vii) Ensure wounded and sick are collected and cared for, (viii) No meddling in civil administration, land disputes or quarrels, (ix) Ensure a high standard of discipline, and (x) Uphold Dharma.

National Human Rights Commission

Every human being has the inherent right to life. In India, the right to life is to be protected by law; and no one can be arbitrarily deprived of his life. The notion of human rights includes elimination of discrimination based on caste, religion, race, colour, sex, language, political or other opinion, social origin, property, birth or other status. It also includes the freedom from arbitrary and unlawful detention; to be produced to the magistrate within 24 hours of arrest; the right to a fair trial by an impartial court; the right to legal representation; humane treatment; and not subjected to cruel, inhuman and degrading treatment or punishment.

The National Human Rights Commission (NHRC) was set up under the provisions of the Protection of Human Rights Act (PHRA), 1993. In terms of s. 2 of the Act, "human rights" means the rights relating to life, liberty, equality and dignity of the individual guaranteed under the Constitution or embodied in the International Covenants and enforceable by courts in India. The "international covenants", in this context, means the International Covenant on Civil and Political Rights (ICCPR), and the International Covenant on Economic, Social and Cultural Rights (ICESCR) adopted by the UN General Assembly on 16 December, 1966.

Inquiry into Complaints

A complaint to the NHRC may be made in Hindi, English or any other language recognized by the Constitution of India, and may be sent through post, telegram, fax or e-mail. Urgent complaints may also be lodged beyond the working hours of the Commission. No fee is charged on complaints. The complainants can ascertain the status of their complaint through the Commission's website.

The complaints are processed by the Law Division of the Commission. On receipt of a complaint, a case number and a file number is assigned to it. Thereafter, details of the complaint are recorded and an acknowledgement is mailed to the complainant. The complaints are later placed before a single-member bench, or before a full Commission, for directions. If any complaint requires an investigation to be conducted by the Commission, this is done by the investigation division. The Commission, under s. 17 of the PHRA may either:

a. Disposes of cases with directions to the authorities concerned to take necessary action;

b. Issues notices and seeks detailed reports from the authorities concerned, and issues appropriate directions/ recommendations thereafter; or

c. Dismiss the complaints, if it does not fall within the preview of the Commission.

Steps after Inquiry

Where the inquiry discloses the violation of human rights or negligence in the prevention of violation of human rights by a public servant, the NHRC may recommend to the concerned government or authority the initiation of proceedings for prosecution or such other action as it may deem fit against the concerned person or persons. It may approach the Supreme Court or the high court for such directions, orders or writs as that Court may deem necessary. The NHRC may also recommend to the concerned government or authority for the grant of immediate interim relief to the victim or the members of his family. It may send a copy of its inquiry report together with its recommendations to the concerned government, which has to forward its comments on the report, including the action taken or proposed to be taken thereon, to the Commission, within a fixed period. [PHRA s. 18].

Procedure with Respect to the Armed Forces

The term armed forces as defined under section 2(a) of the PHRA means the naval, military and air forces and includes any other armed forces of the Union. The NHRC may, on its own motion or on the basis of petitions made to it on allegations of human rights violations by the armed forces, seek a report from the Central Government. On receipt of the report, it may either not proceed with the complaint or, make its recommendations to the Government. It is the responsibility of the Central Government to investigate complaints in a fair and objective manner. The Central Government is required to inform the NHRC of the action taken on the recommendations within three months. The NHRC is empowered to make its recommendations to the Ministry of Defence for compliance. There have been a number of cases where the NHRC has asked the Ministry of Defence to award ex-gratia to the victims/next of kin of the human rights violations. The NHRC is to publish its report together with its recommendations and the action taken by the Government on such recommendations. A copy of the report is also given to the petitioner. [PHRA s. 19]. The Directorate of Discipline and Vigilance at Army Headquarters is responsible for processing cases of human rights violations with the NHRC.

Human Right (HR) Cell and Handling of HR Violation Cases in the Army

With the increasing deployment of the army in Counter Insurgency operations since 1993, cases of alleged violations of human rights were on the increase. International and national media were giving a lot of coverage to such reports which in most cases were biased and false. No Parliament Session was complete without the MPs raising questions on the state of human rights with particular reference to J&K and North East regions. While addressing the importance of human rights and its protection, the government was also contemplating establishing a National Human Rights Commission (NHRC). Thus, a necessity was felt for having an organization in the army to monitor all alleged excesses, analyse them, and provide appropriate response so that a correct picture emerges and credibility of our actions maintained.

The HR Cell was established at Army HQ in May 1993 to monitor, analyse and respond to alleged human rights violations/excesses by the Army personnel. The HR Cell was a part of AG's Branch and functioned under ADG Discipline & Vigilance. The Cell consisted of the Director of the rank of Colonel, assisted by a Joint Director of the rank of Lt Col. Similarly, there were HR Cells at every Command & Corps HQs, which were headed by an officer of the rank of Colonel.

In January 2020, the Government created a new appointment of Additional Director General (ADG) Human Rights under the Vice Chief of the Army Staff. The human rights cell is the nodal point to examine any human rights violation reports. The ADG (HR) will have an Indian Police Service officer of the SSP/SP rank on deputation in his branch to provide investigative expertise. The IPS officer will also facilitate the necessary coordination with the home ministry and other organizations. An ADG (Vigilance) has been appointed as part of the restructuring. The ADG (V) and ADG (HR) will take forward the commitment of the Army for transparency and probity.

The post of ADG (HR) is part of several reforms announced by the Army. With the Army serving in sensitive conflict areas, charges of human rights violations come up but don't get the attention always. The Indian Army has always maintained that its human rights record is impeccable but such a body will help in looking into the charges in a professional manner and will also function as an internal watchdog.

Commission of Inquiry

The Commission of Inquiry Act, 1952, empowers the State as well as the Central Government to appoint commission of inquiry. Some of the State Governments have been instituting Commission of Inquiry under the Act, to enquire into the incidents arising out of counterinsurgency operations and other related activities of the Indian Army when deployed in the states in aid to civil power. Such inquiries may have wider ramifications on the Army's ability to conduct operations effectively.

In 2004, the State of Manipur had issues a Notification under the Act for the investigation of an incident by a Commission of Inquiry in which the Army personnel deployed in the aid to civil power were involved. Two

Writ Petitions were thereafter filed in the Guwahati High Court against the investigation of the matter by the Commission of Inquiry as it directed that the Army personnel to appear before it to give evidence. It was highlighted in the petition that the State Governments do not have the power under section 3 of the Commission of Inquiry Act, 1952, to order an inquiry into such incidents which are included in List 1 of the Seventh Schedule (of the Constitution) at appropriate Entries No. 2 and 2A. In such matters the Central Government is the appropriate authority to order an inquiry. The Guwahati High Court [in the case of *Col Jagmohan Singh v. The State of Manipur* AIR 2006 Gau 33] held that the Notification dated 12 July 2004 issued by the State of Manipur appointing the Commission was beyond its competence.

The High Court held that the State of Manipur is not the appropriate Government having any administrative control over the armed forces deployed in the State. The members of the Armed Forces are entitled to protections under Section 6 of the AFSPA of 1958 which provide that no prosecution, suit or other legal proceeding shall be instituted, except with the previous sanction of the Central Government. The Central Government being the appropriate Government and having absolute control over the armed forces deployed in a disturbed area has to deal with the report and take follow-up action as may be necessary in accordance with the provisions of law. Since the subject-matter of dispute is a definite matter of public importance, the Union Government is required to take appropriate decision without least possible delay. The High Court directed to the State of Manipur to hand over the report of the Commission of Inquiry to the Union Government in the Ministry of Home Affairs. The Union Home Ministry, represented by the Secretary would examine the report take appropriate action against the Army personnel, if any, indicted in the report.

The Army Headquarter had earlier advised the Command Headquarters that immediately on appointment of a Commission of Inquiry by the State Governments, a Writ Petition may be filed in the High Court challenging its jurisdiction to institute an inquiry against the members of the Army. Accordingly witnesses and documents may be denied to the Commission by seeking exclusion for production.

[Army Headquarter letter No. 46440/AG/DV-1(P) dated 14 May 1997]

In cases where the formation commanders feel that it is essential to participate in the inquiry to clear the name of the Army, based on the facts and ground reality, then details of the case along with recommendations of Cdrs-in-chief should be forwarded to the Army Headquarters for decision on a case to case basis.

[Army Headquarter letter No. 46440/AG/DV-1(P) dated 16 April 2007]

CHAPTER 14

THE RIGHT TO INFORMATION

In pursuance of the international trend and of domestic demand, the Government of India enacted the Right to Information Act, 2005. The Act came into force in two stages, with effect from 21 June 2005—(Sections 4(1), 5(1), 5(2), 12. 13, 15, 16, 24, 27 and 28 and 12 October 2005—(all other provisions of the Act). It is applicable all over India except the state of Jammu and Kashmir. The gap, however, is covered as the state has its own access law. The Act prescribes mandatory disclosure of certain information to citizens. It creates a legal-institutional framework for setting out the practical regime of right to information for every citizen to secure access to information under the control of public authority.

Information

The term 'information' has been defined under Section 2 (f) of the Act as "any material in any form, including: records, documents, memos, e-mails, opinions, advices, press-releases, circulars, orders, logbooks, contracts, reports, papers, samples, models, data material held in any electronic form and information relating to any private body which can be accessed by a public authority (PA) under any other law for the time being in force." It is necessary that the information must exist in a material form and hence personal opinions, which are not on record, cannot be asked for as they do not exist in a material form. The applicant cannot ask for interpretation of the Acts, Rules or opinions.

If a record has been destroyed as per the record management policy of the PA or it has been stolen or is untraceable despite best efforts put in, the public information officer (PIO) cannot provide them. The PIO is responsible to a citizen only for that information which is available or ought to be available. He does not have to create or generate fresh information.

The term 'record' as contained in Section 2 (i) of the Act includes: any document, manuscript and file; any microfilm, microfiche and facsimile copy of a document; any reproduction of image or images embodied in such microfilm (whether enlarged or not), and any other material produced by a computer or any other device. The term 'right to information', as defined under Section 2 (j) is not limited to record but includes:

(a) the right to inspection of work, documents, records;

(b) taking notes, extracts or certified copies of documents or records;

(c) taking certified samples of material;

(d) obtaining information in the form of diskettes, floppies, tapes, video cassettes or in any other electronic mode or through printouts where such information is stored in a computer or in any other device.

The Chief Information Commission (CIC), by way of series of decisions, has held that a combined reading of Sections 2(f), (i) & (j) indicates that a citizen has the right of access to the file notings unless it relates to matters covered under Section 8 of the Act.

Authorities

The Act lays down specific obligations on the Central as well as State Governments, Competent Authorities and Public Authorities, as defined by the Act. It also provides for designation of Public Information Officers (PIO) and Assistant Public Information Officers (APIO) in all Public Authorities to attend to requests from citizens for information within stipulated time limits. It provides for appeal to officers senior in rank to PIOs against the decisions of PIOs. It also mandates the constitution of a CIC and State Information Commissions (SIC) to inquire into complaints, hear second appeals, and guide implementation of the Act.

Ambit of applicability

The Act says that the information can be obtained from Public Authority, which is defined under Section 2 (h) of the Act. Under the Act all constitutional, statutory bodies, bodies created by government notifications and local self-government bodies are Public Authorities. In addition, bodies owned, controlled or substantially financed directly or indirectly by government are Public Authorities. The Act, covers important institutions like the two Houses of Parliament, the State Legislatures, the Supreme

Court, High Courts and subordinate courts, constitutional authorities like the Election Commission, Comptroller and Auditor General of India and the Union Public Service Commission.

Suo Moto Publication at Regular Intervals

Sections 4 of the Act stipulates that every Public Authority shall maintain all its records duly catalogued and indexed in a manner and the form which facilitates the right to information under the Act. It also states that the authority shall ensure that all records that need to be computerized are computerized and connected through a network all over the country to facilitate access of information anywhere and anytime. Section of the Act lays down a detailed list of information which should be published by the Public Authority. It mandates the Public Authority to publish the following:

(a) Details of the organizational structure, hierarchy among the officers, remuneration and decision making power of employees and norms for doing so;

(b) Directory of all employees, with details of PIO and AA

(c) Details of budget of the Organization, subsidy scheme and details of recipients;

(d) Description of Rules, Regulations, Instructions, Manuals, Records and statement of categories of documents held by it or under its control;

(e) Particulars of consultation mechanism with public and of consultative bodies like Boards, Committees, and Councils etc;

(f) Details of Information available in electronic form, and (g) Location of facilities where citizens can access the information.

However, the list is only illustrative and not exhaustive. Section 4 (1) (c) of the Act requires that every Public Authority shall publish all relevant facts while formulating important policies or announcing the decisions which affect the public. Section 4 (1) (d) requires that it shall provide reasons for administrative or quasi-judicial decisions to affected persons. The information has to be disseminated taking into account cost effectiveness, local language and the most effective method of communication in that local area, like notice boards, news papers, public announcements, media broadcasts, the internet or any other means.

Information Providers

Under section 5 of the Act, all organization/institutions have to nominate a Public Information Officer (PIO) to provide information. PIO has a duty to assist requesters. If no response is received in 30 days then it can be deemed as refusal and requester can go in for first appeal and subsequently second appeal. Citizen can make direct complaint to Chief Information Commissioner (CIC) at State/Central level.

Under Section 6 of the Act, the request for information can be made in writing or through electronic means in English or Hindi or in the official language of the area in which the application is being made. There is no requirement that application should be on a Particular format or that it should be typed. The applicant must always be polite while asking for information. The applicant is not required to give reason for requesting the information or any other personal details except those that may be necessary for the purpose of contacting him/her. The applicant is required to specify the particulars of the information being sought and the application is to be accompanied by the prescribed fee, unless the applicant is a 'below poverty line' cardholder, in which case he has to attach a copy of his card.

It may happen that applicant may apply to the PIO in a particular Public Authority but the information is either held by another Public Authority or the subject matter is more closely connected with the functions of another Public Authority, in full or part. The PIO to whom the application is made cannot return it but has to, under Section 6 (3) of the Act, transfer it to the concerned Public Authority, within 5 days of receipt of application, under intimation to applicant. The other Public Authority will be subject to time limit for disposal from the date of receipt of the application.

Disposal of Request for Information

The PIO are to receive requests from persons seeking information after payment of the fee prescribed in the Act. Such requests shall be disposed of either by providing the information as requested or by rejecting the request for reasons to be specified within the time period stipulated under the Act. Section 7 (1) of the Act requires that the information requested shall be furnished as expeditiously as possible, but the maximum time limit is as under: -

(a) 48 hours of receipt in cases where the information sought for concerns the life or liberty of a person. Such situations may relate to information pertaining to electricity disconnection or about an unsafe building

(b) 30 days of receipt in general cases

(c) 35 days if the application is submitted to the APIO or transferred by PIO to the appropriate Public Authority under Section 6(3), as described before

(d) 40 days where information is about a Third Party

(e) 45 days when information pertains to human right violations of excluded agencies notified in Schedule II of the Act.

The period intervening the dispatch of Intimation to the applicant and the deposit of further fees towards the cost of providing the information is excluded from the stipulated time limit. Further, where information is to be provided, PIO has to intimate the amount of fees to be paid, the details of fees levied and that the decision of levying a certain amount of fee can be appealed against. If decision on the request for information is not given within the period specified, it is deemed to have been refused and the applicant can than either file the first appeal to appellate authority (AA) or file a complaint before information commissioner (IC).

Where a request has been rejected, the PIO by a written order, has to communicate to the person making the request (i) the reasons for such rejection, (ii) the period within which an appeal against such rejection may be preferred; and (iiii) the particulars of the appellate authority. A speaking order is necessary so as to enable the applicant in deciding to file an appeal or not. In case of an appeal filed against the decision of the PIO, a speaking order by the PIO would support his decision as the burden is on the PIO to prove that he acted reasonably and diligently. It also enables the AA/IC in adjudicating the case.

Section 7 (9) of the Act provides that information shall be provided in the form in which it is sought unless it would disproportionately divert the resources of the Public Authority or would be detrimental to the safety or preservation of the record in question. The information provided to an applicant, to the extent possible, has to be in the form, which is easily understandable to him or her.

Fees

Fees are prescribed for grant of access to information under the rule making powers of the government and the competent authorities. The Act prescribes that the fee: (i) should be reasonable and not so high to discourage the requestor, (ii) is not levied on persons below poverty line. Additional fee for providing information is to be intimated in writing with calculation details and the decision on fee is appeal able. The information is to be given free of cost, if it is not supplied in the prescribed time limit.

The Central Government has framed the RTI (Regulation of Fee and Cost) Rules 2005. It prescribes the following rates: (i) Rs.10/- as application fee, (ii) Rs.2/- per page of A4/A3 size paper, (iii) Actual charge or cost price of larger size paper, (iv) Actual cost or price for samples or models, (v) Rs.50/- per floppy diskette, (vi) Publication at priced cost or Rs. 2/- for each page photocopy, (vii) Inspection of records free for the first hour, (viii) Rs. 5/- for every subsequent hour (or fraction). The fees is payable by Cash/DD/Banker's Cheque/Indian Postal Order.

Severability

This is an innovative and interesting feature of the Act. If an application consists of some information which cannot be disclosed under the Act, it does not mean that the PIO can reject the same. Section 10 ensures that access would be given to non-exempted information, if such information can reasonably be separated. In such case, the PIO has to inform: (i) that only part of the record requested is being provided (ii) the reasons for the decision (iii) the name and designation of the person giving the decision (iv) the details of the fees (v) the right of the applicant to challenge the decision.

Third Party Information

Third Party is defined under the Act to mean a person other than the requestor and the Public Authority to whom the request is made. Section 11 of the Act provides for calling of representation if any, from the Third Party against furnishing of any information supplied by and treated by it as confidential. If the information has been demanded by the third part, PIO is to give a written notice to the Third Party, within 5 days of receipt of the application inviting his objection to disclosure, if any. The Third Party has 10 days to respond. The maximum time limit to supply information in such cases stretches from 30 days to 40 days. The Third Party is entitled to prefer an appeal against the decision of the PIO.

Except in the case of 'trade or commercial secrets protected by law', disclosures involving Third Party information may be allowed, if the public interest in disclosure outweighs any possible harm or injury to the interests of such Third Party. If the Third Party is a private individual, the PIO has to be very cautious and should properly weigh the consequences, as privacy of an individual is important and protected under Section 8 (1) (j) of the Act. The PIO, despite objection of Third Party, can disclose the information if he thinks, for reasons to be recorded, that public interest prevails over the interest of Third Party.

Exemptions

The Act not only lays down the principles of sharing the information, it also specifies the information which cannot be disclosed. Section 8 of the Act provides a list of 10 categories of exempted information, as follows:

(a) **Strategic Interests of the State**: Information the disclosure of which would prejudicially affect the sovereignty and integrity of India, the security, strategic, scientific or economic interests of the State, relation with the foreign State or lead to incitement of an offence should not be disclosed. For example information relating to military operations, location of military units in war and peace, supply order of defence equipments, number and extent of shortage of air force pilots, movement of army officers, etc., is barred.

(b) **Contempt of Court**: Information expressly forbidden to be published by any court of law or tribunal or the disclosure of which may constitute contempt of court cannot be shared. However, it has been made clear that matter being sub-judice is no ground to deny the information about it unless the court explicitly prohibits the disclosure of the same.

(c) **Parliamentary Privilege**: Information, the disclosure of which would cause a breach of privilege of Parliament or State Legislature is protected from disclosure. Documents to legislative Committees have been held to be the property of the legislature and therefore cannot be shared.

(d) **Commercial Confidence**: Information including commercial confidence, trade secrets or intellectual property where disclosure would harm the competitive position of a third Party, is not to be given, unless there is a larger public interest in disclosure of such information. Information about Supply orders, Pricing, Patents, R&D, details of security and surety submitted to Bank are all protected, as they are likely to cause harm to the competitive position of a Party.

(e) **Fiduciary Relationship**: Information available to a person in his fiduciary relationship, unless the competent authority is satisfied that the larger public interest warrants the disclosure of such information.

(f) **Diplomatic Correspondence**: Information received in confidence from a foreign Government cannot be disclosed.

(g) **Protecting of Source**: Information, the disclosure of which would endanger the life or physical safety of any person or identity the source of information or assistance given in confidence for law enforcement or security purposes, is exempted from disclosure. Hence Source Reports or Investigation reports having information about witnesses or officers examined can only be disclosed without identifying them.

(h) **Impeding the Investigation**: The Information which would impede the process of investigation or pertains to apprehension or prosecution of offenders is protected from disclosure. The term investigation is not limited to criminal investigation but has to be construed broadly to include civil investigation, departmental enquiry/proceeding, enquiries, etc.

(i) **Cabinet Decisions**: Cabinet Papers including records of deliberations of the Council of Ministers, Secretaries and other officers cannot be demanded. However, after the decision, its reasons and the material on the basis of which the decisions were taken can be made public. If the cabinet matter pertains to a subject which is protected under any of the clauses of Section 8, than they remain protected even after the decision is taken.

(j) **Privacy**: Personal information, which would cause unwarranted invasion of the privacy of the individual, is to be protected unless larger public interest justifies the disclosure of such information. Thus the information about bank accounts, sources of funds, partnership details, and hospital records etc., of other persons cannot be obtained. However, the Maharashtra SIC in a recent decision has directed hospital authorities to disclose the medical record of a politician who was shifted from jail to the hospital during his imprisonment. The SIC was of the view that because of the tendency of influential people taking advantage of law, there is a public interest in disclosing this personal information.

However, the exemptions under Section 8 of the Act are further diluted by the following provisions: (i) any information that cannot be denied to Parliament and State Legislature should not be denied to a citizen; and (ii) the Public Authority is free to disclose any information, even if otherwise protected from disclosure, if there is public interest in disclosure.

Under Section 9 of the Act, without prejudice to the provisions of section 8, a CIPO or a State PIO, may reject a request for information where such a request for providing access would involve an infringement of copyright subsisting in a person other than the State.

Exemption to Certain Organizations

Section 24 (1) provides that the Act shall not apply to the following intelligence and security organizations established by the Central Government. The Organizations are:

1. Intelligence Bureau.
2. Research and Analysis Wing of the Cabinet Secretariat.
3. Directorate of Revenue Intelligence.
4. Central Economic Intelligence Bureau.

5. Directorate of Enforcement.
6. Narcotics Control Bureau.
7. Aviation Research Centre.
8. Special Frontier Force.
9. Border Security Force.
10. Central Reserve Police Force.
11. Indo-Tibetan Border Police.
12. Central Industrial Security Force.
13. National Security Guards.
14. Assam Rifles.
15. Shastra Seema Bal
16. Special Branch (CID), Andaman and Nicobar.
17. The Crime Branch: CID, CB, Dadra and Nagar Haveli.
18. Special Branch, Lakshadweep Police.
19. Special Protection Group
20. Defence Research and Development Organization
21. Border Road Development Board
22. Financial Intelligence Unit, India

At the time of commencement of the Act, only 18 institutions were included but 4 were added subsequently. The three wings of the Indian Armed Forces, the Army, the Navy and the Air Force are not exempted institutions. State Governments have notified their own agencies. Even excluded institutions need to appoint PIO and AA as information pertaining to allegations of corruption and human rights violations is still to be provided. In the case of information sought in respect of allegations of violation of human rights, the information has to be provided within 45 days but only after getting the approval of the IC.

Appeals

The Act provides two channels of appeals against the decision of a PIO or 'first' appeal to a designated 'officer senior in rank' to the PIO – the Appellate Authority (AA) and a 'second' appeal to the IC. The AA hears appeals both against the order of PIO and deemed refusal. Appeals can be preferred within 30 days from the receipt of such a decision or from the expiry of stipulated time limit in case of deemed refusal. The AA may admit the appeal after the expiry of the period of 30 days if the appellant was prevented by sufficient cause from filing the appeal in time. The AA should dispose of the appeal within 30 days of the receipt of the appeal. Where appeal cannot be decided within 30 days, AA must record the decision for the delay, and decide it within 45 days from the date of filing of appeal. AA cannot entertain any fresh request for information in the appeal proceedings.

Second appeal against the decision of the AA shall lie with the IC, within 90 days from the date on which the decision should have been made or was actually received. However, the IC may admit the appeal after the expiry of the period of 90 Days, if the appellant was prevented by sufficient cause from filing the appeal in time. No time limit for disposal has been prescribed for IC.

The IC has the power to require the Public Authority to take any such steps as may be necessary to secure compliance with the provisions of the Act, including (i) by providing access to information, if so requested, in a particular form, (ii) by appointing a PIO, if not appointed, (iii) by publishing certain information or categories of information, (iv) by making necessary changes to its practices in relation to the maintenance, management and destruction of records, (v) by enhancing the provision of training on the right to information for its officials, and (vi) by providing it with an annual report.

The most effective power of the IC is its competence to impose penalties against PIO, recommend disciplinary action against erring public servants and compensate the requestor. The decisions of the IC are binding. Section 23 of the Act bars the jurisdiction of the lower courts. Only the writ jurisdiction of High Court and Supreme Court can be invoked by parties aggrieved by the decision of the IC. The appeal procedure before CIC is governed by the Central Information Commission (Appeal Procedure) Rules, 2005. An appeal should be accompanied by attested copies of the Orders appealed against and copies of documents relied upon.

Penalty

Penalty can be imposed against the erring PIO in cases where the PIO has, without any reasonable cause: (i) refused to receive an application, (ii) has not furnished information within the stipulated time, (iii) malafidely denied the request for information, (iv) knowingly given incorrect, incomplete or misleading information, (v) destroyed information which was the subject of the request, or (vi) obstructed in any manner in furnishing the information. The PIO is personally liable to pay penalty. The IC however, is legally bound to give the PIO a reasonable opportunity of being heard. The scale of the penalty to be imposed is Rs. 250 each day till application is received or information is furnished subject to the total amount of such penalty not exceeding Rs. 25,000. While Penalty can be imposed only against PIO, compensation and damage can be ordered against AA also. Penalty goes into the account of Commission but compensation and damages are Payable to the complainant or the appellant. However, as a general rule, actions taken in good faith are protected under Section 21 of the Act.

Information Commission

Information Commission (IC) is the guardian of the Act. Section 12 and Section 15 of the Act provide for the constitution of the Central Information Commission and the State Information Commissions respectively to exercise powers conferred on it by Chapter V (Sections 18-20) of the Act. The IC consists of the 'Chief Commissioner' and such numbers of 'Commissioners', not exceeding ten, as may be considered necessary. The Commissioners have to be eminent persons in the field of law, science and technology, social service, management, journalism, mass media, administration and governance. They should not to be associated with politics and business. They have been given a very high status in protocol in terms of the superior status of the Commission.

In order to ensure that they are independent of the government, following safeguards are provided:

(a) Selection of the Commissioners by a collegium including Leader of Opposition.

(b) The general superintendence, direction and management of the affairs of the Commission vest in the Chief Information Commissioner/ State Chief Information Commissioner who shall be assisted by the respective Information Commissioners.

(c) Commission exercises its powers without being subjected to directions by any other authority.

(d) Removal of the Commissioners is possible only on grounds of misbehavior and incapacity after inquiry by a Supreme Court Judge on a reference by the President/ Governor, as the case may be.

In addition to appeal, IC can also entertain complaints directly from any person: -

(a) Who could not submit a request to a PIO because no PIO has been appointed, or because the PIO has refused to accept application or appeal for forwarding to the appropriate authority;

(b) Who did not receive response to a request for information or access to information within the stipulated time limit;

(c) Who has been required to pay an amount of fee which he or she considers unreasonable;

(d) Who believes that he or she has been given incomplete, misleading or false information under the Act; and

(e) In respect of any other matter relating to requesting or obtaining access to records under the Act.

Section 18 of the Act further stipulates that while inquiring into a complaint, the Commission shall have the same powers as are vested in a civil court while trying a suit under the Code of Civil Procedure, 1908. These powers are with respect of summoning and enforcing the attendance of persons, compelling them to give evidence on oath, producing the documents or things, receiving evidence on affidavit, requisitioning public record etc. No public record can be withheld from it on any grounds. The

Commission also has the power to issue directions to Public Authority. The annual report of the Commission has to be laid before the appropriate legislature.

Responsibility for Government

Under the Act, the Government is obliged to develop educational programmes for the public, especially the disadvantaged. It also has the responsibility of training all the stakeholders. The Act calls on the Governments to prepare 'User Guides'.

Implications for the Armed Forces

The right to information is implicitly guaranteed by the Constitution. However, with a view to set out a practical regime for securing information, the Parliament has given a powerful tool to the members of the armed forces to get information from the Government as a matter of right. This law is very comprehensive and covers almost all matters of governance and has the widest possible reach, being applicable to Government at all levels-including the three wings of the armed forces.

Method for Obtaining Information

The queries are required to be addressed directly to the Additional Director General of Public Information. The queries are then sent to the appropriate agency. The timeframe for the query to be answered is 30 days, but sometimes it takes longer if it has to go through many agencies. The query which is answered in a written hard copy can sometimes prove to be a little expensive as the information seeker is asked for an additional amount if the answer is to be accompanied with photo-copies of documents supporting the answer. The list of PIOs and Appellate Authorities under the Army Headquarters are following.

S.No.	Formation	Organisation
1	RTI Cell at IHQ of MoD	(i) Appellate Auth - Provost Marshal (ii) CPIO (DDG RTI) - DDG AE to perform the duties of DDG RTI in addition to his own duties (iii) PIO (Dir RTI) - One Col from AEC

S.No.	Formation	Organisation
2	HQs Comd less HQ ARTRAC	(i) Appellate Auth - COS/ Brig Adm (ii) PIO - Brig/Col (Edn)
3	Cat 'A' Establishments	(i) Appellate Auth-Dy Comdt/CI (ii) PIO - Col GS/Col from AEC
4	HQs Corps	(i) Appellate Auth - COS/ Brig Adm (ii) PIO - Col Edn
5	Div HQ	(i) Appellate Auth - Dy GOC (ii) PIO - SO1/SO2 (Edn)
6	Brigade HQ	(i) Appellate Auth - Dy Cdr (ii) PIO - Edn Offr
7	Area HQ	(i) Appellate Auth - Dy GOC (ii) PIO - Col GS
8	Sub Area HQ	(i) Appellate Auth - Stn Cdr (ii) PIO - Col GS
9	Regimental Centres	(i) Appellate Auth - Dy Comdt (ii) PIO - GSO-1(Trg)
10	Record Offices	(i) Appellate Auth - Dy Comdt (ii) PIO - CRO/SRO

All queries under Right of Information Act must accompany an application stating the type of information required along with a local DD/IPO of Rs 10/- only in favour of GSO-1, RTI Fund payable at New Delhi. The GSO-1, RTI is accounts officer to receive fees/cost of information under the Act. An individual is also required to a proof for being a citizen of India. For any further query (only relating to RTI Act), the following officials could be approached. The Appellate Authority for Integrated HQ of Ministry of Defence (ARMY) is Provost Marshal.

Additional Directorate General of Army Education
RTI Cell, G-6, D-1 Wing, Sena Bhawan
Integrated Headquarter of MoD (Army)
DHQ PO, New Delhi 110011

The Present Trend

The former Chief of the Army Staff, General J J Singh, kicked up a storm by seeking exemption from the Right to Information Act citing national security interest as the chief reason. But the government did not agree with him. The Act has opened the door to people seeking information ranging from commercial information with vendor details to defence deals, acquisitions and procurements. The services headquarters, which earlier traditionally denied the information, are now forced to reveal the same to the serving as well as retired personnel, their dependents and other stake holders. Multifarious queries are being posed by officers of all the ranks ranging from Lieutenant to Major Generals. Non-commissioned ranks too have been filing queries mainly pertaining to pay and allowance, posting and promotions. The bulk of the queries from officers are mainly about postings, promotions, progress in disciplinary cases, policy matters, proceedings of court of inquiry, etc. Sixty percent of the queries are said to be from ex-servicemen, while five percent are from serving officers and men, and the remaining from civilians.

Some of the interesting cases decided by the Chief Information Commissioner, directing the Ministry of Defence to provide the information to the applicants are as follows.

a. The CIC directed that complete court of inquiry proceedings to be provided to a retired Subedar Major. File No.CIC/LS/A/2009/001037, decided on 24 June 2010.

b. The CIC directed that documents to be provided to applicant with the aim of uncovering a large scale corruption prevalent in GREF. File No.CIC/LS/A/2010/000291, decided on 24 June 2010.

c. The CIC directed that applicant should be allowed to access the personal file of her deceased husband (of Indian Navy) to check nomination details. File No.CIC/LS/A/2010/000292, decided on 24 June 2010.

d. The CIC directed that the appellant, who was the Superintending Engineer in E-in-C's Branch be supplied with copies of his ACR of certain years. File No.CIC/LS/A/2010/000348, decided on 24 June 2010.

e. The CIC directed that the applicant Nb Sub RM Bandyopadhyaya, be provided with posting profile of another JCO. It was alleged that the said JCO has been pampered by the Army HQ by way of giving him choice postings in violations of rules/norms and the said information was required for the sake of transparency in the management of postings in the Army. File No.CIC/LS/A/2010/000558, decided on 25 June 2010.

f. The CIC directed that the applicant, a serving Lt Col be provided with the information: (i) the provisions (rules/policies) under which he was attached to another station, (ii) the name, appointment and the designation of the superior military authority by whose orders he was attached, (iii) the copy of the letter of authority of such superior military authority by whose orders he was attached, and (iv) the copies of letters/file notings connected to the above order. Complaint No CIC/WB/C/2007/00247 dated 11 June 2007, decided on 24 March 2008.

g. The CIC directed that all the documents relating to the medical treatment to an air force officer be supplied to his father—the applicant. The CIC also commented on the casual way of handling the application by the PIO and higher authorities of the Indian Air Force. Appeal No. CIC/WB/A/2007/00645 dated 28 Jun 2007, decided on 26 March 2008.

h. The CIC directed to provide the appellant, a Lt Col: (i) reason for his premature posting, (ii) particulars of subordinate authority who initiated move for his premature posting and under what grounds, and (iii) status of his application sent to the COAS. Appeal No. CIC/WB/A/2007/00326 dated 5 March 2007, decided on 29 Feb 2008.

The Delhi High Court's Ruling

In the following cases the Army Headquarter refused to give information as directed by the CIC and instead went in appeal to the Delhi High Court.

Captain Kohli, Shaurya Chakra, while serving in 18 RR, had died in 2006 in Jammu and Kashmir. The matter was investigated by a Court of Inquiry under the Army Rule 177 and his death was stated to be a case of alleged suicide. His mother, Mrs Veena Kohli, on 20

May 2007, filed an application with the Central Public Information Officer (CPIO) for seeking copies of the FIR, ballistic report, post-mortem report, inquest proceedings, forensic and pathological reports conducted after the officer's death. The CPIO by an order dated 28 August 2007 rejected the request of Mrs Kohli accepting the stand taken by the Army Headquarter that in terms of Army Rule 184, she is not entitled to the report of the Court of Inquiry as she was not subject to the Army Act. It was also stated by the Army that the death had occurred in J&K and the RTI Act was not applicable there.

An aggrieved Mrs Kohli approached the Central Information Commission (CIC), pleading that the RTI Act was also applicable to the Army, as it was a Central Government organization.

In its order of 03 February 09, the CIC held that "Central Government establishments, wherever located, would squarely come under this Act and cannot get exemption merely because they are located in some areas of the country to which this enactment does not extend." The CIC also said that the court of inquiry proceedings are not excluded from the RTI Act and they have to be disseminated under it. The CIC asked the Army to hand over the court of inquiry, post-mortem and other reports related to the death of Capt Kohli to his mother. The commission made it clear that the proceedings can be held back in cases where the disclosure of an inquiry can have ramifications on national security.

Not satisfied with the order of the CIC of 3 Feb 09, the Union of India filed a writ petition [W.P. (C) 7604/2009] in the Delhi High Court. The Delhi High Court on 28 July 2010 ruled that the Army Headquarters were not precluded from the transparency law and were obligated to disclose information to the family of those posted in the state. Directing the Army to hand over court of inquiry, post-mortem and other reports relating to the death of Capt Sumit Kohli to his mother Mrs Veena Kohli, the court made it clear that the RTI Act was not applicable to J&K because the state, due to its peculiar conditions, had to have its separate law for public disclosure.

The Delhi High Court held: "This, by no stretch of imagination, can mean that where the offices and establishments of the Central Government, including the Army, are located in the state of J&K,

no application can be made under the RTI Act to such offices and establishments under the RTI Act to seek the information held by them. Further, the mere fact that Army personnel are in the state of J&K, does not preclude such personnel, or their relatives, from seeking information concerning themselves through an application made under the RTI Act to the Army." The High Court dismissed the writ petition of the government and directed that costs of Rs. 5000/- to be paid to the respondent within a period of two weeks.

The right to information is expected to improve the quality of decision making by the military hierarchy and other government authorities in administrative matters, by removing unnecessary secrecy surrounding the decision-making process. It would enable individuals to be kept informed about the functioning of the decision-making process as it affects them and to know the kinds of criteria that are to be applied in making these decisions. It is hoped that this would enhance the quality of governance in the armed forces by giving all citizens further opportunity to participate in informed way. By securing access to relevant information citizens would be able to participate in the process of decision making and policy formulation on issues concerning them.

Official Secrets Act v. RTI Act

The Official Secrets Act, 1923, is a replica of the erstwhile British Official Secrets Act. It deals with espionage, but has the damaging 'catch all' Section 5, which makes it an offence to part with any information received in the course of official duty to non- officials. In fact, the Act has been used time and again to suit the purposes of the government. One such infamous case is the Bhopal Gas Tragedy, in which the leakage of methyl isocynate gas from the Union Carbide factory in Bhopal claimed several thousand lives and maimed and handicapped at least the next three generations. Not only did the government refuse to make public details of the monetary settlements with the Union Carbide, but several participants at a workshop on the medical aspects of the victims were arrested for taking notes under the provisions of the Official Secrets Act.

There have been several futile attempts to amend the Official Secrets Act. A Working Group was formed by the Government of India in 1977 to look into required amendments to the Act to enable greater dissemination of information to the public. This group recommended that no change was required in the Act as it pertained only to the protection of national safety and not to the prevention of the legitimate release of information to the public. Section 22 of the RTI Act provides that in case of conflict, the provisions of the Act would override the Official Secrets Act, 1923, as well as any legal instrument. The inclusion of the word 'instrument' means an obligation to bring all rules, guidelines, manuals, etc., in conformity with the Act.

A statutory right to information is one of the most significant reforms in public administration in India in the last 80 years. It empowers every citizen the enforceable right to question, examine, audit, review and assess government acts and decisions, to ensure that these are consistent with the principles of public interest and justice. It would promote openness, transparency and accountability in administration, by making the government more open to public scrutiny. The RTI Act is a complete code. If information cannot be denied under Section 8 and 9, it cannot be denied under any other law as RTI overrides all of them. The Act casts responsibilities on all competent authorities, appropriate governments, public authorities and other functionaries. All government departments, including the Army, Navy and the Air Force, are covered by the Act except security and intelligence agencies.

The RTI Act has remained a powerful tool with the serving community and veterans and their families to obtain information and documents concerning their service, medical board proceedings relating to the issues of disability and pensioner issues, and also to move the authorities into action with respect to routine grievances. The RTI Act has ensured transparency in official establishments dealing with such cases. Even innocuous documents such as old service records of veterans are only made available through the RTI Act. At the same time, the armed forces have been raising their concern to the Government and requesting for the exemption of armed forces from RTI on the line of Central Armed Police Forces (CAPF). A number of veteran organizations have expressed their reservation and are opposing the complete exemption of armed forces. If Armed Forces are withdrawn from the ambit of the RTI Act, not only will discrepancies in defence procurements, promotions, human rights violations, etc, get swept under the carpet but it would also block information regarding the personnel's service and pensioner issues.

CHAPTER 15

INTERNATIONAL HUMANITARIAN LAW AND GENEVA CONVENTIONS

International Humanitarian Law

International humanitarian law (IHL), also known as the law of war or the law of armed conflict is a branch of international law which limits the use of violence in armed conflicts. It protects persons who are no longer participating in hostilities, and also defines the rights and obligations of the parties to a conflict in the conduct of hostilities. The rules of IHL strike a careful balance between concerns for humanity and military necessity.

The main purpose of the laws of armed conflict is to protect combatants and non-combatants from unnecessary suffering and to safeguard the fundamental human rights of persons who are not or no longer taking part in the conflict. In every armed conflict, members of the armed forces, including accompanying civilians, are subject to relevant international humanitarian law and Indian domestic law, which includes military law. Armed conflicts in modern times are becoming more and more complex due to two main reasons. First, the distinction between international and non-international wars is increasingly getting blurred; and second, technical developments in weapons are continuing to increase their destructive power and range. The field is rapidly advancing. Military robots have been taking to the skies, the seas and even to space. Another issue of concern is that in the last 50 years, civilian casualties in armed conflicts have increasingly outnumbered military casualties.

The law of armed conflict provides for the protection and humane treatment of combatants and non-combatants. The law imposes duties upon combatants and grants rights to individuals. All personnel must be aware of the basic rules of the law of armed conflict, including the practical application of the principles of military necessity, proportionality, distinction and humanity.

Laws of Armed Conflict: Historical

In 1859, Henri Dunant, a Swiss citizen, witnessed the aftermath of the Battle of Solferino. He was horrified by the sight of thousands of wounded soldiers lying helpless and abandoned with no one to care for them. This experience led him to suggest the setting up of voluntary relief societies who could be trained, during peacetime, to care for the wounded in time of war. He also called for an international agreement to be drawn up to protect the wounded and those who look after them from further attack. In 1863, Henri Dunant arranged an unofficial international conference at which it was agreed that each country should form a relief organization capable of assisting the Army Medical Services in wartime. This was the beginning of the Red Cross.

In 1864 governments were invited to send representatives to a diplomatic conference. As a result 12 nations signed a treaty stating that in future wars they would care for all sick and wounded military personnel, regardless of nationality. They would also recognize the neutrality of medical personnel, hospitals and ambulances identified by the emblem of a red cross on a white background. The treaty was called the Geneva Convention. This Convention was concerned only with soldiers wounded on the battlefield. Over the years, however, it has been expanded to cover everyone caught up in conflicts but not actually taking an active part in the fighting.

The four Geneva Conventions

There are now four Geneva Conventions, which were drawn up on 12 August 1949. They cover armed forces on land and at sea, prisoners of war, and civilians. These Conventions have been accepted by virtually every State in the world. India has ratified the four Geneva Conventions in 1960.

1. The First Geneva Convention for the Amelioration of the Wounded and Sick in Armed Forces in the Field.
2. The Second Geneva Convention for the Amelioration of the Condition of Wounded, Sick and Shipwrecked Members of Armed Forces at Sea.

3. The Third Geneva Convention Relative to the Treatment of Prisoners of War.

4. The Fourth Geneva Convention Relative to the Protection of Civilian Persons in Time of War.

In practice, the Geneva Conventions are of virtually universal application and are generally considered to embody customary law. The Geneva Conventions extend to internal armed conflicts a minimum of humanitarian protection. In addition, two Protocols (a Protocol is an addition or amendment to a Convention) were drawn up in 1977. The First Protocol extends the Conventions, taking into consideration modern means of warfare and to give further protection to civilians. The Second Protocol provides a code of minimum protection for the combatants and the civilian population during non-international armed conflict. The Third Protocol, drawn up in 2005 relates to adoption of an additional distinctive emblem. India is not a signatory to the Protocols.

The Conventions are long and complicated, but they are a series of 'do's' and 'don'ts' to apply during conflict to protect vulnerable and defenceless individuals. Their underlying principle behind these conventions is that the human dignity of all individuals must be respected at all times. Everything possible must be done, without any kind of discrimination, to reduce the suffering of people who have been put out of action by sickness, wounds or captivity whether or not they have taken direct part in the conflict.

The four Geneva Conventions

The **First and the Second Geneva Conventions** are similar, covering land and sea respectively. The main difference between the two is that the Second concerns the wounded, sick and shipwrecked members of the armed forces at sea while the First relates to the wounded and sick in armed forces in the field. The principle underlying the two Conventions are identical and the same rules apply to protected persons and property, taking into account the different conditions prevailing on land and at sea.

The main points of these two Conventions are:

- The sick, wounded and shipwrecked must be cared for adequately.
- Belligerents must treat members of the enemy force who are wounded, sick or shipwrecked as carefully they would their own.

- All efforts should be made to collect the dead quickly; to confirm death by medical examination; to identify bodies and protect them from robbery.
- Medical equipment must not be intentionally destroyed and medical establishments and vehicles must not be attacked, damaged or prevented from operating even if, for the moment, they do not contain patients.

The Third Geneva Convention covers members of the armed forces who fall into enemy hands (Prisoners of War). They are in the power of the enemy State, not of the individuals or troops who have captured them. Prisoners of war must be:

- Treated humanely with respect for their persons and their honour.
- Enabled to inform their next of kin and the Central Prisoners of War Agency of their capture.
- Allowed to correspond regularly with relatives and to receive relief parcels.
- Allowed to keep their clothes, feeding utensils and personal effects.
- Supplied with adequate food and clothing.
- Provided with quarters not inferior to those of their captor's troops.
- Given the medical care their state of health demands.
- Paid for any work they do.
- Repatriated if certified seriously ill or wounded, (but they must not resume active military duties afterwards).
- Quickly released and repatriated when hostilities cease.

Prisoners of war must not be:

- Compelled to give any information other than their name, age, rank and service number.

- Deprived of money or valuables without a receipt (and these must be returned at the time of release).
- Given individual privileges other than for reasons of health, sex, age, military rank or professional qualifications.
- Held in close confinement except for breaches of the law, although their liberty can be restricted for security reasons.
- Compelled to do military work, nor work which is dangerous, unhealthy or degrading.

The Fourth Geneva Convention covers all individuals “who do not belong to the armed forces, take no part in the hostilities and find themselves in the hands of the Enemy or an Occupying Power”. Protected civilians must be:

- Treated humanely at all times and protected against acts or threats of violence, insults and public curiosity.
- Entitled to respect for their honour, family rights, religious convictions and practices, and their manners and customs.
- Specially protected, for example in safety zones, if wounded, sick, old, children under 15, expectant mothers or mothers of children under 7.
- Enabled to exchange family news of a personal kind.and helped to secure news of family members dispersed by the conflict.
- Allowed to practise their religion with ministers of their own faith.

Civilians who are interned have the same rights as prisoners of war. They may also ask to have their children interned with them, and wherever possible families should be housed together and provided with the facilities to continue normal family life. Wounded or sick civilians, civilian hospitals and staff, and hospital transport by land, sea or air must be specially respected and may be placed under protection of the red cross/ crescent emblem.

Protected civilians must not be:

- Discriminated against because of race, religion or political opinion.

- Forced to give information.
- Used to shield military operations or make an area immune from military operations.
- Punished for an offence he or she has not personally committed.
- Women must not be indecently assaulted, raped, or forced into prostitution.

Protection of Emblem

The distinctive emblems defined in the Geneva Conventions are the red cross, the red crescent or the red crystal on a white background. In order to retain their protective status in wartime, these emblems may not be used either in peace or war except to indicate or to protect the medical personnel, establishments and material protected by the Conventions. (National Societies may, in accordance with their national legislation, make use of the emblem for their other peacetime activities.) In wartime they must not use the emblem to signify that 'protection' is conferred by it, unless specifically authorized to do by their governments.

Administration of Prisoners of War

The humane treatment of prisoners of war is one of the main characteristics of civilized war. The international humanitarian law relating to treatment of prisoners of war is contained in the Geneva Convention Relative to the Treatment of Prisoners of War, 1949 (GC III). Articles 43 to 46 of Additional Protocol I of 1977 deal with combatant and prisoner of war status and issue of spies and mercenaries.

GC III applies to all armed conflicts between the parties to the convention, whether war has been declared or not, and even if one of the parties refuses to recognize a state of war. It also applies to all parties or total occupation of the territory of a party, even if the occupation is not resisted. The parties undertake to respect and ensure respect for the convention in all circumstances, including those in which one or more of the participants are not parties to the GC III. A party may withdraw from the GC III, but such denunciation of the treaty, if made during a conflict in which the party is involved, cannot take effect until peace has been concluded and after operations connected with the release and repatriation of the persons protected by the convention has been terminated. The denunciation has effect only in respect of the party denouncing.

Who is a Prisoner of War?

The following categories of personnel become prisoners of war under Article 4A of GC III, when they fall into the power of enemy:

(1) Members of the armed forces of a Party to the conflict, as well as members of militias or volunteer corps forming part of such armed forces.

(2) Members of other militias and members of other volunteer corps, including those of organized resistance movements, belonging to a Party to the conflict and operating in or outside their own territory, even if this territory is occupied, provided that such militias or volunteer corps, including such organized resistance movements, fulfil the following conditions:

   (a) that of being commanded by a person responsible for his subordinates;

   (b) that of having a fixed distinctive sign recognizable at a distance;

   (c) that of carrying arms openly;

   (d) that of conducting their operations in accordance with the laws and customs of war.

(3) Members of regular armed forces who profess allegiance to a government or an authority not recognized by the Detaining Power.

(4) Persons who accompany the armed forces without actually being members thereof, such as civilian members of military aircraft crews, war correspondents, supply contractors, members of labour units or of services responsible for the welfare of the armed forces, provided that they have received authorization, from the armed forces which they accompany, who shall provide them for that purpose with an identity card.

(5) Members of crews, including masters, pilots and apprentices, of the merchant marine and the crews of civil aircraft of the Parties to the conflict, who do not benefit by more favourable treatment under any other provisions of international law.

(6) Inhabitants of a non-occupied territory, who on the approach of the enemy spontaneously take up arms to resist the invading forces, without having had time to form themselves into regular armed units, provided they carry arms openly and respect the laws and customs of war.

Under Article 4B of GC III, the following categories of personnel shall also be treated as prisoners of war:

(1) Persons belonging, or having belonged, to the armed forces of the occupied country, if the occupying Power considers it necessary by reason of such allegiance to intern them.

(2) The persons belonging to one of the categories enumerated in Article 4, who have been received by neutral or non-belligerent Powers on their territory and whom these Powers are required to intern under international law.

Medical personnel and chaplains while retained by the detaining power to assist prisoners of war, are not considered as prisoners of war. They shall, however, receive as a minimum the benefits and protection of the Geneva Convention III, and shall also be granted all facilities necessary to provide for the medical care of, and religious ministration to prisoners of war (Article 33, GC III).

Protection: General Provisions

Prisoners of war are in the hands of the enemy power, but not of the individuals or military units who have captured them. Irrespective of the individual responsibilities that may exist, the detaining power is responsible for the treatment given to them. Prisoners of war may only be transferred by the detaining power to a power which is a party to the Convention and after satisfying itself of the willingness and ability of such transferee power to apply the GC III. When prisoners of war are transferred under such circumstances, responsibility for the application of the Convention rests on the power accepting them while they are in its custody.

Prisoners of war must at all times be humanely treated. Any unlawful act or omission by the detaining power causing death or seriously endangering the health of a prisoner of war in its custody is prohibited, and will be regarded as a serious breach of the Convention. In particular, no prisoner of war may be subjected to physical mutilation or to medical or scientific experiments of any kind which are not justified by the medical, dental or hospital treatment of the prisoner concerned and carried out in his interest. They must at all times be protected, particularly against acts of violence or intimidation and against insults and public curiosity. Measures of reprisal against prisoners of war are prohibited.

Prisoners of war are entitled to respect for their persons and their honour. Taking into consideration the provisions of GC III, relating to rank and sex, and subject to any privileged treatment which may be accorded to them by reason of their state of health, age or professional qualifications, all prisoners of war are to be treated alike, without any adverse distinction based on race, nationality, religious belief or political opinions. Women prisoners are to be treated with the regard due to their sex. The power detaining prisoners of war is bound to provide free of charge for their maintenance and for the medical attention required by their state of health. Prisoners of war under no circumstances can renounce in part or in entirety the rights secured to them by the GC III.

Questioning of prisoners

Every prisoner of war, when questioned on the subject, is bound to give only his surname, first names and rank, date of birth, and army, regimental, personal or serial number, or equivalent information. If he wilfully infringes this rule, he may render himself liable to a restriction of the privileges accorded to his rank or status. No physical or mental torture, nor any other form of coercion, is to be inflicted on prisoners of war to secure from them information of any kind whatever. Prisoners of war who refuse to answer may not be threatened, insulted, or exposed to unpleasant or disadvantageous treatment of any kind. Prisoners of war who, owing to their physical or mental condition, are unable to state their identity, are to be handed over to the medical service.

Evacuation

Prisoners of war must be evacuated, as soon as possible after their capture, to camps situated in an area far enough from the combat zone for them to be out of danger. Only those who, owing to wounds or sickness, would run greater risks by being evacuated than by remaining where they are, may be temporarily kept back in a danger zone. They shall not be unnecessarily exposed to danger while awaiting evacuation from a fighting zone.

The evacuation of prisoners of war must be effected humanely and in conditions similar to those for the forces of the detaining power in their changes of station. The detaining power must supply them sufficient food, drinking water, necessary clothing and medical attention; and must ensure their safety during evacuation. If during evacuation, the prisoners of war must pass through transit camps; their stay in such camps must be brief.

Internment

The Detaining Power may intern prisoners of war and impose on them the obligation of not leaving, beyond certain limits, the camp where they are interned, or if the said camp is fenced in, of not going outside its perimeter. Prisoners of war may not be held in close confinement except where necessary to safeguard their health. Prisoners of war may be partially or wholly released on parole or promise, however, they cannot be compelled to accept liberty on parole or promise. Upon the outbreak of hostilities, each Party to the conflict is to notify the adverse Party of the laws and regulations allowing or forbidding its own nationals to accept liberty on parole or promise.

The Quarters, Food and Clothing

Prisoners of war must be quartered under conditions as favourable as those for the forces of the detaining power who are billeted in the same area, making allowance for the habits and customs of the prisoners and in no case prejudicial to their health. The premises provided for the use of prisoners of war must be protected from dampness and adequately heated and lighted, in particular between dusk and lights out. All precautions must be taken against the danger of fire. Separate dormitories must be provided for women prisoners of war in mixed camps.

The daily food rations must be sufficient in quantity, quality and variety to keep prisoners of war in good health and to prevent loss of weight or the development of nutritional deficiencies. Sufficient drinking water must also be supplied to prisoners of war. They should also be associated with the preparation of their meals and may be employed in the kitchens. Adequate premises should be provided for messing. Collective disciplinary measures affecting food are prohibited.

Clothing, underwear and footwear must be supplied to prisoners of war in sufficient quantities by the detaining power, making allowance for the climate of the region where the prisoners are detained. The regular replacement and repair of the clothing articles must be ensured. In addition, prisoners of war who work must be provided appropriate clothing, wherever the nature of the work demands.

Canteens must be established in all camps, where prisoners of war may procure foodstuffs, soap and tobacco and articles of daily use. The tariff must never exceed local market prices. The profits made by canteens must be used for the benefit of the prisoners; and their representative be associated with the management of the canteen and its fund.

Hygiene and Medical Attention

The detaining power is bound to take all sanitary measures necessary to ensure the cleanliness and healthfulness of camps and to prevent epidemics. Prisoners must have for their use, day and night, conveniences which conform to the rules of hygiene and are maintained in a constant state of cleanliness. In camps in which women prisoners of war are accommodated, separate conveniences are to be provided for them. Prisoners must be provided with sufficient water and soap for their personal toilet and for washing their personal laundry.

Every camp must have an adequate infirmary where prisoners of war may have the required attention and appropriate diet. Prisoners suffering from serious disease, or whose condition necessitates special treatment, a surgical operation or hospital care, must be admitted to any military or civilian medical unit where such treatment can be given. Special facilities should be afforded for the disabled, in particular to the blind. Prisoners must not be prevented from presenting themselves to the medical authorities for examination. The detaining authorities must, upon request, issue to every prisoner who has undergone treatment, an official certificate indicating the nature of his illness or injury, and the duration and kind of treatment received. A duplicate of this certificate should be forwarded to the Central Prisoners of War Agency.

Prisoners must have opportunities for taking physical exercise, including sports and games. Sufficient open spaces must be provided for this purpose in all camps. Regular medical inspections of prisoners must be held at least a month, which should include the checking and the recording of the weight of each prisoner. The general state of health, nutrition and cleanliness of prisoners must be undertaken to detect contagious diseases, especially tuberculosis, malaria and venereal disease.

The medical personnel and chaplains while retained by the detaining power with a view to assisting prisoners shall not be considered as prisoners of war. They must receive as a minimum the benefits and protection under the Geneva Convention III, and must be granted all facilities necessary to provide the medical care, and religious ministration to prisoners of war.

The fitness of prisoners for work must be periodically verified by medical examinations at least once a month, with particular regard to the nature of the work which prisoners are required to do. If any prisoner considers himself incapable of working, he must be permitted to appear before the medical authorities. Medial authorities may recommend that the prisoners who are unfit for work, be exempted.

Prisoners have the right to make requests regarding their conditions of captivity to the military authorities in whose power they are. Prisoners' representatives may send periodic reports on the situation in the camps and the needs of the prisoners of war to the representatives of the protecting powers.

Discipline

Every prisoner of war camp must be put under the immediate authority of a responsible commissioned officer (camp commander) belonging to the regular armed forces of the detaining power. This officer must have a copy of the Geneva Convention III and ensure that its provisions are known to the camp staff and the guard. He must be personally responsible for of application the Convention.

Prisoners of war, with the exception of officers, must salute camp commander. Officer prisoners are bound to salute camp commander regardless of his rank, and officers of higher rank. The wearing of badges of rank and nationality, as well as of decorations, must be permitted. The Geneva Convention III and its Annexes, regulations, orders, notices and publications relating to the conduct of prisoners of war must be placed in the camp, in the prisoners' own language, in places where all may read them.

The use of weapons against prisoners of war, especially against those escaping or attempting to escape, constitutes an extreme measure, and must always be preceded by warning.

Special provisions for officer POW (Article 44 and 49)

- Officers and prisoners of equivalent status shall be treated with the regard due to their rank and age.
- In order to ensure service in officers' camps, ORs of the same armed forces shall be assigned in sufficient numbers. Such ORs (orderlies) shall not be required to perform any other work.
- Supervision of the mess by the officers themselves shall be facilitated in every way.
- If officers ask for suitable work, it may be assigned to them; however, as far as possible, they will not be compelled to work. (Article 49).

Relations with the Exterior

As soon as prisoners of war have fallen into its power, the detaining power must inform them and the powers to which they belong, through the protecting power. Immediately upon capture, or not more than one week after arrival at a camp, every prisoner of war must be enabled to write direct to his family, and to the Central Prisoners of War Agency (Article 123), about his capture, address and state of health. The prisoners must be allowed to send and receive letters and cards, which may be subject to necessary censorship.

Prisoners must be allowed to receive by post or by any other means individual parcels or collective shipments containing, foodstuffs, clothing, medical supplies and articles of a religious, educational or recreational character, including books, devotional articles, scientific equipment, examination papers, musical instruments, sports outfits and materials allowing them to pursue their studies or their cultural activities.

Penal and Disciplinary Sanctions

A prisoner of war is subject to the laws and regulations of the armed forces of the detaining power. That power shall be justified in taking judicial or disciplinary measures in respect of any offence committed by a prisoner of war against such laws or regulations. However, no proceedings or punishments contrary to the Chapter III of the third Geneva Convention are permitted. In deciding whether proceedings concerning alleged offence shall be judicial or disciplinary, the detaining power must ensure that the competent authorities exercise the greatest leniency and adopt, wherever possible, disciplinary rather than judicial measures.

A prisoner of war must be tried only by a military court, unless the existing laws of the detaining power expressly permit the civil courts to try a member of the armed forces of the detaining power in respect of the alleged offence committed by the prisoner of war. A prisoner must never be tried by a court which does not follow the essential guarantees of independence and impartiality and does not afford the accused the rights of defence provided in Article 105 of the third Geneva Convention. A prisoner must not be punished more than once for the same act or on the same charge. Collective punishment for individual acts, corporal punishment, imprisonment in premises without daylight and, in general, any form of torture or cruelty, are forbidden. A prisoner must not be deprived of his rank by the detaining power, or prevented from wearing his badges.

Officers, non-commissioned officers and men who are prisoners of war undergoing a disciplinary or judicial punishment, must not be subjected to more severe treatment than that applied in respect of the same punishment to members of the armed forces of the detaining power of equivalent rank. A woman prisoner of war must not be sentenced to a punishment more severe, or treated whilst undergoing punishment more severely, than a woman member of the armed forces of the detaining power dealt with for a similar offence. Disciplinary punishments must not be inhuman, brutal or dangerous to the health of prisoners of war.

Punishment Summarily Awarded to a POW

The disciplinary punishments applicable to POW are the following:

- A fine, not to exceed 50 % of the advances of pay which the POW would receive under Articles 60 and 62.
- Discontinuance of privileges granted over and above the treatment provided for by the third Geneva Convention.
- Fatigue duties not exceeding two hours daily (not to officers).
- Confinement.

The duration of any single punishment shall not exceed thirty days.

Pay and Allowances to POW

- Article 60 (Advance of pay): The Detaining Power shall grant POW a monthly advance of pay, the amount of which shall be fixed as per the rank of prisoner. However, the parties to the conflict may by special agreement modify the amount of advances of pay due to prisoners of various ranks.
- Article 62 (Working Pay): POW shall be paid a fair working rate of pay as fixed, by the detaining authorities.
- Working pay shall be paid by the detaining authorities to POW detailed for duties in connection with the administration, installation or maintenance of camps, and to the prisoners who are required to carry out spiritual or medical duties.
- The working pay to the prisoners' representative and his assistants shall be paid from the 'canteen profits' fund. The scale of this working pay shall be fixed by the prisoners' representative and approved by the camp commander. If there is no such fund, the detaining authorities shall pay these prisoners a fair working rate of pay.
- Article 63 (Transfer of Fund): POW shall be permitted to receive remittances of money addressed to them individually or collectively.

- Article 64 and 65 (Prisoners' Account): The Detaining Power shall hold an account for each POW, and every item entered in the account of a POW shall be countersigned by him, or by the prisoners' representative acting on his behalf.
- Article 66 (Winding up of accounts): On the termination of captivity of a POW or his repatriation, the Detaining Power shall give him a statement, signed by an authorized officer of that Power, showing the credit balance then due to him.

Escape

According to Article 91, GCIII, the escape of a prisoner of war shall be deemed to have succeeded when: (1) he has joined the armed forces of the Power on which he depends, or those of an allied Power; (2) he has left the territory under the control of the Detaining Power, or of an ally of the said Power; (3) he has joined a ship flying the flag of the Power on which he depends, or of an allied Power, in the territorial waters of the Detaining Power, the said ship not being under the control of the last named Power.

Prisoners of war who have made good their escape and who are recaptured, are not be liable to any punishment in respect of their previous escape. A prisoner who has made an unsuccessful attempt to escape is liable only to a disciplinary punishment, even if it is a repeated offence. The record of disciplinary punishments must be maintained by the camp commander, which must be open to inspection by representatives of the protecting power.

Article 75 of the Additional Protocol I of 1977 contains more far reaching provisions to protect prisoners captured during armed conflicts. Whatever their status, such prisoners are entitled to humane treatment. It is generally accepted that Article 75 reflects customary international law. The use of torture and inhuman or degrading treatment is prohibited. The authorities are entitled to question a prisoner but there is no obligation on the prisoner to answer the questions put. Coercing a prisoner to confess is unlawful. Article 75(4) is particularly significant. It provides:

> No sentence may be passed and no penalty may be executed on a person found guilty of a penal offence relating to the armed conflict except pursuant to a conviction pronounced by an impartial and

regularly constituted court respecting the generally recognized principles of regular judicial procedure.

Judicial Proceedings

A prisoner of war must not be tried or sentenced for an act which is not forbidden by the law of the detaining power or by international law, in force at the time the said act was committed. No moral or physical coercion may be exerted on a prisoner to induce him to admit himself guilty of the act of which he is accused. He may not be convicted without having had an opportunity to present his defence and the assistance of a qualified counsel.

Prisoners of war and the protecting powers must be informed of the offences which are punishable by the death sentence under the laws of the detaining power. Other offences shall not thereafter be made punishable by the death penalty without the concurrence of the power on which the prisoners of war depend. If the death penalty is pronounced on a prisoner of war, the sentence must not be executed before the expiration of a period of at least six months from the date when the protecting power receives, at an indicated address, the detailed communication provided for in Article 107of GC III.

The prisoner is entitled to assistance by one of his prisoner comrades, to defence by a qualified advocate or counsel of his own choice, to the calling of witnesses and, if he necessary, to the services of an interpreter. He must be advised of these rights by the detaining power before the trial. Failing a choice by the prisoner, the protecting power must provide an advocate or counsel for his defence at trial. Prisoner must have the right to appeal against a sentence, in the same manner as the members of the armed forces of the detaining power. He must be informed of his right to appeal and of the time limit within which he may do so.

Release

Prisoners of war who are seriously wounded and sick may be accommodated in neutral countries. Each of the parties to the conflict may, in addition, conclude agreements with a view to the direct repatriation or internment in a neutral country of able-bodied prisoners who have undergone a long period of captivity. No prisoner on whom a disciplinary punishment has been imposed and who is eligible for repatriation or for accommodation in a neutral country, may be kept back on the plea that he has not undergone his punishment. Prisoners of war must be released and repatriated without delay after the cessation of active hostilities.

A Central Prisoners of War Information Agency must be created in a neutral country. The International Committee of the Red Cross may propose to the powers concerned the organization of such an Agency.

The Geneva Conventions Act, 1960

In order to give effect to the four Geneva Conventions of 1949, the Government of India has legislated the Geneva Conventions Act, 1960. When a grave breach of any of the provisions of Conventions is committed by any person, irrespective of his nationality, whether outside or inside the Indian territory, he is liable to be tried in India. Such an offender may be brought to trial before a Court of Session or a Court of Chief Metropolitan Magistrate in India. The Act provides for a detailed procedure which would ensure a fair trial to the accused. The Act also contains elaborate provisions which prohibit the misuse of the Red Cross and such other emblems and also provides for penalty for such misuse or abuse.

Command Responsibility

The principle objective of the armed forces is to fight and win wars. The highly peculiar features of the armed forces are centralized command, hierarchy, and discipline. The centralized command structure ensures that a continuous chain of command links the lowest rank to the supreme commander of the armed forces. The commanders at various hierarchical levels are responsible to ensure that while participating in an armed conflict, the forces under their command follow the laws of war or the IHL. The responsibility for the success or failure of a military mission falls squarely on the commander's shoulders. But, the commander's responsibility extends to more than just mission success.

The modern doctrine of command responsibility can be defined as the responsibility of commanders for war crimes committed by subordinate members of their armed forces or other persons subject to their control. This responsibility is based on a failure to prevent or punish subordinates for their unlawful actions. The concept of 'command responsibility' in the armed conflicts embraces two issues. In the first place, it concerns the responsibility of a commander who has given an order to a subordinate to commit an act which is in breach of the law of armed conflict or whose conduct implies that he is not averse to such a breach being committed.[i] It also covers the plea of the subordinate that he is not responsible for any breach because he was acting in accordance with the orders of or what he presumed to be the wishes of his commander, a plea that is more commonly described as that of "compliance with superior orders". The subordinate putting forward such a plea contends that the superior alone is responsible.

The Geneva Convention of 1949 lays down that each belligerent party bears responsibility under international law for the conduct of all members of its armed forces, and the State is obliged to maintain discipline, law and order at all times. All members of armed forces are subject to the military and criminal code of the States they serve, and in case of infraction they are liable to be prosecuted before military or civil courts of that State. For example, the Third Geneva Convention (Article 129) states: "The High Contracting Parties undertake to enact any legislation necessary to provide effective penal sanctions for persons committing, or ordering to be committed, any of the 'grave breaches' of the present Convention." The 'grave breaches' to which Article 129 relates are further listed in Article 130 as (i) willful killing, (ii) torture or inhuman treatment, including biological experiments, (iii) causing great suffering or serious injury to body or health, and (iv) compelling a prisoner of war to serve in the forces of the hostile Power, or depriving a POW of the rights of fair and regular trial.

---

i A command to be lawful must satisfy the following requirements:

(a) A superior officer must give it personally.

(b) It must be a specific command to an individual.

(c) It must be capable of execution by the individual to whom it is addressed.

(d) It must be justified by the AA as well as civil law and by usages.

(e) It must relate to military duty, disobedience of which must tend to impede, delay or prevent some military proceedings.

(f) The disobedience must have reference to the time at which the command is to be obeyed. If the command demands a prompt and immediate compliance, hesitation or unnecessary delay in obeying it may be sufficient to constitute the offence. [AA s. 41 notes]

Article 3 of the Geneva Conventions (Common Article 3) states that in cases of armed conflict not of an international character occurring in the territory of one of the High Contracting Parties, each Party to the conflict shall be bound to apply as a minimum the provisions to protected persons: those not taking active part in hostilities; members of armed forces who have laid their arms; members of armed forces who are *horse de cambat* by sickness, wounds, detention etc. The acts prohibited against these persons are: (i) violence to life and person, in particular murder of all kinds, mutilation, cruel treatment and torture; (ii) taking of hostages; (iii) outrages upon personal dignity, in particular, humiliating and degrading treatment; and (iv) the passing of sentences and the carrying out of executions without previous judgment pronounced by a regularly constituted court affording all the judicial guarantees which are recognized as indispensable by civilized peoples.

In some cases, a military commander may be responsible for war crimes committed by subordinate members of the armed forces, or other persons subject to their control. Thus, for instance, when troops commit atrocities against the civilian population in a territory or against POW, the responsibility may rest not only with the actual perpetrators but also with the commander. Such a responsibility arises directly when the acts in question have been committed in pursuance of an order of the commander concerned. The commander is also responsible if he has actual knowledge, or should have known, through reports received by him, that troops subject to his command are likely to commit or have committed a war crime and he fails to take the necessary action to punish violators.

The doctrine of command responsibility has been codified in Article 28 of the Rome Statute of the International Criminal Court (ICC). Article 28(a) of the Statute imposes individual responsibility on military commanders for crimes committed by forces under their effective command and control. It states:

> A military commander shall be criminally responsible for crimes within the jurisdiction of the Court committed by forces under his effective command and control, as a result of his or her failure to exercise control properly over such forces, where:

(i) That military commander either knew or, owing to the circumstances at the time, should have known that the forces were committing or about to commit such crimes; and

(ii) That military commander failed to take all necessary and reasonable measures within his power to prevent or repress their commission or to submit the matter to the competent authorities for investigation and prosecution.

It is felt that this provision will serve as a deterrent, giving incentive to a commander to be aware of what his subordinates are doing. The offences dealt with under the Rome Statute are genocide, war crimes and crimes against humanity. The ICC is complementary to national jurisdictions and will intervene only where States are unable or unwilling to act. India is not a party to the Rome Statute.

Commander's Duty in a War

In the armed forces, it is the commanders' duty to ensure observance of the law of war. Every military leader is responsible for giving instruction to his men and for their behaviour in action. The commander himself must ensure that (i) his subordinates are aware of their obligations under the law of war, and (ii) necessary measures are taken to prevent violations of the law of war. The commander must ensure that his subordinates respect the law of war. The commander must give appropriate guidance (e.g. rules of engagement) to subordinates with regard to specific circumstances (i) to assure uniform action and behaviour, and (ii) to prepare subordinate commanders to take themselves the measure required by the situations. He must also ensure that in case of a breach of the law of war (i) the breach ceases, and (ii) disciplinary or penal action is taken. The military legal system provides that a violator can be tried immediately by a simple legal system, before a court martial. The most important factor in the reduction of war crimes is an assertive and proactive command structure that aggressively seeks to prevent its subordinates from committing atrocities. The doctrine of command responsibility plays a fundamental role in regulating the behaviour of superiors and their subordinates in times of war.

International Crimes

International criminal law defines certain types of conducts as crimes under international law. The establishment of various international judicial bodies in the recent past and the establishment of ICC to punish those who have committed genocide, war crimes and the crime against humanity has been a significant development in the field of international criminal law. The ICC has been functional since 2003 to promote the rule of law and ensure that the gravest international crimes do not go unpunished. In this section definition of the crime of genocide, war crimes, crime against humanity and torture has been included.

I. Genocide

Genocide is a crime under international law. Rome Statute of the ICC, Article 6 states 'genocide' means any of the following acts committed with intent to destroy, in whole or in part, a national, ethnical, racial or religious group, as such:

(a) Killing members of the group;

(b) Causing serious bodily or mental harm to members of the group;

(c) Deliberately inflicting on the group conditions of life calculated to bring about its physical destruction in whole or in part;

(d) Imposing measures intended to prevent births within the group;

(e) Forcibly transferring children of the group to another group.

II. War Crimes

War Crimes means:

(a) Grave breaches of the Geneva Conventions of 12 August 1949, namely, any of the following acts against persons or property protected under the provisions of the relevant Geneva Convention:

(i) Wilful killing;

(ii) Torture or inhuman treatment, including biological experiments;

(iii) Wilfully causing great suffering, or serious injury to body or health;

(iv) Extensive destruction and appropriation of property, not justified by military necessity and carried out unlawfully and wantonly;

(v) Compelling a prisoner of war or other protected person to serve in the forces of a hostile Power;

(vi) Wilfully depriving a prisoner of war or other protected person of the rights of fair and regular trial;

(vii) Unlawful deportation or transfer or unlawful confinement;

(viii) Taking of hostages.

(b) Other serious violations of the laws and customs applicable in international armed conflict, within the established framework of international law, namely, any of the following acts:

(i) Intentionally directing attacks against the civilian population as such or against individual civilians not taking direct part in hostilities;

(ii) Intentionally directing attacks against civilian objects, that is, objects which are not military objectives;

(iii) Intentionally directing attacks against personnel, installations, material, units or vehicles involved in a humanitarian assistance or peacekeeping mission in accordance with the Charter of the United Nations, as long as they are entitled to the protection given to civilians or civilian objects under the international law of armed conflict;

(iv) Intentionally launching an attack in the knowledge that such attack will cause incidental loss of life or injury to civilians or damage to civilian objects or widespread, long-term and severe damage to the natural environment which would be clearly excessive in relation to the concrete and direct overall military advantage anticipated;

(v) Attacking or bombarding, by whatever means, towns, villages, dwellings or buildings which are undefended and which are not military objectives;

(vi) Killing or wounding a combatant who, having laid down his arms or having no longer means of defence, has surrendered at discretion;

(vii) Making improper use of a flag of truce, of the flag or of the military insignia and uniform of the enemy or of the United Nations, as well as of the distinctive emblems of the Geneva Conventions, resulting in death or serious personal injury;

(viii) The transfer, directly or indirectly, by the Occupying Power of parts of its own civilian population into the territory it occupies, or the deportation or transfer of all or parts of the population of the occupied territory within or outside this territory;

(ix) Intentionally directing attacks against buildings dedicated to religion, education, art, science or charitable purposes, historic monuments, hospitals and places where the sick and wounded are collected, provided they are not military objectives;

(x) Subjecting persons who are in the power of an adverse party to physical mutilation or to medical or scientific experiments of any kind which are neither justified by the medical, dental or hospital treatment of the person concerned nor carried out in his or her interest, and which cause death to or seriously endanger the health of such person or persons;

(xi) Killing or wounding treacherously individuals belonging to the hostile nation or army;

(xii) Declaring that no quarter will be given;

(xiii) Destroying or seizing the enemy's property unless such destruction or seizure be imperatively demanded by the necessities of war;

(xiv) Declaring abolished, suspended or inadmissible in a court of law the rights and actions of the nationals of the hostile party;

(xv) Compelling the nationals of the hostile party to take part in the operations of war directed against their own country, even if they were in the belligerent's service before the commencement of the war;

(xvi) Pillaging a town or place, even when taken by assault;

(xvii) Employing poison or poisoned weapons;

(xviii) Employing asphyxiating, poisonous or other gases, and all analogous liquids, materials or devices;

(xix) Employing bullets which expand or flatten easily in the human body, such as bullets with a hard envelope which does not entirely cover the core or is pierced with incisions;

(xx) Employing weapons, projectiles and material and methods of warfare which are of a nature to cause superfluous injury or unnecessary suffering or which are inherently indiscriminate in violation of the international law of armed conflict, provided that such weapons, projectiles and material and methods of warfare are the subject of a comprehensive prohibition.

(xxi) Committing outrages upon personal dignity, in particular humiliating and degrading treatment;

(xxii) Committing rape, sexual slavery, enforced prostitution, forced pregnancy, enforced sterilization, or any other form of sexual violence also constituting a grave breach of the Geneva Conventions;

(xxiii) Utilizing the presence of a civilian or other protected person to render certain points, areas or military forces immune from military operations;

(xxiv) Intentionally directing attacks against buildings, material, medical units and transport, and personnel using the distinctive emblems of the Geneva Conventions in conformity with international law;

(xxv) Intentionally using starvation of civilians as a method of warfare by depriving them of objects indispensable to their survival, including wilfully impeding relief supplies as provided for under the Geneva Conventions;

(xxvi) Conscripting or enlisting children under the age of fifteen years into the national armed forces or using them to participate actively in hostilities.

(c) In the case of an armed conflict not of an international character, serious violations of article 3 common to the four Geneva Conventions of 12 August 1949, namely, any of the following acts committed against persons taking no active part in the hostilities, including members of armed forces who have laid down their arms and those placed *hors de combat* by sickness, wounds, detention or any other cause:

(i) Violence to life and person, in particular murder of all kinds, mutilation, cruel treatment and torture;

(ii) Committing outrages upon personal dignity, in particular humiliating and degrading treatment;

(iii) Taking of hostages;

(iv) The passing of sentences and the carrying out of executions without previous judgement pronounced by a regularly constituted court, affording all judicial guarantees which are generally recognized as indispensable.

(d) Paragraph 2 (c) applies to armed conflicts not of an international character and thus does not apply to situations of internal disturbances and tensions, such as riots, isolated and sporadic acts of violence or other acts of a similar nature.

(e) Other serious violations of the laws and customs applicable in armed conflicts not of an international character, within the established framework of international law, namely, any of the following acts:

(i) Intentionally directing attacks against the civilian population as such or against individual civilians not taking direct part in hostilities;

(ii) Intentionally directing attacks against buildings, material, medical units and transport, and personnel using the distinctive emblems of the Geneva Conventions in conformity with international law;

(iii) Intentionally directing attacks against personnel, installations, material, units or vehicles involved in a humanitarian assistance or peacekeeping mission in accordance with the Charter of the United Nations, as long as they are entitled to the protection given to civilians or civilian objects under the international law of armed conflict;

(iv) Intentionally directing attacks against buildings dedicated to religion, education, art, science or charitable purposes, historic monuments, hospitals and places where the sick and wounded are collected, provided they are not military objectives;

(v) Pillaging a town or place, even when taken by assault;

(vi) Committing rape, sexual slavery, enforced prostitution, forced pregnancy, enforced sterilization, and any other form of sexual violence also constituting a serious violation of Article 3 common to the four Geneva Conventions;

(vii) Conscripting or enlisting children under the age of fifteen years into armed forces or groups or using them to participate actively in hostilities;

(viii) Ordering the displacement of the civilian population for reasons related to the conflict, unless the security of the civilians involved or imperative military reasons so demand;

(ix) Killing or wounding treacherously a combatant adversary;

(x) Declaring that no quarter will be given;

(xi) Subjecting persons who are in the power of another party to the conflict to physical mutilation or to medical or scientific experiments of any kind which are neither justified by the medical, dental or hospital treatment of the person concerned nor carried out in his or her interest, and which cause death to or seriously endanger the health of such person or persons;

(xii) Destroying or seizing the property of an adversary unless such destruction or seizure be imperatively demanded by the necessities of the conflict.

The International Criminal Court shall have jurisdiction in respect of war crimes in particular when committed as part of a plan or policy or as part of a large-scale commission of such crimes. [Rome Statute of the ICC, Article 8].

III. Crimes against Humanity

Crime against humanity means any of the following acts when committed as part of a widespread or systematic attack directed against any civilian population, with knowledge of the attack:

(a) Murder;

(b) Extermination;

(c) Enslavement;

(d) Deportation or forcible transfer of population;

(e) Imprisonment or other severe deprivation of physical liberty in violation of fundamental rules of international law;

(f) Torture;

(g) Rape, sexual slavery, enforced prostitution, forced pregnancy, enforced sterilization, or any other form of sexual violence of comparable gravity;

(h) Persecution against any identifiable group or collectivity on political, racial, national, ethnic, cultural, religious, gender as defined in paragraph 3, or other grounds that are universally recognized as impermissible under international law, in connection with any act referred to in this paragraph or a crime within the jurisdiction of the Court;

(i) Enforced disappearance of persons;

(j) The crime of apartheid;

(k) Other inhumane acts of a similar character intentionally causing great suffering, or serious injury to body or to mental or physical health.

For the purpose of above paragraph:

- "Attack directed against any civilian population" means a course of conduct involving the multiple commission of acts referred to in paragraph 1 against any civilian population, pursuant to or in furtherance of a State or organizational policy to commit such attack.
- "Extermination" includes the intentional infliction of conditions of life, inter alia the deprivation of access to food and medicine, calculated to bring about the destruction of part of a population.
- "Enslavement" means the exercise of any or all of the powers attaching to the right of ownership over a person and includes the exercise of such power in the course of trafficking in persons, in particular women and children.
- "Deportation or forcible transfer of population" means forced displacement of the persons concerned by expulsion or other coercive acts from the area in which they are lawfully present, without grounds permitted under international law.
- "Torture" means the intentional infliction of severe pain or suffering, whether physical or mental, upon a person in the custody or under the control of the accused; except that torture shall not include pain or suffering arising only from, inherent in or incidental to, lawful sanctions.
- "Forced pregnancy" means the unlawful confinement of a woman forcibly made pregnant, with the intent of affecting the ethnic composition of any population or carrying out other grave violations of international law.
- "Persecution" means the intentional and severe deprivation of fundamental rights contrary to international law by reason of the identity of the group or collectivity.
- "The crime of apartheid" means inhumane acts of a character similar to those referred to in paragraph 1, committed in the

context of an institutionalized regime of systematic oppression and domination by one racial group over any other racial group or groups and committed with the intention of maintaining that regime.

- "Enforced disappearance of persons" means the arrest, detention or abduction of persons by, or with the authorization, support or acquiescence of, a State or a political organization, followed by a refusal to acknowledge that deprivation of freedom or to give information on the fate or whereabouts of those persons, with the intention of removing them from the protection of the law for a prolonged period of time. [Rome Statute of the ICC, Article 7].

IV. Crime of Aggression

For the purpose of the Rome Statute, "crime of aggression" means the planning, preparation, initiation or execution, by a person in a position effectively to exercise control over or to direct the political or military action of a State, of an act of aggression which, by its character, gravity and scale, constitutes a manifest violation of the Charter of the United Nations.

For the purpose of above para, "act of aggression" means the use of armed force by a State against the sovereignty, territorial integrity or political independence of another State, or in any other manner inconsistent with the Charter of the United Nations. Any of the following acts, regardless of a declaration of war, shall, in accordance with United Nations General Assembly resolution 3314 (XXIX) of 14 December 1974, qualify as an act of aggression:

(a) The invasion or attack by the armed forces of a State of the territory of another State, or any military occupation, however temporary, resulting from such invasion or attack, or any annexation by the use of force of the territory of another State or part thereof;

(b) Bombardment by the armed forces of a State against the territory of another State or the use of any weapons by a State against the territory of another State;

(c) The blockade of the ports or coasts of a State by the armed forces of another State;

(d) An attack by the armed forces of a State on the land, sea or air forces, or marine and air fleets of another State;

(e) The use of armed forces of one State which are within the territory of another State with the agreement of the receiving State, in contravention of the conditions provided for in the agreement or any extension of their presence in such territory beyond the termination of the agreement;

(f) The action of a State in allowing its territory, which it has placed at the disposal of another State, to be used by that other State for perpetrating an act of aggression against a third State;

(g) The sending by or on behalf of a State of armed bands, groups, irregulars or mercenaries, which carry out acts of armed force against another State of such gravity as to amount to the acts listed above, or its substantial involvement therein.

The crime of aggression is defined in Article 8 of the Rome Statute of the ICC. In essence, three elements are required for crime of aggression: (i) The perpetrator must be a political or military leader, i.e. a "person in a position effectively to exercise control over or to direct the political or military action of a State"; (ii) The Court must prove that the perpetrator was involved in the planning, preparation, initiation or execution of such a State act of aggression; and (iii) Such a State act must amount to an act of aggression in accordance with the definition contained in UN GA Resolution 3314, and it must, by its character, gravity and scale, constitute a manifest violation of the UN Charter.

Torture

The international human rights law, which is applicable both in times of peace and in times of emergency and armed conflict, absolutely prohibits torture. The Universal Declaration of Human Rights, 1948, adopted by the United Nations General Assembly condemns torture and other cruel, inhuman or degrading treatment. In addition to the absolute prohibition of torture or other forms of cruel, inhuman or degrading treatment or punishment under Article 7 of the International Covenant on Civil and Political Rights, 1966, the prohibition of torture also has been firmly rooted in international human rights law, international criminal law and customary international law. The most important among all international instruments is the UN Convention against Torture and Other Cruel,

Inhuman or Degrading Treatment or Punishment (CAT) which was adopted by the General Assembly on 10 December 1984 and entered into force on 26 June 1987.

The most innovative aspect of the CAT is the obligation of States to combat impunity of perpetrators of torture by enacting torture as a crime under their domestic criminal law with appropriate penalties and by assuming the responsibility of establishing various types of jurisdiction, including for the first time in a human rights treaty the obligation of universal jurisdiction.

What is torture?

The term "torture" means any act by which severe pain or suffering, whether physical or mental, is intentionally inflicted on a person for such purposes as obtaining from him or a third person information or a confession, punishing him for an act he or a third person has committed or is suspected of having committed, or intimidating or coercing him or a third person, or for any reason based on discrimination of any kind, when such pain or suffering is inflicted by or at the instigation of or with the consent or acquiescence of a public official or other person acting in an official capacity. It does not include pain or suffering arising only from, inherent in or incidental to lawful sanctions. [CAT Art. 1].

Definitions of torture cover any act which:

- causes severe pain or suffering;
- is intentionally inflicted on a person;
- is done to obtain information or a confession, punishment for an act he or a third person has committed or is suspected of having committed, or to intimidate or coerce him or a third person, or for any reason based on discrimination of any kind; and
- is done at the instigation of, or with the consent or acquiescence of, a public official or other person acting in an official capacity.

The term "torture" encompasses a variety of methods including severe beatings, electric shock, sexual abuse and rape, prolonged solitary confinement, hard labour, near drowning, near suffocation, mutilation, and hanging for prolonged periods. Torture is not limited to acts causing physical pain or injury but also includes acts that cause mental suffering, such as through threats against family or loved ones.

Rights at Stake

International human rights law protect a number of key rights relating to torture and inhuman or degrading treatment. This includes:

(a) **Right to be protected from torture:** Every State is required to take effective legislative, administrative, judicial, or other measures to prevent acts of torture in its territory. Acts of torture must be offences under criminal law. There is no justification to the use of torture in exceptional situations, e.g. during a state of war, internal political instability, or any other public emergency. Following an order from superior authorities also does not justify torture (CAT Art. 1and 2).

(b) **Duty to prosecute torturers:** All governments are responsible for the prosecuting offenders under the international criminal prosecution system that applies to torture. The principle of universal jurisdiction obliges all countries where alleged offenders are found to either extradite those who torture for prosecution by the government that is more directly affected (i.e., the country where the offences were committed, or the country of citizenship of the victims or the abusers), or to initiate prosecution themselves. (CAT Art. 5 and 6).

(c) **Right not to be expelled, returned or extradited to another state where one may face danger:** The State Parties are not to expel, return or extradite a person to another State where there are substantial grounds for believing that he would be in danger of being subjected to torture. (CAT Art. 3). This article creates an unconditional right of a person not to be expelled, returned or deported to another country where torture is a likely result.

(d) **Right of victims to obtain redress, fair compensation, including rehabilitation and the right of victims to make a complaint, to have it impartially investigated, and to be protected from retaliation for making complaints:** There are five types of reparation: financial compensation, medical care and rehabilitation, restitution (seeking to restore the victim to his or her previous situation), guarantees of non-repetition, and forms of satisfaction such as restoration of their dignity and reputation and a public acknowledgment of the harm they have suffered. (CAT Art. 13 and 14).

With the growing complexities of modern armed conflict, the law of war is also becoming more complicated. The States which have signed and ratified the laws of war are bound to "respect and to ensure respect for the treaties in all circumstances". The application of the laws of war from strategic level down wards becomes a matter of internal order and discipline. It addresses command responsibility. The military commander must ensure that forces under their command adhere to the following fundamental principles of IHL which could be helpful in preventing international crimes:

- Attacks must be confined to military objectives, and neither civilians nor civilian property may be attacked. If there is a doubt about whether a target is a civilian or military one, it must be assumed to be civilian.
- An enemy who has surrendered or who cannot take part in fighting any longer may not be killed or wounded.
- The wounded and sick must be cared for by whichever party to the conflict has taken them under its control. Medical personnel and equipment are exempt from attack.
- Prisoners of war and civilians who are in the power of an enemy must have their rights protected.
- There are practical constraints on the methods and means of warfare that are allowed. In particular, those which cause unnecessary losses or sufferings are illegal.
- Reprisals are forbidden.
- Unavoidable civilian casualties are acceptable, but every effort should be made to keep them to a minimum, and they should be proportionate to the military advantage expected to be gained.

CHAPTER 16

MILITARY CONTINGENTS IN PEACEKEEPING

Peacekeeping has been the technique most frequently used by, and associated with the United Nations (UN) to end conflicts and to preserve peace. Since the end of the cold war, peacekeeping operations have become more complex. In the first forty years, peacekeepers functioned mainly as buffer zones between warring parties and monitored cease-fires. Nowadays, they are increasingly engaged in internal rather than international conflicts and perform a multitude of tasks. Among others, they act as civilian administrators, oversee elections and monitor human rights. These changes have raised new legal problems. Today, nearly 100,000 UN peacekeepers—soldiers and military officers, police and civilian personnel monitor and observe peace processes that emerge in post-conflict situations and assist conflicting parties in implementing the peace agreements they have signed.

UN Peacekeeping Missions

Peacekeeping operations have traditionally been associated with Chapter VI of the UN Charter dealing with the 'Pacific Settlement of Disputes'. However, the Security Council need not refer to a specific chapter of the Charter when passing a resolution authorizing the deployment of a peacekeeping operation and has never invoked Chapter VI. In recent years, the Security Council has adopted the practice of invoking Chapter VII of the Charter when authorizing the deployment of peacekeeping operations into volatile post-conflict settings where the State is unable to maintain security and public order.

Mandate and Authority

The UN has traditionally defined peacekeeping as missions 'involving military personnel, but without enforcement powers, undertaken by the UN to help maintain or restore international peace and security in areas of conflict (ceasefires, separation of forces, etc.), or to ensure the safe delivery of humanitarian relief.' The authority for enforcement is dealt with in Chapter VII of the Charter and includes the use of armed forces to maintain or restore international peace and security in situations in which the Security Council has determined the existence of a threat to peace, breach of peace or act of aggression.

Under the UN Charter, the Security Council normally creates and defines peacekeeping missions. It does this by providing the mission with a mandate—a description of the mission's tasks. To establish a new peacekeeping mission, or change the mandate or strength of an existing mission, nine of the Security Council's 15 Member States must vote in favour. However, if any one of the five permanent members—China, France, the Russian Federation, the United Kingdom or the United States—votes against the proposal, it fails. Most peacekeeping operations are established and implemented by the UN itself, with the troops supplied by member states serving under UN operational command.

Each UN peacekeeping mission is a separate entity and operates under different circumstances. Troops from different countries have different national military rules. The task of the missions is always different and, therefore, the Status of Forces Agreement (SOFA) may differ from mission to mission. The SOFAs and status of mission agreements (SOMAs) are bilateral or multilateral treaties that define the legal position of military forces and civilian personnel deployed by one or more states or by an international organization in the territory of another state with the latter's consent. They normally deal with such issues as the entry and departure of foreign personnel, the carrying of arms, taxation, the settlement of claims, and the modalities for the exercise of civil and criminal jurisdiction over members of the visiting force or mission. The UN and other international actors have also developed distinct arrangements regulating the immunities and privileges of peace support operations.

The peacekeeping forces have status, privileges and immunities which are granted to UN personnel while carrying out peacekeeping operations under the:

(a) UN Convention on Privileges and Immunities of 13 February, 1946;

(b) UN Convention on Safety of UN and its Personnel, adopted by the General Assembly on 9 December, 1994;

(c) Secretary General's 2003 bulletin, Special Measure for Protection from Sexual Exploitation and Sexual Abuse; and

(d) Ten Rules: For the code of personal conduct for blue-helmet.

Role of Peacekeepers

The range of tasks assigned to UN peacekeeping operations has expanded significantly in response to shifting patterns of conflict and to best address emerging threats to international peace and security. Although each UN peacekeeping operation is different, there is a considerable degree of consistency in the types of mandated tasks assigned by the Security Council. These could be (i) conflict prevention, (ii) peacekeeping, (iii) peace enforcement, or (iv) peace-building. However, in today's scenario, the boundaries between these roles have become increasingly blurred. Peace operations are rarely limited to one type of activity.

Peacekeeping operations commonly support local authorities in the following: (i) the implementation of a peace agreement; (ii) the maintenance of stability through military and police interventions; (iii) disarmament, demobilization and reintegration of former combatants; (iv) the supervision of ceasefires and troop withdrawal and manning of buffer zones; (v) the return of refugees and internally displaced persons to their homes; (vi) the delivery of humanitarian services to those in need; (vii) restructuring and reform of local armed forces and police; (viii) the maintenance of law and order; (ix) strengthening of court and judicial systems and prison facilities; (x) the promotion and protection of human rights; (xi) the conduct and monitoring of elections (for example, UN peace missions have supported elections in seven post-conflict countries—Afghanistan, Burundi, Haiti, Iraq, Liberia, the DRC and Timor); and (xii) the promotion of development and economic reconstruction.

International Humanitarian Law

International Humanitarian Law (IHL) also known as "the law of war" or "the law of armed conflict" is designed to protect persons who do not participate, or are no longer participating, in hostilities; and it maintains the fundamental rights of civilians, victims and non-combatants in an armed conflict. IHL also restricts the means and methods of armed conflict. It is relevant to UN peacekeeping operations because these missions are often deployed in post-conflict environments where violence may be ongoing or conflict could reignite. Additionally, in post-conflict environments there are often large civilian populations that have been targeted by the warring parties, prisoners of war and other vulnerable groups to whom the Geneva Conventions or other humanitarian law would apply in the event of further hostilities. UN peacekeepers need to have a clear understanding of the principles and rules of IHL and observe them in situations where they apply.

Modern IHL is contained in the four Geneva Conventions of 1949 and their two Additional Protocols of 1977, as well as in rules regulating the means and methods of combat. IHL also includes conventions and treaties on the protection of cultural property and the environment during armed conflict, as well as the protection of victims of conflict.

In 1995 the ICRC convened a group of experts tasked with identifying the core IHL provisions applicable in UN peacekeeping operations. Its proposed core principles came in form of the "Secretary-General's Bulletin on the Observance by United Nations Forces of International Humanitarian Law" [No. ST/SGB/1999/13 of 6 August 1999]. The Bulletin, vide Section 10, has entered into force on 12 August 1999. The instructions contained in the Secretary-General's Bulletin are applicable to UN peacekeeping forces under UN command and control, when in situations of armed conflict they are actively engaged therein as combatants. They apply in Chapter VII operations or in Chapter VI operations in self-defence, to the extent and for the duration of their engagement.

Secretary-General's Bulletin on IHL

The ten-section Bulletin includes the principles of distinction between civilians and combatants and between civilian objects and military objectives, means and methods of warfare, treatment of civilians and persons *hors de* combat, treatment of detainees, and protection of the wounded, the sick and medical and relief personnel. Fundamental principles and rules of IHL applicable to UN forces conducting operations under UN Command and Control are as follows.

Section 1 - Field of Application

The fundamental principles and rules of IHL are applicable to UN forces when in situations of armed conflict they are actively engaged as combatants, to the extent and for the duration of their engagement: (i) Enforcement actions and (ii) Peacekeeping operations when the use of force is permitted in self-defence.

This does not affect the protected status of members of peacekeeping operations under the 1994 Convention on the Safety of United Nations and its Personnel or their status as non-combatants, as long as they are entitled to the protection given to civilians under the international law of armed conflict.

Section 2 - Application of National Law

It does not constitute an exhaustive list of principles and rules of IHL binding upon military personnel, and do not replace the national laws by which military personnel remain bound throughout the operation.

Section 3 - Status-of-forces Agreement (SOFA)

In the SOFA concluded between the United Nations and a State in whose territory a UN force is deployed, the United Nations undertakes to ensure that the force shall conduct its operations with full respect for the principles and rules of the general conventions applicable to the conduct of military personnel.

The UN also undertakes to ensure that members of the military personnel of the force are fully acquainted with the principles and rules of those international instruments. The obligation to respect the said principles and rules is applicable to UN forces even in the absence of a SOFA.

Section 4 - Violations of International Humanitarian Law

In case of violations of IHL, members of the military personnel of a UN force are subject to prosecution in their national courts.

Section 5 - Protection of the Civilian Population

1. The UN force shall make a clear distinction at all times between civilians and combatants and between civilian objects and military objectives. Military operations shall be directed only

against combatants and military objectives. Attacks on civilians or civilian objects are prohibited.

2. Civilians shall enjoy the protection afforded by this section, unless and for such time as they take a direct part in hostilities.

3. The UN force shall take all feasible precautions to avoid, and in any event to minimize, incidental loss of civilian life, injury to civilians or damage to civilian property.

4. In its area of operation, the UN force shall avoid, to the extent feasible, locating military objectives within or near densely populated areas, and take all necessary precautions to protect the civilian population, individual civilians and civilian objects against the dangers resulting from military operations. Military installations and equipment of peacekeeping operations, as such, shall not be considered military objectives.

5. The UN force is prohibited from launching operations of a nature likely to strike military objectives and civilians in an indiscriminate manner, as well as operations that may be expected to cause incidental loss of life among the civilian population or damage to civilian objects that would be excessive in relation to the concrete and direct military advantage anticipated.

6. The United Nations force shall not engage in reprisals against civilians or civilian objects.

Section 6 - Means and Methods of Combat

1. The right of the UN force to choose methods and means of combat is not unlimited.

2. The United Nations force shall respect the rules prohibiting or restricting the use of certain weapons and methods of combat under the relevant instruments of international humanitarian law. These include, in particular, the prohibition on the use of asphyxiating, poisonous or other gases and biological methods of warfare; bullets which explode, expand or flatten easily in the human body; and certain explosive projectiles. The use of certain conventional

weapons, such as non-detectable fragments, anti-personnel mines, booby traps and incendiary weapons, is prohibited.

3. The UN force is prohibited from employing methods of warfare which may cause superfluous injury or unnecessary suffering, or which are intended, or may be expected to cause, widespread, long-term and severe damage to the natural environment.

4. The UN force is prohibited from using weapons or methods of combat of a nature to cause unnecessary suffering.

5. It is forbidden to order that there shall be no survivors.

6. The UN force is prohibited from attacking monuments of art, architecture or history, archaeological sites, works of art, places of worship and museums and libraries which constitute the cultural or spiritual heritage of peoples. In its area of operation, the UN force shall not use such cultural property or their immediate surroundings for purposes which might expose them to destruction or damage. Theft, pillage, misappropriation and any act of vandalism directed against cultural property is strictly prohibited.

7. The UN force is prohibited from attacking, destroying, removing or rendering useless objects indispensable to the survival of the civilian population, such as foodstuff, crops, livestock and drinking-water installations and supplies.

8. The UN force shall not make installations containing dangerous forces, namely dams, dikes and nuclear electrical generating stations, the object of military operations if such operations may cause the release of dangerous forces and consequent severe losses among the civilian population.

9. The UN force shall not engage in reprisals against objects and installations protected under this section.

Section 7 - Treatment of civilians and persons hors de combat

1. Persons not, or no longer, taking part in military operations, including civilians, members of armed forces who have laid down their weapons and persons placed hors de combat by reason of sickness, wounds or detention, shall, in all circumstances, be

treated humanely and without any adverse distinction based on race, sex, religious convictions or any other ground. They shall be accorded full respect for their person, honour and religious and other convictions.

2. The following acts against any of the persons mentioned in section 7.1 are prohibited at any time and in any place: violence to life or physical integrity; murder as well as cruel treatment such as torture, mutilation or any form of corporal punishment; collective punishment; reprisals; the taking of hostages; rape; enforced prostitution; any form of sexual assault and humiliation and degrading treatment; enslavement; and pillage.

3. Women shall be especially protected against any attack, in particular against rape, enforced prostitution or any other form of indecent assault.

4. Children shall be the object of special respect and shall be protected against any form of indecent assault.

Section 8 - Treatment of detained persons

The UN force shall treat with humanity and respect for their dignity detained members of the armed forces and other persons who no longer take part in military operations by reason of detention. Without prejudice to their legal status, they shall be treated in accordance with the relevant provisions of the Third Geneva Convention of 1949, as may be applicable to them mutatis mutandis. In particular:

(a) Their capture and detention shall be notified without delay to the party on which they depend and to the Central Tracing Agency of the ICRC, in particular in order to inform their families;

(b) They shall be held in secure and safe premises which provide all possible safeguards of hygiene and health, and shall not be detained in areas exposed to the dangers of the combat zone;

(c) They shall be entitled to receive food and clothing, hygiene and medical attention;

(d) They shall under no circumstances be subjected to any form of torture or ill-treatment;

(e) Women whose liberty has been restricted shall be held in quarters separate from men's quarters, and shall be under the immediate supervision of women;

(f) In cases where children who have not attained the age of sixteen years take a direct part in hostilities and are arrested, detained or interned by the United Nations force, they shall continue to benefit from special protection. In particular, they shall be held in quarters separate from the quarters of adults, except when accommodated with their families;

(g) ICRC's right to visit prisoners and detained persons shall be respected and guaranteed.

Section 9 - Protection of the wounded, the sick, and medical and relief personnel

1. Members of the armed forces and other persons in the power of the UN force who are wounded or sick shall be respected and protected in all circumstances. They shall be treated humanely and receive the medical care and attention required by their condition, without adverse distinction. Only urgent medical reasons will authorize priority in the order of treatment to be administered.

2. Whenever circumstances permit, a suspension of fire shall be arranged, or other local arrangements made, to permit the search for and identification of the wounded, the sick and the dead left on the battlefield and allow for their collection, removal, exchange and transport.

3. The UN force shall not attack medical establishments or mobile medical units. These shall at all times be respected and protected, unless they are used, outside their humanitarian functions, to attack or otherwise commit harmful acts against the United Nations force.

4. The UN force shall in all circumstances respect and protect medical personnel exclusively engaged in the search for, transport or treatment of the wounded or sick, as well as religious personnel.

5. The UN force shall respect and protect transports of wounded and sick or medical equipment in the same way as mobile medical units.

6. The UN force shall not engage in reprisals against the wounded, the sick or the personnel, establishments and equipment protected under this section.

7. The UN force shall in all circumstances respect the Red Cross and Red Crescent emblems. These emblems may not be employed except to indicate or to protect medical units and medical establishments, personnel and material. Any misuse of the Red Cross or Red Crescent emblems is prohibited.

8. The UN force shall respect the right of the families to know about the fate of their sick, wounded and deceased relatives. To this end, the force shall facilitate the work of the ICRC Central Tracing Agency.

9. The UN force shall facilitate the work of relief operations which are humanitarian and impartial in character and conducted without any adverse distinction, and shall respect personnel, vehicles and premises involved in such operations.

Use of Force

Peacekeeping is a non-coercive instrument, based on the consent and cooperation of the parties. Force is not the means which it utilizes to achieve its mandate. However, peacekeepers at all times retain the right to self-defence, in which case force may be used as a last resort. The right to self-defence ends with the threat that gave rise to it. Retaliation is not self-defence. The peacekeeper's right to self-defence does not end with the defence of his own life. It includes defending one's comrades and any persons entrusted to one's care, as well as defending one's post, convoy, vehicle, or armed and ammunition. Each peacekeeping operation is expected to function as a single, integrated unit and an attack on any one of its members or sub-units engages the right to self-defence of the operation as a whole.

The environments in which UN peacekeeping operations are deployed are often characterized by the presence of militias, criminal gangs and other spoilers who may actively seek to undermine the peace process or pose a threat to the civilian population. In such situations, the Security Council has given UN peacekeeping operations "robust" mandates authorizing them to "use all necessary means" to deter forceful attempts to disrupt the political process, protect civilians under imminent threat of physical attack, and/or assist the national authorities in maintaining law and order. By proactively using force in defence of their mandates, these UN peacekeeping operations have succeeded in improving the security situation and creating an environment conducive to reconstruction.

The UN and International Responsibility

The UN has, in general, assumed responsibility for the activities of UN peacekeeping forces. The UN perceives its international responsibility to be an aspect of its international legal personality and its capacity to bear international rights and obligations. The UN Secretariat has stated, "As a subsidiary organ of the UN, an act of a peacekeeping force is, in principle, imputable to the Organization, and if committed in violation of an international obligation entails the international responsibility of the Organization and its liability in compensation." On the basis of this premise, the UN has acknowledged its responsibility for the conduct of peacekeepers participating in the UN Operations.

Action against Peacekeepers

The military personnel while serving as United Nations peacekeepers remain subject to their national laws. They are subject to the exclusive jurisdiction of the contributing States in respect of any criminal offences which may be committed by them in the host country. In return for an absolute immunity from local jurisdiction in the State of operation, the State of nationality is expected to prosecute members of its national contingents before its national courts. Section 4 of the Secretary General's Bulletin also provides: "In case of violations of IHL, members of the military personnel of a UN force are subject to prosecution in their national courts."

Actions against Persons attacking UN Peacekeepers

The Rome Statute was adopted on 17 July 1998. It has created a permanent tribunal, the ICC, to deal with all crimes of serious concern to the international community as a whole. Anyone intentionally directing an attack against personnel, installations or material, involved in an UN peacekeeping mission, can be charged for 'War Crime' under Article 8, 2 (b) (iii) of the Rome Statute and punished by the International Criminal Court: "Intentionally directing attacks against personnel, installations, material, units or vehicles involved in a humanitarian assistance or peacekeeping mission in accordance with the Charter of the UN, as long as they are entitled to the protection given to civilians or civilian objects under the IHL."

Peacekeeping is a tool of conflict prevention, management and resolution. They have no enemies and are not there to win a war. The key characteristic of peacekeeping is the minimum use of force, only as a last resort and only in self-defence. The chain of command for UN peace operations runs from the UN Security Council through the UN Secretary-General and his representatives in the field to the military contingents supplied by UN member states. Their effectiveness depends on voluntary cooperation.

Protection of Civilians

During armed conflict civilians face threats of violence and death. Despite being protected under international humanitarian and human rights law, they continue to be the victims of violence and are sometimes deliberately targeted by belligerents. The failure of the UN peacekeeping missions to provide security in complex crises such as Somalia, and to protect civilians from mass atrocities in Rwanda and Bosnia, highlighted the shortcoming in the peacekeeping operations. Besides damaging the standing of the UN, it also discredited the effectiveness of peacekeeping operations in general. In order to bring the reform in the system, the UN has attempted to improve the overall effectiveness of the peacekeeping operations, including their capabilities to protect civilians.

Modern peacekeeping missions are multidimensional, addressing the full spectrum of peace-building activities, from providing secure environment to monitoring human rights and rebuilding the capacity of the State under conflict. As a part of this evolution, UN peacekeeping missions have been explicitly mandated to protect civilians who are under imminent threat of physical violence. The 1999 UN peacekeeping operation in Sierra Leone (UNAMSIL), was the first such mission provided with explicit mandate to afford protection to civilians. Today, the majority of the nearly 100,000 uniformed UN peacekeepers deployed worldwide operate with such mandates, for the protection of civilians during armed conflict.[i]

---

i For further details see: Victoria Holt and Glyn Taylor, Protecting Civilians in the Context of UN Peacekeeping Operations: Successes, Setbacks and Remaining Challenges, 2009, available at: http://www.peacekeepingbestpractices.unlb.org/pbps/LibraryProtecting%20Civilians%20in%20the%20Context%20of %20UN%20PKO.pdf

Appendix

Court Martial: Procedure

Convening of GCM/DCM (AR 37)

- Power to convene GCM & DCM (AA s. 109, 110).
- Composition (AA s. 113,114, AR 40, RA para 460)
- Responsibility of convening officer (RA para 452)
- Reference to JAG branch (RA para 459).
- Disqualification of officers (AR 39 and 40, MML Vol I, Ch IV/21).
- Which court to try (RA para 452 and MML Vol. I, Ch IV, para 24)
- Preparation of defence and warning for trial (AR 33, 34)

↓

Inquiry by the court as to legal composition (AR 41)

↓

Inquiry by the court: amenability of the accused (AR 42)

↓

Appearance of prosecutor/Accused (AR 43)

- Choice of prosecutor, duty (RA para 458, 464)
- Defending officer and friend of accused (AR 95)
- Counsel in GCM/DCM (AR 96)
- Defence counsel (RA para 479)

↓

Challenge by the Accused (AA s. 130 and AR 44)

↓

Swearing or affirmation of court (AR 45, 46 and 47)

↓

Arraignment of the accused (AR 48)

↓

Objection by the accused to charge (AR 49) and amendment of charges (AR 50)

↓

Special Plea as the jurisdiction of the court (AR 51)

Plea allowed. Court to receive evidence and forward proceedings to Convening Authority.

Convening authority to:

(i) Release the accused, or (ii) Constitute a new court for trial

↓

Plea overruled by the Court

↓

General Plea of 'Guilty' or 'Not Guilty'

The court to explain effect of 'plea of guilty'

Not to accept plea of guilty in cases of death punishment (AR 52)

- Pleads Guilty. Summary of evidence to be read in the court. The court to take evidence to enable to determine the sentence.
- Accused to make statement and give evidence in mitigation of punishment and witness to character (AR 54)

↓

Plea in Bar of Trial (AR 53)

- **If plea in bar is proved with evidence, the court shall record its finding and notify confirming authority and shall adjourn. If finding is not confirmed, the court to re-assemble and proceed.**

Plea overruled or not confirmed

↓

Accused at any time withdraw plea of 'not guilty' and plead 'guilty' (AR 55)

↓

- Plea of Not Guilty and procedure (AR 56)

- The court to ask the accused about opportunity for preparing his defence
- The prosecutor may make an opening address.
- The prosecution witnesses give evidence (cross and re-examination).
- The prosecutor may also appear as witness and cross-examined.
- Power to summon witnesses (AA s. 135)

↓

Plea of No Case (AR 57)

That the prosecution has not established a prima facie case on the charge(s), If the court allows the Plea—it shall record a finding of 'Not Guilty' and announce the finding in open court as subject to confirmation.

Plea of No Case fails

↓

Examination of accused and defence witnesses (AR 58)
Accused may give unsworn statement or give evidence on oath/ affirmation (AR 58)

↓

Prosecutor to make closing address and accused/ his counsel entitled to reply (AR 59)

↓

Summing up by Judge Advocate (AR 60)

↓

Consideration of finding in closed court (AR 61 and AA s. 132)

↓

The court to give brief reasons in support of findings (AR 62)
The court is empowered to find guilty of offence not charged with (AR 62 (9) and AA s 139)

Finding on each charge to be announced in open court

↓

Procedure on acquittal (AR 63)

On Conviction (AR 64)

Court will take evidence on general character of accused, age, service, rank and acts of gallantry or distinguished acts.

Accused may also address court in mitigation of punishment

↓

Court determines single punishment in respect of all offences of which accused is found guilty (AR 65)

Power of punishment GCM (AA s. 118, 132(2) and DCM (AA s. 119)

Sentence of court martial (RA para 468)

↓

Court may make recommendation to mercy (AR 66)

↓

Announcement of sentence in open court and forwarding of proceedings for confirmation (AR 67)

Sentence subject to confirmation as Finding and sentence not valid unless confirmed (AA s 153)

↓

Review of Proceedings by Judge Advocate, JAG (AR 69)

- Power to confirm finding and sentence (AA s 154-159)
- Power of confirming officer to mitigate, remit or commute that punishment. (AAs 158)
- Grounds on which confirmation can be withheld (AA s.153, note 4)

↓

Revision of finding and sentence (AA s 160 and AR 68 and notes)

↓

Confirmation (AA s. 153 and notes, AR 70, RA para 472)

Remedy against order, finding or sentence of court martial (AA s 164 and RA para 365):

(a) Pre-confirmation petition [to authority empowered to confirm], and

(b) Post-confirmation petition [to authority superior to one who confirmed]

↓

Promulgation (AR 71 and RA para 473)

Annulment of Proceedings (AA s. 165, AR 202, RA para 365(l)).

Summary General Court Martial

1. Power to convene SGCM (AA s. 112).
2. Composition (AA s. 115).
3. Procedure for trial (AR 151-165): see AR 164 for application of rules.
4. Summoning of witnesses (AA s. 135).
5. Power to try and award punishment (AA s. 118 and 132(3).
6. Power to confirm finding and sentence (AA s. 153, 157 and RA para 472).
7. Revision (AA s. 160 and AR 68)
8. Remedy against order, finding and sentence (AA s. 164 and RA para 365).
9. Annulment of proceedings (AA s. 165, AR 202, RA para 365(l)).

Summary Court Martial

1. To be held by the CO. The proceeding to be attended throughout by two officers/JCOs/or one of either. They are not sworn/affirmed (AA s. 116 and RA para 447).
2. Power to try persons, offences and award punishment (AAs. 120).
3. Procedure for trial (AR 106-130) and summoning of witnesses (AA s. 135).
4. Finding and sentence not required to be confirmed; except when the CO has less than 5 years of service, or held on active service, sentence to be approved by Brigade Commander.
5. Scale of punishment to be awarded (RA para 448).

6. Transmission of proceedings to Brigade/Div Commander (AA s. 162 & AR 200, AR 133).
7. Promulgation (AR 131-132).
8. Remedy against finding and sentence (AA s. 164 and RA para 365).
9. Annulment of proceedings (AA s. 165, AR 202, RA para 365(l)).

Index

B

C

D

E

F

G

H

I

P

R

T

U

W

www.ingramcontent.com/pod-product-compliance
Lightning Source LLC
Chambersburg PA
CBHW031320230926
51848CB00001B/25